Sacred Dors
On the Path of the Dragon

Peter Knight

Sacred Dorset
On the Path of the Dragon

©1998 Peter Knight

ISBN 186163 058 1

ALL RIGHTS RESERVED

No part of this publication may be reproduced, stored in a retrieval system or transmitted in any form or by any means, electronic, mechanical, photocopying, scanning, recording or otherwise without the prior written permission of the author and the publisher.

Cover design by Paul Mason

Published by:

Capall Bann Publishing
Freshfields
Chieveley
Berks
RG20 8TF

Contents

Chapter One In Search of Dragons   3
    The Veneration of Nature   4
    The Oncoming of Christianity   6
    Perceiving Sacred Dorset   9
Chapter Two Sanctuary - The Sacredness of Place   **10**
Chapter Three Land of Myth and Fairie   **19**
    Of Dragons and Men   19
    Magical Beasts   25
    Fairies   27
    Dorset Fairy Folklore   29
    The Demise of the Fairies   34
Chapter Four Sacred Symbols   **35**
    Dragons and Saints   35
    The Heraldic Dragon   41
    Survivals   41
    The Celtic Cross   42
    Runes   47
    The Cult of the Head   49
    The Mystic Spiral   52
    Mazes and Labyrinths   58
    The Circle   62
    Survivals   70
Chapter Five Rites of Fertility   **71**
    Phallic Symbolism   72
    Ancient Phallic Megaliths   74
    Phallicism of the Celts and Romans   76
    Christian Phallicism   79
    The Horned Fertility Cults   81
    The Bull   81
    The Ram   84
    The Stag   85
    Cernunnos - Lord of the Animals   85
    Cernunnos and the Devil   89
    Survivals of Fertility Rites and Superstitions   94
Chapter Six Waters of Purification   **98**
    Rivers and Streams   101
    Lakes and Ponds   103
    Wells and Springs   104
    Of Golden Tables and Coffins   107
    Holy and Curative Wells and Springs   108
    Other Wells and Springs of Note   116
Chapter Seven Heights of Aspiration   **120**
    Dorset High Places   122

Maiden Castle   128
Chapter Eight Brother Sun - Sister Moon   **135**
Brother Sun   136
Some Dorset Solar Alignments   140
The Dorset Cursus   141
Sister Moon   155
Some Dorset Lunar Alignments   158
Dorset Solar and Lunar Monuments   160
Chapter Nine The Goddess in the Landscape   **163**
The Goddess of the Megaliths   165
Into the Womb of the Goddess   174
Medieval Legacy of the Goddess   175
The Triple Goddess   179
Goddess Landscapes - Mindshift and Perception   182
Journeying With the Goddess   184
Chapter Ten Graves of the Giants   **195**
Buried Treasure   196
Of Giants and Gods   197
Musical Mounds   198
Barrows of the Mysterious   200
Barrows of the Dead and the Living   204
Chapter Eleven Sacred Trees - The Spirit of the Green Man   **209**
Trees in Folklore and Myth   210
Trees and Dragon Lore   218
The Sacred Yew   218
Tree Spirits   221
Some Dorset Tree Spirits   223
Dragon Trees   228
The Green Man and the Wodehouse   236
The Green Man in Dorset   236
The Wodehouse - Wild Man of the Woods   240
Survivals   242
Chapter Twelve Paths of the Dragon   **245**
Of Leys and Dragons   252
Chapter Thirteen Awakening The Dragon   **260**
The Dragon Stirs   260
Seeking Out Dragons and Goddesses   265
Awakening the Dragon Within   267
Pilgrimage   268
Appendix One Ancient Stones of Dorset - Supplemental   **272**
Biblical Accounts and Folklore   272
Some Dorset Place Names   273
Additional Dorset Stone Site Information   273
Appendix Two Further Information   **279**
Bibliography   280
Index

Peter Knight holds talks and seminars on ancient sites and spiritualities and is a tutor on such subjects for the Adult Education Service. He is a member of the Wessex Dowsers and his interests include folklore, ancient cultures and related subjects. He is 43 and lives in Bournemouth with his wife Ghermaine and their daughter Leela Zen.

Dedication

This book is lovingly dedicated to my wife Ghermaine, to whom I owe so much
and to Leela Zen, our daughter and companion on the path

Acknowledgments

As with my previous volume, some special 'thank you' wishes and acknowledgements are due to people who have assisted my project. I apologise for anyone I have omitted, as this is due to lack of memory rather than intent.

Once again I thank Gordon Harris for placing his valuable map of leys at my disposal once more; Ken Bailey for photos and site information, plus permission to include extracts from two of his poems; Martin Driscoll and John Edmunds (site information); Mike Clark of the New Forest Dowsers for new information on Knowlton and the Verwood stone; John Bush of Winterborne Zelston for informing me of new stones; Michael Hodges of Christchurch for correcting an error in my previous work; Mr D Partridge of Corfe Mullen for information on two new stones in this area; David Kingston for the loan of crop circle photographs; I thank Belinda Lopez for information and photos on stones near Shaftesbury. Thanks also to Kevin Minn for information on a ley marker stone at Edmundson, and Val Ghose of Frampton, for confirming the survival of Jackman's Cross.

I thank George Terence Meaden for permission to use an extract from "*Stonehenge - The Secret of the Solstice*"; Ebury Press for granting permission to quote from "*Phallic Worship*"; White Eagle Publishing Company for the use of a quote from "*The Light in Britain*".

Once again, I thank my wife Ghermaine (formerly Gemma), who accompanied me on several trips and patiently awaited my return from others. She read every word of the manuscript, offering valuable advice and correcting innumerable errors, took some of the plate photographs, provided two drawings and some insights and comments in the text.

I finally thank those at Capall Bann, the publishers, who had faith in the project, when others had not.

To The Reader - A Preface

This volume is presented to the reader essentially as a companion to *"Ancient Stones of Dorset"* (Power Publications, 1996). Much material was amassed during research for the above work, yet which fell beyond the scope of it, making this follow-up book perhaps inevitable. I make no apologies for the many references to the previous work and indeed such cross-referencing is, I believe, a useful feature of any "series". It has enabled me to avoid repetition of material, something I feel every author should strive to accomplish.

The production of *"Sacred Dorset"* did not carry the pressure of production of the previous work, due mainly to the fact that I have made no attempt to compile a "definitive list" of any kind, something I now realise is impossible to do. Within these pages I merely present examples from Dorset and beyond to develop and expand themes and personal avocations. I welcome the space here to fully develop my ideas on subjects such as earth energies, hill forts, folklore, ancient symbologies and so on, more than was possible in the first book, which was restricted to sites and folklore of ancient stones. The opportunity also occurs within this volume to happily include some ancient stones not included in my initial book, plus too update the reader with information which has come to light since its publication.As with the previous work, I welcome comments and suggestions from readers that might assist the production of future editions.

With Love and Light,

Peter Knight
Bournemouth, Summer Solstice, 1998

By the same author:

Ancient Stones of Dorset, Power Publications, 1996

Chapter One

Introduction - In Search of Dragons

---

*The real magic lies not in seeking new
landscapes but in having new eyes.
French novelist Marcel Proust (1871 - 1922)*

The dragon being sought throughout these pages is symbolic of former magical ages
long gone. Times when legends were born and myths respectfully nurtured.

Yet such wonders can, on an individual level, be rekindled and experienced today.
All that is needed is a mind-shift, a change of perception. Such a change allows us
to approach and experience the landscape, and its sacred sites, as a place of mystical
enchantment, indeed the very domain of the Earth Goddess with Her entourage of
mystic companions.

To our ancestors, many centuries past, the earth was alive with all manner of myth,
folklore and tales of wonder and magic that kept an otherwise precarious everyday
life from becoming uninspired and grey. Can we say that today's technology has
lead us up a path of happiness and spiritual contentment? - I think not! The wonder
and mystique has retreated from life and we are no longer in contact with the earth in
a way we have been. We buy our food packaged in plastic from supermarkets; we
travel across the land in polluting mechanical devices; we sleep under roof tiles
rather than the stars. We have separated ourselves as a species from the Earth Spirit.
The great Irish poet and nature mystic George William Russell saw through the veil
into the otherworld and wrote of his experiences. In *"The Candle of Vision"*, written
in 1918, he describes this magical realm thus:

*"in that land I saw fountains as of luminous mist.....a shining folk. They were, I
believe, those who in the ancient world gave birth to legends of nymph and dryad."*

3

I believe the magical landscape of Russell and the Ancients is all around us and fully accessible to those who have "new eyes", as Proust suggests above. An enriched imagination and a sense of the spirituality of Nature can take us beyond the 20th century mind-trap into which we have imprisoned ourselves.

The enchanted landscape of fairy tale and myth has not disappeared, it is our technological consciousness and life-style that has detached Man from that enchantment.

Fig 1. A 1608 rendition of a dragon, a common style of portrayal

The Veneration of Nature

When we consider cave art found across Europe, which go back to circa 30,000 BC, it is safe to assume that worship of the earth, in the form of the Goddess, is very ancient indeed. Figurines, carvings and other relics portraying female deity are found in virtually every ancient civilisation.

The Greeks saw nature as alive and developed a nature philosophy. They saw spirit in every stone, river and tree. The seas were home to naiads, the forests the domain of the satyrs.

The Romans, Greeks and Celts had a whole pantheon of Goddesses associated with aspects of the primal Earth Goddess; Chapter 9 delves into the symbology of the Goddess in more detail.

To ancient people (as indeed to the Aborigine cultures of today) the earth was a living sculpture onto which myths were carved. Onto the outlines and hills of the landscape legends would be captured. These people were part of the landscape, not separate from it. It is perhaps but a small step from the personification of an object such as a stone, hill or tree, to that object being regarded as deity. To venerate an object is to worship the deity it represents.

Many think it impossible to believe that we find the true meanings of the Neolithic and Bronze age monuments. At the talks I give to local groups and societies I impress on those present that to view the landscape and its sites with an altered perception will get us some way into the mind of our distant ancestors. In "*Stonehenge - The Secret of the Solstice*", Terence Meaden shares my view:

"I believe it is possible to retreat in time, to think to some extent as our forebears did and, by uncovering some of the elements of the Neolithic religion, to recreate the basic ideas which inspired the planning of the monument."

Who were the Ancient Britons,
and by what races were the tumuli
of Dorset and Britain built?
Charles Warne, 1866

I believe that Britain is a particularly magical part of the earth, a view held by many mystics. The old name for these lands is Albion, which derives from *Albus*, Latin for "white". This could either refer to the famous white cliffs of the south coast or equally to the pure and higher virtues and famed spirituality of the people, or at least the priesthood of the land.

The Britons of course became subject to Roman law after AD 43. The Romans were generally tolerant of religions and cults that fell within its empire, the exception to this being the Druids and the early Christians, who they deemed had a threatening influence to the stability of the empire. Observance, not devotion, to the Roman gods was all they seem to have expected, which meant the Celtic gods and goddesses could still be venerated. These deities were in fact assimilated into the Roman pantheon as in them the Romans saw many classical counterparts. The horned Celtic god, Cernunnos is represented in a carving at Roman Cirencester. Epona, the horse goddess is on a figurine found in Wiltshire. Taranis was found in a temple at Forley Heath, Surrey. At Bath the Celtic goddess Sulis became the water goddess Sulis Minerva.

5

It should be noted that by Roman and Celtic times a predominance of male over female deities had taken place. The Earth Goddess was gradually losing her grip to the male warrior gods. This was due to the rise of male dominated, land conquering regimes that were often no more than extensions of male egos driven on by the lust for power. The nature religions were fading - and a new god arrived from across the seas.

The Oncoming of Christianity

Plate 1. The 8th century cross at Glamis, Scotland, a replica of which is now in the County Museum, Dorchester.

When the early Christian missionaries arrived on these shores they were certainly not met by a people eagerly searching for salvation or a new religion. Pagan practices, centred around nature gods and goddesses, had been going on since prehistoric times. The fact that several Church councils had to issue many decrees

6

on how to convert the "stubborn heathen Britons" (as late as 9th} century!) testifies to the strong and deeply imbedded spirituality of pre-Christian Britain.

A change in policy by Pope Gregory in AD 601 proved ultimately to be the "winner" as far as converting the British was concerned. Knowing that the native population visited and revered stones, wells, trees, etc., he made politically effective order that these should not be destroyed, but instead sprinkled with holy water and turned into Christian places of worship.

Early Christian art contains a fusion of classical, pagan and more overtly Christian symbology. This tells us that the old and the new coexisted quite healthily in the early years following the adoption of Christianity as the "official" religion. Plate 1 shows a Celtic cross and other symbols carved on a stone block. Certainly the cross predominates, with fine interlacing typical of the period. Yet classical and pagan symbology is also in evidence. In the top right hand corner is a centaur, the classical half-man, half-horse figure. Lower to the right is a deer or stag head, another pagan symbol. Below the left arm of the cross, above two fighting figures, is a cauldron into which two figures are being dipped. This could be seen as representing baptism, but could equally be related to the very similar scene depicted on the Gundestrup Cauldron, dating from 1st century BC pagan Denmark, which has been interpreted as initiation, re-birth or indeed sacrifice.

Dragons were originally regarded as guardians of knowledge, as depicted in Chinese legends. Nearer to home, the Celts had many benevolent dragons woven into their folklore. To the early Christians the dragon was not regarded as an evil force and in fact the symbol of John the Apostle is a chalice containing a dragon. However, the beast was gradually seen to represent the old ways of paganism and thus became the object of propaganda.

Bible quotes relating to the dragon representing evil and the devil were used to further the anti-pagan campaign. The dragon-slayers, such as St George and St Michael, were symbolic of the triumph of good over evil, the old religions being subdued.

In the Book of Revelations we read:

"three unclean spirits like frogs came out of the dragon.....spirits of evil."

The die was cast. The dragon came to represent envy, sin and pestilence. Plate 2 shows a much weathered rendition of St Michael slaying the dragon and more examples across Dorset of dragon symbology occur throughout this book.

Plate 2. St Michael slaying a dragon at Stinsford church, near Dorchester.

Other relics representing the suppression of the old religions can be found if one looks closely enough. A dragon being suppressed by a bishop can be seen on the church font at Avebury, a major sacred site. The 12th century font at Castle Frome, Herefordshire, sits on top of an oppressed creature.

Here in Dorset we have some examples. At Puncknowle the 12th century font is mounted on top of a Celtic-style figure. At Toller Fratrum the font, of the same age, has carved on it a creature with two heads. The font at Melbury Bubb has lots of pagan imagery, all turned up-side-down (see *Ancient Stones of Dorset*, Plate 113).

These examples lead us to seek out more surviving symbols of pre- and early Christian times. But we are also enticed to seek out the actual Earth Spirit, and its sacred places, that the relics merely represent.

8

Perceiving Sacred Dorset

*Time, ages and circumstance have not been
able to disperse the real stories of the past;
some day and at some magical hour the truth
will be revealed. I feel that England has been
awaiting this hour.*
J Foster Forbes, The Unchronicled Past , 1938

How many people go to Rempstone Stone Circle, near Corfe Castle, yet fail to see that one stone is head-shaped with eyes, mouth and large nose? How many thousands of people walk through Charminster Cemetery, in Bournemouth, without noticing the splendid green man carving, an ancient pagan symbol, high up on the chapel? Few people, I would dare say, stand on the top of Pilsdon Pen, Dorset"s highest point, realising they are on a ley alignment that goes all the way to Stonehenge.

Still fewer travellers would have noticed the dragon heads in a tree next to the busy road down to Swanage at Ulwell. Many people may know that gargoyles were supposedly put up around churches to protect the congregation from evil, but how many fully realise the ancient and sacred symbolism wrapped up in these stone edifices.

A reappraisal of the landscape, sacred sites and those ancient relics that have survived time and Man, can open up to anyone a taste of magic and mystery that our distant ancestors saw. Much of the material presented within these pages is described in a way that will hopefully enable the reader to develop a sense of awe for the achievements of the ancient people of this sacred land, and also a reverence of the land itself. For this is the crux of the ancient spiritualities: the earth was, as still is, *alive*. Not just the obvious living creatures such as trees, animals and birds, but also every rock, and river, every cloud and hill. Even the sun and the moon that shine down are endowed with spirit and life-force.

It is this "earth consciousness" that can, I believe, return to us a magic and purpose that is so sadly lacking in today's society.

Chapter Two

Sanctuary - The Sacredness of Place

"Every great locality has its own pure
daimon (attendant spirit).
D H Lawrence, "The Spirit Of Place".

As well as regarding landscape generally as the abode (and indeed the very body) of the Earth Goddess, ancient cultures, without exception, visited and worshipped at localities they deemed special. These places were where energies or spirits could be approached, experienced and interacted with.

Australian aborigines in their Dream Time would see totem animals, spirits and even their ancestors in rocks, trees and topographical features at places which had been known about and visited for generations.

In ancient Greece, temples would be placed on the landscape at places thought to be favourable to conversing with the gods. Moreover, the temples were built so that an inter-relationship was achieved between sites and the surrounding landscape. Many Greek temples are positioned within sight of hills the shape of breasts and horns. These features were an integral part of the site and perhaps even the ceremonies that took place.

In *"Symbolic Landscapes"*, Paul Devereux describes two goddess temples: Delphi and Eleusis are described as possessing "a powerful poetic atmosphere". The surrounding hills are in fact "focused by the sites". In other words, *the sites are part of the landscape.*

On a trip to the Egyptian pyramids, I personally experienced a sense of something magical, sacred and timeless. An equal sense of awe and humbleness was felt when I stood on top of Table Mountain, looking down onto the sprawling city of Cape Town, yet feeling safe, and conscious that I was on a "holy mountain".

Fig 2. Romantic 18th century drawing of a Druid in a sacred grove, complete with henge. A sense of 'the magic of place' has been achieved. (F Grose, 'Antiquities of England and Wales")

Nearer home, places like Stonehenge, Glastonbury Tor and Avebury never fail to instill in me something almost intangible, a feeling of the sanctity of place, a timeless quality.

In Dorset, too, we encounter many places which can be deemed sacred. Knowlton is one such place. Plate 3 shows a view through the entrance of the Neolithic henge, with the Norman church and sacred yew trees beyond. Our distant ancestors found here a locus where powerful earth energies were, as still are, experienced. When I leave the car and step into the henge it is like stepping back in time. Perhaps sacred places are indeed time portals in a sense. But maybe they are more than this. They are, I believe, doors through which Self can know Self, capsules of eternity into which our imaginations can be projected.

The Nine Stones, a stone circle near Dorchester, is another such locality. This Bronze Age circle nestles beneath the branches of a huge beech tree. My wife, Ghermaine, sees the tree as "housing the stones, watching over them. They sit under

Plate 3. Knowlton Henge, with church and yew trees within. (For details see 'Ancient Stones of Dorset' pages 48-52)

its protective branches". Over 3,000 years separate the creation of the circle from the birth of the beech. Yet this guardian tree is an integral component of the place, the spirit of the tree unavoidable. Sacred places evolve due to the fusion of many different facets of Man and Nature.

"If Nature is your teacher,
your soul will awaken".
Goethe's "Faust".

Many sacred places around Dorset will be described in subsequent chapters, but I will cover a few here to give a sense of why sites are "sacred", as well as mentioning some localities which will not be encountered later.

Many, if not most, of Dorset"s older chapels and churches owe their origins to an older sacred locality or shrine. St Catherine's Hill, Abbotsbury, is crowned by a chapel, yet the hill was no doubt venerated prior to this. Its tor-shaped outline would have been seen as the breast or recumbent body of the Goddess. Woodbury Hill once had a chapel, possibly dating back to the 12th century. Yet this place was regarded as sacred long before the building of the chapel. A holy, healing well was once present on the hill.

The church at Church Knowle stands on a round prehistoric mound of earth, a sure sign of the Christianisation of an older pagan sacred site, the "site evolution" process of ley hunters.

Another example of a site literally evolving is Maumbury, in Dorchester. Originally a Neolithic henge, it was expanded into a huge amphitheatre by the Romans. The site"s original sacredness is confirmed by ritual phallic objects found there (see Chapter 5). Dowsing confirms powerful energy lines passing through the site and even today, with the traffic just yards away, one can stand or indeed sit within its banks and feel something of the sacredness of the place.

"The body of the Earth has special regions
through which the traffic of perception seemed
most clearly to take place."
George William Russell, 1932

Just like their prehistoric forebears, the Romans had an acute sense and eye for a sacred locality. At Bath they built extensively on an existing hot spring sacred to the

Plate 4. The Nine Stones circle shaded by the huge beech.

14

Plate 5. The church at Church Knowle, west of Corfe Castle, stands on a much older circular mound.

Celts. Here in Dorset Romano-British temples were erected high on hills at Maiden Castle and Jordan Hill. With breathtaking views of the surrounding landscape one truly feels as if one is half way to the gods. At Maiden Castle a shrine was built on the site of an earlier hut, more evidence of site continuity. At Witchampton a Romano-British temple was built close to the river Allen.

The site of Studland Church appears to have been used by the Romano-British, as a burial site was found there. At Puncknowle one can see laid out in the churchyard small votive stones, with depressions for offerings to the Romano-British gods. At Kingston, south-west of Corfe Castle, a small alter stone was found, marking another Roman place of worship. Fig. 3 is a drawing of the stone, which is now on display in the County Museum, Dorchester.

A shrine from the Romano-British age has been uncovered at Norden. Two altars, steps down to a holy well and a carved shale head uncovered there all point to a sacred place nearly two thousand years old.

Many more examples of man-made monuments will be covered later. But we must realise that sacred sites are not just those places man has deemed special enough to warrant the erection of monuments and shrines. Let us now look at Nature's own handiwork.

Fig. 3. Romano-British altar stone from Kingston, now in the County Museum.

---

*"Our destination is never a place,
but rather a new way of looking at things."
Henry Miller.*

Plate 6. Thorncombe Wood, near Dorchester, on an atmospheric misty day.

The Sacred Places of Nature

Sacred places are by no means chosen or created by mortal man. We merely discover them or, more accurately, they are revealed to us. Within the Earth Goddess landscape can be found secret, mysterious and meditative localities where Man would find it impossible to improve or better the atmosphere or solitude. Hills are certainly such places. They are windswept, desolate and enable us to seemingly reach for the gods. We are elevated both physically and spiritually. Chapter Seven is devoted entirely to these "heights of aspiration".

Caves take us into the womb of the Earth Goddess. Even man-made caves, such as at Tilly Whim and Winspit, enable us to "enter the primal belly", as my wife Ghermaine puts it. Here, as in barrow tombs, we can relive similar conditions and emotions that we would last have encountered in our mother's womb, prior to our birth.

Forests and woods have a timeless-ness and mystique about them. Is it any wonder that the Druids made their homes and their shrines in groves, which they regarded as Nature's temples. On entering a wood one can leave the 20th Century behind. The scene before your eyes could be identical to that witnessed by prehistoric man, Roman and Celt alike. One can sense "something", the spirit of the forest. A feeling I often get when exploring a wood or forest is that of being observed: I am being watched by creatures as yet unseen, but who invite me to reach out and perceive them.

One such place is Thornecombe Wood, at Stinsford, near Dorchester. Ghermaine and I went there one foggy winter day. Plate 6 is a view into the mist-shrouded wood. The air was damp, atmospheric and magical: We stood still as we peered back into the mists of time. The ghost of a Roman soldier has been seen in these woods and it seemed as if he would march out of the fog at any moment.

Other types of sacred sites, such as springs and wells, will be dealt with in subsequent chapters. All that needs to be added at this juncture is that sacred places also possess sacred time:-

A sacred place can certainly display many moods and take on quite a multitude of atmospheres depending on the climatic conditions or the time of day or night. Many ancient sites were designed to be used at certain time of day, month or year. In chapter eight we will look at a range of sites that can only be experienced to optimum effect on particular festival dates, or else may need the moon to enliven them, revealing their wisdom for only brief moments.

Certainly our visit to Thornecombe Wood would have been totally different on a bright summer day, and perhaps on such a day we would not have had the *experience* that we did. The landscape is a living being, but has many mood swings: Indeed, at times the Goddess sleeps.

"The beautiful landscape, as we know,
belongs to those who like it".
Zen monk Muso Sosieki, 14th century.

Chapter Three

Land of Myth and Fairie

"In the old days of King Arthur,
of which Britons speak great honour,
All was this land filled with fairy,
The elf-queen with her jolly company"
"Canterbury Tales", Chaucer.

Ancient Wessex is steeped in folklore, myth and legend, and no part of it more so than Dorset. Oral and written lore has been handed down from generation to generation.

The folklore associated with Dorset"s stone sites has been covered previously in *"Ancient stones of Dorset"*, pages 16-26, so most tales need not be repeated in this volume.

Our quest to reveal sacred Dorset will continue with not just our indigenous folklore, but also mythical creatures imported to these lands from overseas via invaders and migrants, who likewise left stories and indeed relics in their wake.

Of Dragons and Men

In 1132 Geoffrey of Monmouth wrote (in his *"Historia Regum Brittaniae"*) of a tale of Merlin and two dragons:-

The story goes that Merlin orders Vortigern, King of the Britons, to drain a pond. At the bottom two dragons appeared, one white, the other red. They fought each other, eventually the white one prevailing. From this apparition Merlin prophesied that the

Saxons (the white dragon) would defeat the British (red dragon). Perhaps this is the legend depicted in Fig. 4 (A).

This tale is typical of countless dragon folklore that has come down to us through history. Dragon myths are universal, occurring across the world. A Hindu myth, from the Rg Veda (1200 BC), tells of Indra, who slew a dragon who lay upon a mountain, "releasing waters from the belly of the mountain". In Egyptian legend Ra and Seth defeated a serpent named Apep. Germanic myths often refer to dragons guarding treasure. The dragon Fafnir, whom Siegfried slew, was a wise and magical being.

Nearer to home, folklore first recorded in 1630 tells us that every night a dragon flies between Dolbury and Cadbury hill, in Devon's Exe Valley. Some have interpreted this tale as a line of earth-force linking the two hills. This theme is expanded in Chapter 12 and 13.

Plate 7. The dragon of Bisterne, above the door of Bisterne Manor

A tale from Bisterne, just one mile east of the Dorset border, is worth looking at in more detail as it is typical of many dragon myths:-

A dragon roamed around the New Forest area, between Bisterne and Burley. It's lair was Burley Beacon and it demanded daily a pail of milk from the villagers, occasionally craving men and cattle. He was covered in scales and belched fire. Eventually Sir Maurice de Berkeley fought the beast in what became know as "Dragon Field". One version says they fought a terrible battle which the knight won, yet died soon afterwards, presumably from his injuries. Another variant tells how he simply put out some milk for the dragon, lay in wait, and killed him whilst he drank, a much tamer end so magnificent beast!

Edward IV conferred a knighthood on Sir Maurice and gave him permission to use the dragon on his badge. If one goes to Bisterne Manor today we can see the dragon above the door, immortalised in the family ensign (see Plate 7).

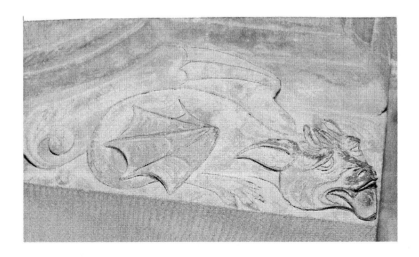

Plate 8. One of the carved dragons in Christchurch Priory

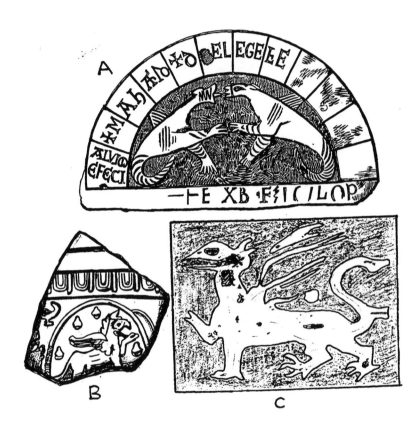

Fig. 4. A: The fighting dragons on the tymparnum at Wynford Eagle church. (From Hutchins, 1774. For a modern photo see 'Ancient Stones of Dorset', plate 111); B: Pottery found at Lady St mary, Wareham: C: Griffin on medieval floor tile from Preston church, now on display in the County Museum.

The only Dorset myth concerning a dragon I could find was of the Christchurch Dragon. An account of 1113 tells how the "whole town had caught fire..... a dragon had come out of the sea......had flown to the city, breathing fire out of it's nostrils". It was seen to have five heads, breathing "sulphurous flames". It evidently destroyed a church and a ship.

The tale in fact has a moral twist. Apparently the whole event was viewed as "God's vengeance" for the wrong doings of the local Dean. Local inhabitants who had previously shown kindness to the travelling medieval monks, the narrators of the story, were spared the dragon's wrath.

The interpretation of the tale is given later in this book in Chapter 13, with its possible connection to earth energies. But a visit to Christchurch priory will reveal that dragons are still in residence. Plate 8 shows a dragon carving (one of two) which adorns the base of one of the Norman arches. If one takes a look at the quire screen (dated 1320) more tiny dragon carvings can be found. Plate 110 shows another, this time in wood. A number of other dragons can be seen in the choir area and as gargoyles outside.

"they very soon came upon a Gryphon,
lying fast asleep in the sun"
From *"Alice"s Adventures in Wonderland"*

A variety of dragon is known as the Griffin, which had the head and wings of an eagle. It derived from the myths of Minos and Greece. One can be found carved on the font at Winchester Cathedral. In Dorset, relics of creatures can also be seen. At Bradford Abbas, near the Devon border, a magnificent griffin is carved in wood on a bench end, along with other beasts. Several griffins are carved in wood in Christchurch priory (see Plate 9).

Excavations at Lady St Mary, Wareham, revealed a collection of Romano-British pottery, richly decorated with mythological characters, amongst them a griffin, shown in Fig.4 (B). A piece of medieval floor tile found in 1855 in the south aisle of Preston church, north-east of Weymouth, also displays a griffin. This is shown in Fig. 4 (C). More tiles with griffins were found at Bindon Abbey.

Other dragon-like creatures appear in churches across Dorset. A fine one is a winged "demon' inside Maiden Newton church, to the left as one enters church. At Shroton church two more dragon images survive.

Fig. 5 A selection of mythical creatures. A. An enlargement of the centaur shown on a Celtic cross in Plate 1. On display in County Museum. B. Mermaid on Roman pottery from Lady St Mary, Wareham. C. Chimaera from the Roman villa at Hinton St Mary. Now in the British Museum. D. The depiction of Veasta in stone by the Ferrybridge Inn, Weymouth.

Magical Beasts

The Centaur, that half-man half-horse creature of Greek mythology was probably introduced to these lands by either early Greek traders or else the Roman conquest. The creature is barbarous for the most part, but it is also sensual and famed for wisdom. These characteristics easily enabled it to be assimilated into Romano-British and Celtic culture.

We have already seen one representation next to a Celtic cross, shown in Plate 1. Fig.5 has an enlargement of it. Another was found on some Roman pottery at Lady St Mary, Wareham.

Another beast of Greek mythology which found its way to Dorset was the Chimaera. This curious creature had the head of a lion, the body of a goat and the tail of a dragon. In 1963-4 a beautiful mosaic pavement was unearthed at the villa at Hinton St Mary (grid ref:784160). Part of the mosaic depicts a scene of Bellerophon spearing a chimaera, which is shown in Fig.5(C).

The mermaid is a creature well known from myths and tales of these shores. The most famous one is probably that of Zennor, in Cornwall. In Dorset, too, these half-fish half-woman beings have sparked the imagination. One was found portrayed on Roman pottery, again at Lady St Mary, Wareham. This is shown in Fig.5(B). High up on a roof boss in Sherborne Abbey is located another, beautifully carved.

Plate 9. 16th century carvings in wood above misericords in Christchurch Priory. On the left are two opposing griffins. To the right is a two-tailed mermaid.

Plate 10. The White Hart at Longham. A reminder of a distant apparition of the magical creature?

Another can be seen as a wooden carved panel in the quire at Christchurch Priory, next to two griffins. These date from 1515 and are shown in Plate 9. At Whitcombe church, SE of Dorchester, a 15th century painting of St Christopher has a mermaid in the background. Another mermaid can be seen in wood on a misericord in Winchester Cathedral.

It is possible that some of these relics represent sightings of a south coast mermaid. Veasta is the name of a mermaid-like creature seen periodically in the sea off Chesil Beach and Portland. It is reported to be 12ft high, half seahorse and half fish, resembling the mermaid of legend. She was first spotted in 1457 and then again in 1757. In 1965 it was again seen by two witnesses at Church Ope Cove. The last recorded appearance was in August 1995 off Chesil Beach by Martin Ball (see *Dorset Life* magazine, No. 218, May 1997). A depiction of Veasta stands in stone by the Ferrybridge Inn, Weymouth (see Fig.5).

The white hart or stag is another illusive beast of the folklore of Britain. In Dorset the magical beast seems to have been sighted. Blackmoor Vale is still known as the Vale of the White Hart, which is said to haunt it. You can find "White Hart" inns and pubs at Longham, Blandford, Burley, Ringwood, Dorchester and elsewhere, probably remembrances of previous apparitions.

As recently as 1962 a white "fairy hind' was seen by Lord Kilmersdon on the Mendip hills and was followed for more than a mile. Perhaps we should not, after all, look on folklore tales of magical creatures as simply the result of the imagination of simple medieval folk.

Another mythical creature of these Isles is of course the Unicorn. This magical beast had a horn thought to have medicinal powers of healing. The animal usually represents purity and was taken on by early Christians as a symbol for the Virgin Mary. In Dorset we have the Unicorn Inn at Bayford. A unicorn can be seen carved on a bench end in the church at East Quantoxhead, Somerset.

Giants will be looked at later in Chapter 10, as they are strongly associated with prehistoric mounds. Dragons will again be encountered in Chapter 12, with an array of gargoyles and other relics, making the link between them and ley lines.

Let us now turn our attention to much smaller creatures of folklore: the fairy folk.

Faíríes

> *"Come follow, follow me,*
> *You fairy elves that be:*
> *Which circle on the greene,*
> *Come follow Mab you queene,*
> *Hand in hand let's dance around,*
> *For this place is fairye ground"*
> *"The Fairy Queen"*, Anon, 1658.

Stories of a race of "little people' are universal and folklore involving them goes back many centuries. There seems to be a vast variety of types and an equally varied array of moods shown by them. Some are mischievous, whilst others offer protection and healing. They are strongly associated with ancient sites, particularly barrows which are often known as fairy mounds.

Dorset has countless fairy tales and sightings. Let us take a look at a few associated with definite localities.

Place names give us clues to previous encounters with fairies. Puck is another name for a fairy, and places with the elements "puck', "poke' or "puk' can be taken as

Fig. 6. Fairies dancing in a circle, from an old English chapbook. Note the door in the mound, the toadstool and the Green Man in the tree.

being associated with them. Poxwell, near Weymouth, was still known as Pokeswell in 1906, meaning "fairy well". Pokesdown, in Bournemouth, is traceable as a name back to 1300. It comes from the Old English and means "hill or down haunted by a puck or goblin". The Puckstone near Studland is named after fairy folk (see *"Ancient Stones of Dorset'*, Plate 32).

Chapmans Pool, on the Purbeck coast, was originally Schortmannes Poole. Literally "short man's pool' this may have derived from dwarf or goblin folklore. A field at Wyke Regis, Weymouth, was known as Camp de Pokulchurche in 1460, meaning"goblin's camp/church'. The Old English word *"bugge'* means hobgoblin and the villages of Bugley and Buckshaw may have derived their names from it. Similarly, the names Pucksbarry and Puckysway on 1451 maps of Winfrith Newburgh stem from folklore.

Doรรet Fairy Folklore

"I feel that the only true tales
are fairy tales".
J Foster Forbes, "The Unchronicled Past", 1938

The village of Stourpaine nestles quietly in a river valley west of Blandford. At the church of the Holy Trinity there is a small door at the foot of the bell tower (Plate

Plate 11. Stourpaine's fairy door.

29

Plate 12. The barrows where fairies danced on Bottlebrush Down.

Fig. 7. The fairy face at Charminster church.
See also Plate 13.

11). Superstition has it that fairies and elves ring the church bells. The door was supposedly made to allow them to go up to the bells. They ring them by using in some way the dew of the grass. It is said that one can see tiny drops of dew that they have dropped as they hurried up the stairs.

It is also said that if the fairies see footprints of a human on the grass then that person shall have bad luck and that the bells will no longer be rung.

At Wimborne St Giles there are two barrows of interest up on Bottlebush Down. They sit on either side of the road, just east of where the Cursus crosses it (grid ref:019159). Plate 12 shows the barrows. It is recorded that a curate of Sixpenny Handley, the late Rev A.R.T. Bruce, lay down to rest on one of the barrows. He was astonished to then see a "crowd of little people" . They wore leather jerkins and danced around him!

 A record of 1629 speaks of the Buckbarrow at Ryme Intrinseca being haunted by a "bug or goblin'. A barrow at Corfe Castle called "Grimberry' was haunted by a grim or goblin. Three local fields also bear this name on a 1772 map (grid ref:966838 to 968834). Are these fields where the locals saw the fairies?

Around Dorset many gargoyles, church carvings and other relics appear to depict fairy-type creatures. Obviously the medieval masons were still superstitious enough to include them in their work. Perhaps they were portraying images from personal experience.

Two images deserve special mention and both are easily found.

In the parish church of St Mary the Virgin, in the village of Charminster, north of Dorchester, is a carving of interest. Tucked away in a corner of the west tower, near to the font, is a small pixie-type face, about 9ft above the floor (see Plate 13 and Fig. 7). It dates from the 16th century and the church guide describes it as a "devil's head', probably due to the horns. But the ears are elf-like and the expression of its

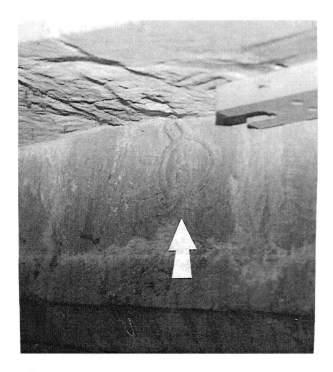

Plate 13. Location of the fairy carving, above the font at the base of the tower, Charminster church.

face is far from evil or menacing. Here, again, the mason has left us a reminder of his otherworldly imagination.

"Nature is imagination itself"
William Blake (1799)

The second example of note is in the Choir of Christchurch Priory. One of the large wooden panels at one end of the stalls displays the face shown in Plate 14. At first sight it may appear to be the devil with horns. But it will be seen that what at first appear to be horns are in fact the creature's ears. A second possibility is that it may be the face of a green man, a woodland spirit, who we will encounter in Chapter 11. Although there is leaf-like foliage coming from behind his head, he does not have any coming out of his nose or mouth, a characteristic of the green man.

Plate 14. The face in wood in Christchurch Priory.

I believe this to be a medieval representation of a fairy-like being. The harsh image and the horn-like ears is due, I believe, to fairies being regarded as the devil's followers by the medieval Church.

This leads us nicely into a tale resulting from the witch trials, where contact with fairy folk was seen to be equally damning as Satan himself.

In 1566 an examination of a Dorset man, John Walsh of Netherbury, resulted in his "confession' which contained references to fairie folk:

"the man is bewitched: He says that he knew it partly by the fairies, and says there are three kinds, white, green, and black.....He speaks with them upon hills, where there are great heaps of earth, as namely as Dorsetshire.....at the noon and midnight he visits them......the black fairies be the worst."

"Oh prythee come and dance with me
Around the ring where fay
And elfish sprites in revelry
Their nightly gambols play" .
"Fairy Rings", old Dorset song.

So called 'fairy lights' have been recorded for centuries and probably witnessed for much longer. Strange lights over water, wells and barrows have been attributed to fairies. We shall look at these more closely when we look into earth energies in Chapter 13.

The Demise of the Fairies

African, Greek, Buddhist, Amerindian and European cultures alike contain fairy folklore. Generally the fairy is a being with a passion for life, dancing and merry making, magical, benevolent yet punishing if crossed. The fairies are shy of human company except at moments of *their* choosing and they appear to have strict moral and ethical codes. Tales and sightings of them clearly fostered the belief of country folk that the land was alive and populated by all manner of magical spirits.

Unfortunately, by the Middle Ages the fairy folk had been demonised, seen as allies of the Devil. All through history, though, it is recorded that the golden age of the fairies was some time previous, always somewhere in past. Yet still the folklore persists, as perhaps do the fairies. The imagination of Shelley, Shakespeare, Yeats, Keats and other romantic poets were all moved to write about "little people'. Perhaps their keen sense and appreciation of magic and Nature took them through the veil into the realms of the fairies; perhaps they wrote from personal experience! To remove this veil between us and the magic of Nature we simply need imagination, belief in things other than the mind has led us to accept and, above all, a respect and humility for the Earth and it's inhabitants, both seen and unseen.

"When a house happens to be built on a
fairy-track, the doors on the front and back,
or the windows if they are in line of the track,
cannot be closed at night, for the fairies
must march through" .
Irish Priest.

Chapter Four

Sacred Symbols

"Old stories tell, how Hercules
A dragon slew at Lerna,
With seven heads, and fourteen eyes,
To see and well discern-a" .
from *"Dragon of Wantley"*, 1699.

Man has used symbols to express his spirituality since prehistoric times, when images were painted inside caves. Over thousands of years Man's expression of the gods and goddesses evolved, and by Greek and Roman times complex symbols had been incorporated into ritual practices. We find relics with phallic symbolism greatly developed alongside a myriad of other designs and icons that were deemed sacred.

It must be realised that an object used to represent a god, goddess or an aspect of them, was itself venerated. The gods of the universe were seen to impress their very characteristics upon an object which acted as their earthly representative - *the object became the deity.*

We will look through the relics that have been left to us from earlier ages in Dorset, and try and see what can be interpreted from them. Goddess symbology and phallic symbolism are dealt with separately in later chapters, such is the wealth of material available. In this chapter we review symbolism not encountered in detail later.

Dragons and Saints

We have already looked at Dorset folklore associated with Dragons. I have indeed suggested that dragons were originally regarded as benevolent beasts. In China they were responsible for controlling the weather and ensuring the rains arrived. The Aztecs had Kukulcan, a god whose sign was the feathered serpent, resembling the European flying dragon. The Romans had both good and bad dragons, yet recognised and respected the beast's strength by using a dragon on their banner for a cohort, a division of approximately 500 men.

The tale of Odysseus has dragons in it. An interesting passage occurs when the hero is returning from Troy:

"You can see the ridges now, where this disgusting great dragon coiled his tail around the hill."

This perhaps gives us a clue of how dragons were associated with the land, even representing aspects of the elements of Nature. In Chapter 13 we shall look into this link between earth energies, ley lines and dragons.

Unfortunately for the poor old dragon, the Church came to associate the beast with the devil, evil and paganism. The dragon came under attack via the Bible and its entourage of dragon-slaying saints.

I think it is somewhat ironic that churches were built dedicated to St Michael, St George and other dragon killers to stamp out pagan practices, yet it is their very architecture that ensures the survival of the dragon's form.

Plate 15. St George and the dragon at Cattistock church.

There are, however, some vestiges of Dragon symbology that show us how the dragon was regarded as a beneficial force even after the dragon-slayers arrived. For instance, at Samford Courtney there is a carving of a dragon with vine foliage coming out of it's mouth, symbolic of the fertilising influence of earth energies. At Knook, Wiltshire, a dragon guards the tree of life. Much seems to be down to local interpretation of legends, as well as the influence perhaps of the masons doing the carving. At Lullington, Somerset, we find a dragon not guarding the tree of life, but *eating* it!

The anti-dragon propaganda was no doubt encouraged by Bible quotes given by energetic priests fostering the temptations of the Devil. There are rich pickings in the Bible for such work:

Isaiah 27:1 - *"The Lord shall slay the dragon that is in the sea."*

Psalms 74:13 - *""thou breakest the heads of dragons.."*

Ezekiel 29:3 - *"The great dragon that lieth in the midst of the rivers, which hath said, my river is mine"*

Revelations 12:7 - *"Michael and his angels fought against the dragon.....the dragon was cast out."*

The Church's anti-dragon, anti-pagan campaign was fostered, no doubt, by the numerous raids by Vikings and Danes, who had the dragon head on the front of their ships. Churches were looted and relieved of large quantities of gold by these "heathens of the dragon".

St George was introduced to Europe via the Crusaders. He is reputed to have been a Roman officer in Palestine in 3rd century AD. In Cattistock church, here in Dorset, a huge painting can be seen above the font. Plate 15 shows the saint killing the dragon.

St Michael is the Bible's champion dragon slayer. In Dorset he is well represented. Churches dedicated to him occur at Stinsford, Gussage St Michael, Anderson, Askerswell, Verwood and elsewhere. We have already seen him in Stinsford (Plate 2) on a much weathered carving. At Gussage St Michael church he is shown on stained glass windows. Plate 16 shows him slaying the beast, whilst Plate 111 shows the dragon again. At St Michael's, Poole Hill, Bournemouth, a large Victorian carving shows a winged archangel Michael slaying a dragon.

Scenes of the saint and the dragon could formerly be seen on the crosses at Rampisham and Leigh (see *Ancient Stones of Dorset*, pages 173 and 191). On the outside of Preston church, near Weymouth, a figure can be spearing a dragon at the

Plate 16. St Michael slaying the dragon in the church at Gussage St Michael.

base of the window arch, next to the porch. High up on the roof boss in bay six of Milton Abbey, the persistent saint is yet again depicted subduing the poor dragon. At Shroton church, north of Blandford, two dragons are depicted with St George. One is on a wall memorial near the door, whilst the other is in the stained glass window above the altar. At Child Okeford a fire-breathing dragon is seen below the saint in one of the north windows. A beautiful stained glass window in Christchurch Priory shows a winged St George slaying a red dragon.

Plate 17. Two dragon-like gargoyles outside St Peters in Dorchester.

There are over 600 English churches dedicated to St Michael, the warrior archangel. A large number are on hill tops and certainly replaced earlier pagan sites. Later on in Chapter 12 we look at the connection between some of the Dorset examples and ley lines, the "dragon paths" themselves.

> *"Here I am, St George*
> *From Britain I did spring,*
> *And I will fight the fiery dragon*
> *My wonders to begin".*
> From mumming play, Oxfordshire.

On a more general level, dragons can be seen adorning many church towers in Dorset, such as Cattistock, Durweston and Mappowder, to name but three.

The ones shown in Plate 17 are relatively close to ground level for inspection. They are outside St Peters in Dorchester. Two excellently carved and unworn ones can be

Fig. 8. Dragon symbology on Dorset heraldry. A: a griffin on the coat of arms of the Daccomb family of Corfe Castle; B: Dragon or wyvern on coat of arms of the Sawbridge-Erle-Drax family of Charborough. (From Hutchins, 1774.)

seen at St John's church in Weymouth (Plate 114). A 17th century coffin lid in the chapel of Bindon Abbey has two wyvern dragons with interlocking tails. At Affpuddle church two weathered dragons can be seen near the base of the tower.

The Heraldic Dragon

In early medieval times heraldry was making its mark. Its growth coincided with the Crusades. Heraldic devices proved necessary to identify both friend and foe during a battle where knights were covered from head to toe in armour. It is ironic that whilst the peasantry were being led to believe that dragons represented evil and the Devil, a counter culture existed amongst the rich and titled that used dragon symbology to represent strength and virtue. Even though he was a Christian, King Arthur of legend continued to use the dragon on his banner. The Christian Emperor Constantine II employed dragon emblems. The Red Dragon, of course, is still today the Welsh emblem.

In Dorset we find titled families that use dragon symbology. A wyvern is on the Tilly coat of arms, whilst a griffin is to be seen on the Botreux arms. Fig. 8 shows two more Dorset examples. The arms of Daccomb of Corfe Castle date from Henry VIII and shows a griffin. A wyvern dragon adorns the Charborough arms.

Survivals

Dragon symbology, perhaps surprisingly, survived into modern times in festivals and ceremonies. In many parts of the country, including Dorset, the dragon was a central figure in hobby horse processions and mumming plays, remnants of ancient fertility rites. In the 1860's antiquarian R. Chambers records: "In rogation [beating the bounds] processions in England there was always carried the image of a dragon". Again this appears to be a reminder of distant fertility festivals, when people paid homage to the earth.

Hobby horse plays were performed in Dorset at Christmas at Bridport and nearby Symondsbury. In the plays characters are killed, then restored to life, which is surely symbolic of the "death" of the old year and the "rebirth" of Nature around the winter solstice. In his excellent book *"Here Be Dragons"*, Ralph Whitlock links the hobby horse to the dragon, citing old records of Salisbury, Norwich and Belgium festivities where the hobby horse was either preceded or accompanied by a dragon.

The persistent dragon refuses to lie down and even today we find his form on many a pub sign, examples being the Green Dragon at Marlborough, Wilts, and at Alderbury, Salisbury. In the churchyard of Wimborne Minster, the cross incorporated into the war memorial has on one side of it a scene with St Michael once again slaying the dragon. This depiction is symbolic of the triumph of good over evil, the evil in this case not being paganism, but our wartime enemies (see

Plate 116). It is perhaps fitting that fine dragon gargoyles adorn the tower of the modern Bournemouth Crematorium, a place of fire and of passing over to the otherworld.

"St Pedroc led the docile creatures down
To the sandy, seashore, where amid the waves
The last Cornish dragon swam away,
Bound for what strand or desert island far
We none of us can tell" .
Cornish dragon tale.

The Celtic Cross

Although now considered an entirely Christian symbol, the cross is, in fact, very ancient. It was used in Bronze Age burial mounds some 4,000 years ago. The Maoris had a cross representing the moon goddess; The tree of life was shown in the form of the tau cross by the Mayans; The Egyptian ankh is a variation of the cross.

Dorset's stone crosses are dealt with extensively in *"Ancient Stones of Dorset"*, but it is the sacred symbology of the Celtic variety which we will look into more closely here, space and time not allowing me to do so previously.

To the pre-Christian pagans the cross symbolised the sun, eternal life and the productive powers of Nature. The cross was regarded as having phallic significance. In AD 336, Iamblichus wrote "crosses are signs of productive energy and provocation to a continuation of the world". It was regarded as such a pagan symbol that the early Church actually forbade the use of the cross amongst its followers!

Fig. 9. Delicate interlacing on a fragment of Celtic cross, set into the wall of the vicarage at Gillingham. (Drawn by the author from a photograph).

42

Plate 18. Modern wheel cross in the Celtic style. Charminster Cemetery, Bournemouth.

Plate 19. Another modern example of the tradition of the Celtic cross in the churchyard at Woodlands, north of Wimborne.

Sense prevailed, though, the Church recognising the spiritual "pulling power" of the symbol, enabling the beautiful Celtic and Saxon crosses to be developed.

The Celtic wheel cross, modern examples of which are shown here, owes nothing to its origin to the crucifixion. It is a solar symbol and was taken on by early Christians as representing Christ as the Divine Light. The centre of the wheel cannot turn, yet everything moves around it. Due to centrifugal forces, the movement is outwards in a turning wheel, here representing the divine radiance.

The cross shaft below was seen as the world axis, the Axis Mundi, connecting heaven to earth. Above this was mounted the wheel cross, originally seen as the solar orb shinning down on the earth, but now representing a different sun, the "Son of God".

Fig. 10. Saxon cross shaft at Whitecombe.

Anyone visiting the fine 12th century font at Toller Fratrum could surely not miss the ornate stone plaitwork around the top of it, and it is the ornamentation of Celtic stonework that is arguably it's most impressive and noteworthy feature. Delicate spirals, plaitwork and knotwork are all characteristics of Celtic art. Plaitwork no doubt comes from weaving of cloth, in itself profoundly symbolic. There are usually no loose ends, symbolising the continuity of spirit throughout time and space. Fig. 9 gives a Dorset example, at Gillingham.

Knotwork is likewise filled with symbolism. The knots are endless and thus cannot be undone. Here the meaning appears to be the knots that bind the soul to this world. Examples are shown in Plate 1, 18 and 19. The oldest shown here is that in Fig. 10. It is a drawing of one of the 10th century fragments of a Saxon cross shaft in Whitcombe church, south of Dorchester. (See also "*Ancient Stones of Dorset*" Plates 96, 127 and 144 for examples at Whitcombe, East Stour and Todber respectively).

Plate 20. Runes on the modern cross at Studland.
(Photograph by Ghermaine Knight).

46

The Celtic tradition continues in Dorset with the inspired incorporation of Celtic knotwork on the new cross at Studland by local mason Trevor Heysom.

A visit to the churchyard of Shroton church is worthwhile. A small open air shrine can be found through a gate in the SW corner. A tall Celtic-style cross, dated 1900, is the focus. Woods behind the enclosure add to the atmosphere of the place.

Runes

Runes are an ancient alphabetic script, much publicised by Tolkien in *"The Lord of the Rings"*. They were used throughout northern Europe and Scandinavia by the Anglo-Saxons and the Vikings. Many Viking runic stones still stand today as a testament to not only their use as an alphabet, but also the magical properties they were thought to possess. Vikings carried runic marks into battle on their helmets and shields. The runes were also used for divination, and indeed they still are today.

In Dorset we find today remains of the ancient runic scripts. In 1841 the greater part of the Saxon Minster at Wareham was demolished. Inscriptions were found on five memorial stones, thought to be of Romano-British age. Barbara York, in *"Wessex in the Early Middle Ages"* is of the view that they come from a Celtic burial ground which proceeded the Saxon Minster. They imply that prominent people with Celtic names were still being commemorated in a Christian manner (for the stones have a mixture of runic and Latin characters) even after the conquest of the area by the, still pagan, Anglo-Saxons. Fig. 11 shows the runic marks which can be seen on display in Lady St Mary, Wareham (see also pages 100-102 of *"Ancient Stones of Dorset"*).

The tradition of the runes happily continues to this day in Dorset. At Studland the new village cross was erected in 1976, mounted on top of the original Saxon cross base. On the south side of the shaft are runic characters, spelling out, according to the guide book obtainable in the church, the inscription "I created this world and I sustain this world" (see Plate 20).

Fig. 11. Runic characters on stones in Lady St Mary, Wareham.

Top: Fig. 12. Stone head from Portisham.
Bottom: Fig 13. Two stone heads from Shipton Gorge, now on display in the
County Museum, Dorchester.

48

The Cult of the Head

The Romano-British, as indeed the Celts before them, held the head to be of spiritual significance, and skulls were likewise ritually revered. Stone heads, sacred skulls and masks symbolised divine power. Water drunk from a skull was supposed to have magical powers and indeed many sacred wells and springs have skulls associated with them, such as at St Decuman's Well, Watchet, in Somerset and a well at Holywell, in Flint. Celtic and Romano-British sites at Steep Holm, Lamyatt and Cadbury (all in Somerset) have yielded stone heads.

Head cults may have endured due to several Celtic myths, in which severed heads speak and converse with heroes or else give prophecies. The skull of an ancestor would also be seen as a link with not only their departed body, but also the soul and spirit of the deceased.

In Dorset, the head was immortalised in stone and several examples are known. Most have ended up on display in the County Museum, and a visit is recommended.

Plate 21. The font at Stoke Abbot, showing heads.

Fig. 14. Some of the heads on the font at Toller Fratrum.

Fig. 12 is one such head of uncertain age in Purbeck stone from Portesham. The phallic nose is a feature of many Celtic stone heads.

Fig. 13 shows two more heads on display at the museum. These have been regarded as Celtic and were found by the Chaplin family in the 1960's at Shipton Gorge. One was in fact sitting on a wall and locals would pat it for good luck. The other was dug up during road widening or house building operations.

The heads both appeared to have been deliberately blackened. This is interesting because real skulls blacken when left in the sun. The blackening of the stones may have been to sympathise with the state of real skulls left out to dry.

The tradition of displaying severed heads for public view was continued by the Church. Many human heads can be found carved in Dorset churches, too numerous to list here. For instance, heads can be seen on corbel tables at the church at Studland and St Nicholas at Worth Matravers. Heads are also found either side of the doors at the parish churches of Belchalwell, Affpuddle and Corfe Castle.

Rodney Castleden, in *"The Cerne Giant"*, gives convincing evidence that the giant's left hand once held a severed head, surviving still as a low knoll.

Another legacy of the reverence of the skull could be the well known legend of the Bettiscombe Skull. It is said to have screamed in the past and to remove it from

Bettiscombe Manor, near the Dorset-Devon border, would bring ill-fortune upon the occupants. The skull has been analysed and found to be around 2000 years old, once belonging to a woman in her twenties. It is thought to have possibly come from Pilsden Pen, a Celtic sanctuary on manor land.

Numerous Christian carvings are those of heads, be they of saints, demons or animals. Gargoyles may have originated from the practice of publicly displaying the heads of defeated enemies and executed criminals. Two 12th century fonts in Dorset show detached heads. Plate 21 shows the Norman font in the church at Stoke Abbot, north of Bridport. Several heads are carved on it, and are in the style of the "grotesque", as opposed to the rendering of more saintly features. One face could possibly be that of a Wodehouse, and it is shown in Plate 107.

The other font is that of Toller Fratrum, just west of Maiden Newton. Fig. 14 shows four of the detached heads, which are carved in a Celtic style, with elongated noses.

"and take my head and bury it at
White Mound, London, facing France,
said Bendigeid Vran.....
And no invasion came from across the
sea while the head was in that concealment" .
From *The Mabinogion.*

In recent years, hundreds of grotesque carved heads have come to light in the West Riding of Yorkshire. Known as the "Bradford Heads", they were carved in a Celtic style, but analysis of many has shown them to be of Victorian age. The head cult seems to have amazingly survived in some form into modern times. And what of countless headless ghosts: more memories of severed head cults? Dorset is full of folklore of ghosts either carrying their decapitated heads, or else solitary spectral heads. One can perhaps speculate a link between these apparitions and ancient head cults.

I recommend the reader to view the "Flying Angel" in the church at Winterbourne Steepleton. It is a Saxon relief 25 x 15 inches in size and is mounted on an internal wall. The angel is in fact holding what looks like a severed head or, more accurately, a skull. Is this an attempt by early Christians to either Christianise or stamp out old pagan reverence of the skull?

Plate 22. "The Flying Angel", a Saxon relief in the church at Winterbourne Steepleton. Note the skull being carried by the angel.

The Mystic Spiral

"At its most abstract level of meanings,
the spiral may have expressed the concept
of life energy, of cosmic energy and life
rhythms with which early man was concerned".
Irish archaeologist Michael Morris, 1974.

There is a traditional folk song in the West Country telling us to "dance the mystic spiral", that it will "take us home". This is a modern legacy of the sacredness of this ancient symbol.

Stones in countless barrows, cairns and temples have spirals engraved on them. An Ice Age mammoth, dating to 16,000 BC, had spirals carved into it's ivory. Other spirals adorn cave paintings across Europe. Nearer home, broken Neolithic pots found at Skara Brae, Scotland, show spiral decoration. A mace head, 4,500 years old from Norfolk, shows spiralling.

Newgrange has the world's finest display of spiral engravings. Dozens of intricately carved spirals and other symbols cover huge stones within and outside the Neolithic barrow. George Terence Meaden has made an exhaustive study of spiral symbology and his results are given in his book "*Goddess of the Stones*". He sees the spiral as a symbol of birth, death and rebirth, a link between life and afterlife.

He concludes that left-handed spirals represent the birth-death-rebirth cycle, but also are symbolic of the Goddess, the feminine, passivity and the moon. Right-handed spirals he sees as also representing the birth-rebirth cycle, but additionally symbolise male gods, the masculine, activity and the sun.

Many see the spiral as representing the opening of the womb of the Goddess. It can also be seen as the universe spiralling out from the Divine centre. A symbol frequently accompanying the spiral is the lozenge. This is taken to represent fertility, the pubic mound and the vulva of the Earth Goddess. In Dorset we have a beautiful example of the ancient reverence of the spiral and lozenge.

In 1971 Tim Roberts picked up a piece of chalk protruding from one of the ramparts of Maiden Castle. The small fragment shows spirals and curvi-triangular markings. Fig. 15 shows the stone, alongside some of the markings on one of the large Newgrange stones. The similarity is immediately apparent. The Maiden Castle

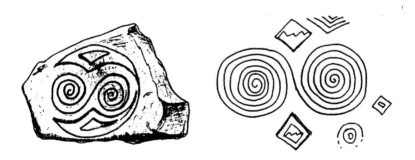

Fig. 15. Spirals on stones from Maiden Castle, Dorset (left) and Newgrange (right). The Maiden Castle stone is on display in the County Museum, Dorchester.

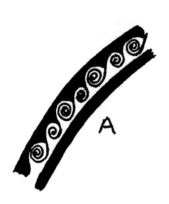

Fig. 16. Romano-British finds from Dorset displaying spirals. A: Mosaic border from Roman villa at Witchampton (now in the British Museum); B: A carved stone from the townhouse at Colliton Park, Dorchester, now in the County Museum.

spirals are left-handed, what Meaden concludes to be Goddess symbology. The Newgrange example is right-handed, symbolic of the male gods. The similar position of the accompanying lozenges is surely no coincidence. A Neolithic enclosure was uncovered on Maiden Castle, so the spiralling may be comparable in age to Newgrange.

The spiral continued to be used into Celtic and Roman times, but on a reduced scale, often little more than decoration. Its use in temples and shrines, however, does show us that its spiritual and ritual power was still appreciated. Fig. 16 shows two Dorset examples of Romano-British finds displaying spirals. On the left is a section of the border surrounding a scene depicting the Goddess Venus on a mosaic pavement at the Roman villa at Witchampton, north of Wimborne. On the right is a drawing of a large stone found at the Romano-British townhouse at Colliton Park, Dorchester (see "*Ancient Stones of Dorset*", pages 13 and 113). A carved head with either spiralling horns or head-dress can be seen.

With the oncoming of Christianity, the spiral appears to have regained some of its former importance. The beautifully decorated Celtic knotwork evolved from the early prehistoric spiral images. The lozenge also continued to be associated with it, as is seen on the cross at Moone, County Kildare, which has both symbols side by side. The spiral of the Earth Goddess became the symbol of the universe radiating from the Father God. Fig. 17 shows a section of the 9-11th century Saxon cross in the church at Todber, SW of Shaftesbury. Spirals such as this are known as "spectacle spirals". Copper and bronze pins dating from the Bronze Age display these double-headed spirals.

In Norman and Medieval times the spiral retained a foothold in the architecture of the Church. Fig. 18 shows just a few of many examples of spirals to be found in churches right across Dorset. Perhaps your next visit to a church may turn up more of these ancient symbols. Fig. 18 shows some interesting points. "A" again displays the double-headed spiral, seen at Todber. But note the triangle above: is this a legacy of the prehistoric triangles and lozenges, discussed earlier?

Fig. 17. Section of the Saxon cross in the church at Todber.

"B" shows a ram's head, with spiralling horns. This perhaps beckons us to look at why Man took on the spiral as a symbol of birth, death and rebirth. Neolithic Man would have seen all around him spirals in Nature, to him the very body of the Goddess. Snails, sea shells, animal horns, whirl-pools and whirl-winds, ammonite fossils, plants and even sleeping snakes took on spiral form. This surely inspired our ancestors to regard the spiral as sacred, hence its depiction on countless figurines and stones.

In Fig. 18 "C" we have a sketch of a 12th century capital found during excavations at Shaftesbury Abbey. The double spiral is again evident, but note not only the face in the scene, but also the phallic nature of the carving: The spirals can be taken as either eyes or testicles. Phallic symbolism is dealt with in more detail in the next chapter.

Several spirals can be seen around the tower of St Mary's church, Charminster. They are the monogram of Thomas Trenchard, who built the 16th century tower.

The spiral has certainly inspired the imagination of people for thousands of years. Even in post-medieval times this enigmatic symbol still pulls at our subconscious. A remarkable gargoyle with a spiral on it's forehead can be seen on the font at Lostwithiel, Cornwall. Glastonbury Tor has a legendary spiral path leading up it. Dowsers for hundreds of years have recorded the spiralling nature of earth energies. The White Well at Glastonbury has a modern spiral as it's focus (Plate 23).

Prior to the birth of our daughter Leela, my pregnant wife Ghermaine suddenly had the strong urge to paint spiral symbols. She was unaware of the goddess-birth-

Fig. 18. Examples of the use of spirals in church architecture. A: The Norman font at Toller Porcorum. B: Ram's head seen on the same font. C: Capital with stylised face incorporating spirals at Shaftesbury Abbey.

rebirth symbology at that time. It appears that the archetypal image must have already been in her psyche and was triggered by her pregnancy.

Fig. 19 is a modern work depicting the primal Goddess. The double spiral of birth, life, death and rebirth is on her belly. It expresses, says Ghermaine ""the cycle of the Goddess and the polarities of the Universe; yin-yang, birth-death, pleasure and pain".

The sensual and surreal quality of this depiction is characteristic of ancient Goddess images and figurines.

Yet the story of the spiral is not yet done. Let us look at it's offspring, the maze.

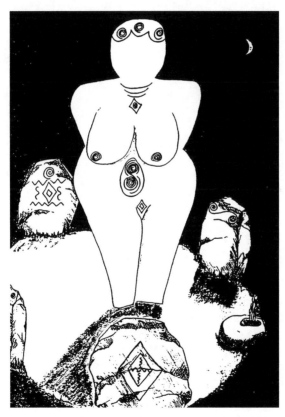

*Fig. 19. 'The Goddess of the Circle', by Ghermaine Knight
(1996 Copyright: G. Knight)*

Plate 23. The spiral at the White Well, Glastonbury. This modern work continues the long tradition of the reverence of the spiral. (Photograph: Ghermaine Knight)

Mazes and Labyrinths

"The nine men's morris is filled up with mud
And the quaint mazes in the wanton green
For lack of tread are indistinguishable" .
Shakespeare, *"A Midsummer Night's Dream"*.

The spiralling maze has been around at least since Bronze Age times. As symbols on caves, stones and other relics they are almost universal. Plate 24 shows a design in the rock face at Rocky Valley, near Tintagel, Cornwall, though many more occur.

Plate 24. Rock carving at Rocky Valley, Cornwall.

The Greeks created the archetypal labyrinth at Knossos, on Crete, around 1600 BC. Legend says it was created to house the Minotaur, a half-man and half-bull beast. The Romans, too, built labyrinths, one being uncovered from the ash at Pompeii.

In many a legend, mazes and labyrinths must often be overcome by heroes. Mazes represent a passage from the profound to the sacred, the trials of life before enlightenment is attained. Before one can obtain this goal one must encounter the darker sides of ourselves, the Minotaur hidden within the maze of our minds.

In southern England we have some surviving examples of ancient mazes. On St Catherine's Hill Winchester, is the Mizmaze which is at least Medieval in age. It is of turf, 96 ft square. On Breamore Down (grid ref:142203) another maze 87 ft in diameter is thought to be of medieval Christian design.

Here in Dorset mazes were built. Just west of Puddletown is Troy Town Farm (grid ref:738939). The name occurs across Britain and is thought to indicate a former maze in the locality. The name is considered to drive from the city of Troy, whose labyrinth-like defences were invincible.

> *"The maze pattern has been shown to*
> *represent "Spiral Castle" or "Troy Town",*
> *where the sacred Sun-King goes after*
> *death and from which, if he is lucky,*
> *he returns" .*
> Robert Graves, *"The White Goddess".*

At Leigh, north west of Cerne Abbas, Ordinance Survey maps still show "Miz Maze" just outside the village (grid ref:619083). Now completely eroded, in the 18th century John Hutchins saw "a circular form, 30 ft in diameter". The former maze has been dated as Medieval, but may possibly be earlier.

At Pimperne, near Blandford, another maze was built. Fortunately for us the antiquarian John Aubrey left us a plan (see Fig.20). In 1686 he wrote that the maze was "much used by the young people on Holydaies and by ye School-boies". The maze was defined by 1 ft high ridges either side of the paths. Regrettably, the whole maze was ploughed up in 1730. Aubrey recognised that antiquity of the origin of mazes and labyrinths. He considered that "......we received these mazes from our Danish ancestors".

Fig. 20. John Aubrey's
17th century plan of the
Pimperne Maze.

Plate 25. One of the several spirals seen inside and without the tower of Charminster church, near Dorchester. (Photograph by Ghermaine knight).

"This is as strange a maze as e"er
men trod" .
William Shakespeare, *"The Tempest"*.

The Circle

The circle has long been regarded as having major significance as a spiritual and ritual symbol. This was probably due to the fact that Man is surrounded in Nature by circular forms. The sun and the moon were highly venerated by cultures right across the world, their glowing circles (for one cannot discern them as three-dimensional with the naked eye) illuminating day and night. Prehistoric cave paintings and pottery show sun and moon symbols. The Neolithic barrow at Newgrange has numerous circles, some of which may have represented the sun or moon. A cut down tree displays circular annular rings and early Man would have perhaps regarded them as signs of the cycles of the Earth Goddess. Ripples on the water radiate outwards in circles, and even the humble spider weaves circular webs.

Plate 26. Sunset at the Grey Mare and Her Colts. The sun's circular orb would have been venerated from the earliest times.

The Egyptian Goddess Isis had a disc on her head-dress, the solar orb. Eastern mandalas and the yin yang symbol are enclosed within circles. Amerindian medicine wheels and sun dances are circular, as too, of course, many prehistoric stone circles here in Britain.

The circle is an image of wholeness and eternity. It has no beginning nor end. It represents the world, the cosmos and, indeed, the perfection of spirit Man aspires to. Buddhists have a symbol of two overlapping circles called the mana, which symbolise the sun and the moon. The solar archetype represents the inner mind and consciousness, the lunar one the outer world of the physical and appearances. The coming together of the two symbolises balance and harmony.

The circle was taken in classical times to represent the divine and many Greek and Roman temples, such as at Delphi, were round constructions, symbolic of the order of the cosmos, reflecting its perfection.

In Britain, the Bronze Age stone circles represent to me a microcosm, man epitomising the universe. Inside is a place apart from the world outside, a sacred, ceremonial and meditative locality. Although most stone circles are not in fact exactly circular (often being ellipses) they still symbolise, like the circle, a sacred enclosed area, its boundaries having no beginning or ending. The central focus of them is an analogy of our own spiritual centre.

Fig 21. An old engraving of cup-and-ring marks from Northumberland

Stonehenge is very nearly circular and represents one of Man's finest attempts to reflect the cosmic order here on earth. Within the henge at Avebury are two smaller circles of stones, possibly depicting the concepts of the sun and moon, yin and yang, the Sky Gods and the Earth Goddess, balance. Silbury Hill, nearby, is circular in plan, as is Old Sarum, Salisbury.

The cup-and -ring marks inscribed on many stones in Britain are the enigmas of archaeology. These strange prehistoric markings are mainly found in northern Britain, but some have been found in the south. In Dorset, faint circular cup marks were found at Badbury Barrow, accompanied by dagger carvings. Fig. 21 shows an 1860 engraving of some cup-and-ring marks from Northumberland and the circular symbology is plain to see.

In Dorset, the henge at Mount Pleasant, just east of Dorchester (see *"Ancient Stones of Dorset"*, pages 136-9) incorporated an elaborate design of concentric circles of wooden posts, allowing astronomical observations of celestial objects, according to John North in *"Stonehenge"*. Fig. 22 shows the central enclosure with the circular plan of the post holes.

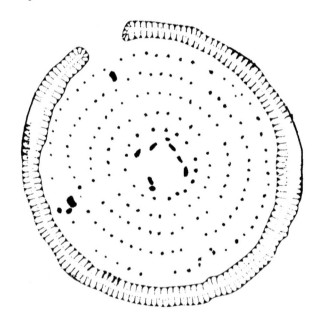

Fig. 22. The circular design of the post holes at Mount Pleasant henge, Dorset.

In Dorset one is rarely far away from round barrows, which are spread over the landscape in huge numbers. These Bronze Age mounds are circular in plan and, according to dowsers, are foci for earth energies. Chapter 10 takes a closer look at barrows.

Within these barrows we in fact find more evidence of the reverence of the circle. The Clandon Barrow sits on Clandon Hill, just west of Maiden Castle (grid ref:656890). In 1882 excavations uncovered on of the richest barrow finds ever in Britain. Among the relics were gold objects, including the shale mace head shown in Fig. 23(A). The two circular discs inlaid into it are of gold. The object was clearly ritual as it is too delicate to have been used seriously as a weapon. In the same barrow was found an incense dish, shown in Fig. 23(B). On it's surface are eight concentric circles. This ritual relic again links the circle with Man's spiritual quest.

A remarkable ancient stone from Eype, Dorset, has inscribed interlocking circles. This stone is discussed in the next chapter (see Fig. 30).

Other pottery of prehistoric age has been recently found by Martin Greene, of Down Farm, Sixpenny Handley. At sites close to the Dorset Cursus he dug up several shards displaying concentric circle decoration.

Moving forward in time, the Romans used circles in many of their splendid mosaics which have been found in Dorset. At the Hinton Parva villa, the mosaic floor has

Fig. 23. Objects found at the Clandon Barrow, Dorset. A: Ritual mace head, with gold discs; B: Incense dish with concentric circles on the top surface

Plate 27. The cross at Staple Cross, Christchurch, showing the unusual circular steps.

three central circles. A circular mosaic design is also seen at Colliton Park, Dorchester. At Hinton St Mary a large mosaic pavement shows several circles enclosing the two main scenes, but additionally has four semi-circles around their depictions. At Witchampton, north of Wimborne, a temple was built with a circular ground plan.

The Celts employed the circle as a sacred symbol. We have already seen three in the bottom right hand corner of Plate 1. It is thought that the wheeled cross originally represented the sun, Christianity later adapting the symbol as the divine representation (Plate 1 shows the circle in the centre of the cross). Derek Bryce, in his excellent *"Symbolism of the Celtic Cross"*, sees the circle of Celtic crosses to symbolise the "motionless mover", the Divine. He considers the outer circle of wheel crosses to represent heaven, surrounding Christ at its centre.

Most of Dorset's stone crosses are mounted on octagonal or square bases or steps. There are a few exceptions to this, however. Plate 27 shows the cross at Staple Cross, at Christchurch (grid ref:173938). Two circular steps can be seen. Medieval crosses at Trent and Milborne Port, and Studland's cross also have circular bases or steps (all these are illustrated in *"Ancient Stones of Dorset"*).

Another example of the circle retaining reverence is the church font. Most of Dorset's fonts are round and symbolise spiritual initiation, as indeed the circle has often done since ancient times.

Ancient temples, such as built by the Romans and Greeks, had circular columns, a tradition carried forward into Christian architecture and used extensively up to the 12-13th century. From the 13th century the more prominent designs became the octagonal type, and even more complicated columns were to follow.

Likewise, early church windows were round, only to be replaced later by the more elaborate Norman and Gothic styles. The magnificent round window at the west front of Chartres Cathedral, France, is a remnant of ancient circle symbology. In Dorset, too, we have some circular windows surviving in churches. The church at East Chelborough is 16th century in origin, and above the door is a large round window. A rare 12th century example is inside Lady St Mary at Wareham. It is set into the east wall of the north aisle and opens into the organ chamber, probably having been moved during its long history. Fig. 24(A) shows the window.

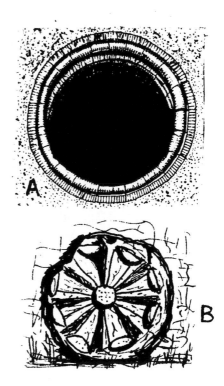

Fig. 24. Circular symbology in Dorset; A: The round window at Lady St Mary, Wareham; B: The Catherine Wheel at the well at Cerne Abbas.

The Catherine Wheel is an ancient solar symbol which was later Christianised after the martyrdom of St Catherine. One can be seen in stone at St Augustine's Well at Cerne Abbas, an ancient sacred site. The solar rays emanating from a centre orb are still evident, as Fig. 24(B) shows. There are eight spokes on the wheel image carved on a prehistoric chamber wall at Longcrew, Ireland. Paul Devereux suggests the rays depict the eight divisions of the solar year of the Celts.

Fig. 25. Examples of Dorset crop circles. The shaded areas are those of the flattened crop. (Drawn from photographs supplied by David Kingston).

The Christian vesica piscis symbol is that of two overlapping circles, reminiscent of the Buddhist mana already discussed. The symbol is seen on the lid of the Chalice Well at Glastonbury (see Plate 28). It is a figure of sacred geometry, having ancient associations with the vulva of the Mother Goddess. The symbol was adopted by the early persecuted Christians in the catacombs. To them it still represented the interpenetration between the material and spirit worlds. At Glastonbury, the abbey is built to sacred geometry of the vesica piscis, the overlapping area of the circles being overlaid by the St Mary Chapel. This is the spiritual focus of the Abbey and is located within the vulva of this ancient Goddess symbol.

Wells, of course, are usually circular in construction. These uterine openings out of the Earth Goddess have often been held as sacred. The Earth Mother was seen to bestow life-giving waters and deserved veneration. Wells are discussed at length in Chapter 6.

Fig. 26. William Stukeley's 18th century drawing of Celtic druids going about their learning, with the sacred circle in the foreground.

Plate 28. The vesica piscis on the well cover at Glastonbury.

69

As we approach the end of our search for sacred circles it would be incomplete were I not to briefly mention crop circles. These enigmatic manifestations are still causing great controversy. Many are no doubt the results of hoaxes, which has been detrimental to the study as a whole. Yet every year highly complex designs appear in fields, in a matter of minutes on occasions; some other force than human seems probable. Many have claimed that it is the earth talking to us, whilst others say they are messages from the Cosmos, responding to our heightening consciousness as a species.

Whatever their origin crop circles certainly are, quite often, true circles. Fig. 25 is a selection that recently formed around Dorset. Inside many of these circles the crops are flattened in a spiralling formation, linking us perhaps with the sacred spiral already discussed. Is the Earth Goddess and Man once again interacting by means of the mystic spiral?

Survivals

"Let us in a lover's round
Circle all this hallowed ground;
Softly, softly trip and go,
The light-foot Fairies jet it so" .
From *"The Fairy Ring"*, 17th century.

In modern times we find festivals and ceremonies that remind us of former rites associated with the sacred circle. The famous Hobby 'Oss still parades through the streets at Padstow in Cornwall every May Day, and a Maypole is set up in the town centre. The Baal Festival held at Whalton, Northumberland, had children dancing around a fire, again on May Day. Janet and Colin Bord show us a photo of children dancing in a circle around a thorn tree at Appleton (*"Earthrites"* page 104).

Today, Maypole dancing reminds us of the ancient symbolic meaning of the circle with its symbolic Divine centre, the "motionless mover" of Derek Bryce. The tradition was once carried out above the Giant at Cerne Abbas as well as other Dorset towns and villages. Circle dancing and healing circles in self-help groups both demonstrate the energising and healing quality of the unbroken, unending circle. In early May a procession takes place through Dorchester to Maumbury Henge, where dancing and celebrations are held.

One type of powerful symbolism has not been dealt with in this chapter due to the wealth of material to be discussed. This is the fertility and phallic symbolism of our ancestors, to which we will now turn.

70

Chapter Five

Rites of Fertility

"Come lasses and lads, take leave of your dads,
And away to the Maypole hie;
For every he has got him a she
With a minstrel standing by;
For Willy has gotten his Jill,
And Jonny has got his Jone,
To jig it, jig it, jig it, jig it,
Jig it up and down" .
Anonymous, May song, 1672

For life to be sustained on this planet it is vital that both the earth and Man are fruitful and of good health. Our ancestors evolved and practised ways to maintain and fertility of land, beast and Man himself.

Objects displaying phallic symbolism have been widely found across the world, including many in Dorset. These date from early prehistoric times right through the Neolithic and Bronze Age. This suggests that, as part of Man's spiritual and cultural development, rituals were enacted to enhance the fertility of the earth and venerate the Earth Mother and other gods responsible for the weather and crops, etc. Crop yield would be improved and hunting would be successful if sympathetic rituals and worship of their deities was undertaken.

There are countless traditions of old fertility rituals being observed. Barren women would visit stones, wells or other sacred places for the purpose of helping them become pregnant, whilst others visited special stones to aid childbirth. At Cerne Abbas young people still visit the Giant in the hope that the supposed fertility powers of his phallus works for them.

The fertility god of the Celts in Dorset, as elsewhere, was the horned or antlered Cernunnos. We will look at this cult figure later, but first let us delve into the world of phallic symbolism and see what it can tell us of ancient fertility rites.

Phallic Symbolism

"The study of phallicism is the study
of religion" .
George Ryley Scott, *"Phallic Worship"*.

It is possible that phallic reverence may have developed from the presence of stalactites and stalagmites in caves, Palaeolithic Man's home. These male symbols grow within a cave, itself the womb of the Earth Goddess. The Goddess's waters create these rock pillars in a dark, moist environment, similar to the womb.

Phallic worship was universally accepted as the concept of fertility, immortality and virility. The serpent was one of the widespread images in ancient times, even in the Garden of Eden representing sexual temptation. The serpent has the ability to cast off it's old skin and even survive after amputation. This led it to be regarded as a

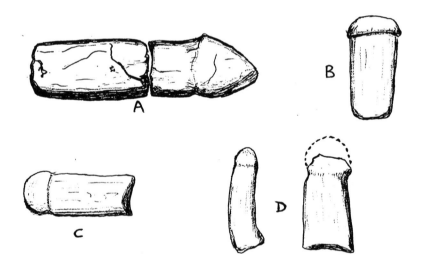

Fig. 27. Prehistoric phallic objects found in Dorset. Objects are on show in the County Museum, Dorchester.

symbol of re-birth and immortality. In Egypt, Osiris is accompanied by a serpent, as too is the Celtic god Cernunnos.

Moses revered the fertilising powers of the serpent. In the second book of Kings we read of the breaking up of "the brazen serpent Moses had made". Ancient Egypt, from whence Moses came, had many phallic and fertility symbols.

It must be realised that phallicism was not the result of primitive people cavorting around partaking pleasures of the flesh per se. The God of the Hebrews tells them throughout the Old Testament to "be fruitful and multiply". Throughout the world, the myths of gods and goddesses are full of romantic and sexual adventures. The Gods were seen to look down with favour upon sexual intercourse, sex being seen to have a spiritual, as well as reproductive, purpose. Man followed his deities seeking to emulate them and gain favour. For instance, in India many temples are adorned with erotic architecture, displaying the coming together of the physical and spiritual.

In Dorset, Neolithic and Bronze Age people used phallic objects to please the fertility gods as well as increase their own sexual potency. Fig. 27(A) shows a long chalk phallus from Neolithic ritual pit at Maumbury Henge. Fig. 27 (B+C) are likewise of chalk, between 3-5" long and were dug up during excavations at Mount Pleasant Henge. They were accompanied by rounded and smooth chalk balls, hinting at fertility ritual use. Similar phallus-ball associations have been found at Grimes Grave, Norfolk. Fig. 27(D) shows two phalluses from the Gussage St Michael II long barrow, close to the Dorset Cursus.

George Terence Meaden, in *"The Stonehenge Solution"*, discusses his observation that many chalk phalluses appear to have been broken prior to burial. He considers that the damage was caused by the objects being ritually dragged along the ground, perhaps at sunrises symbolising the Sky God impregnating the Earth Goddess. Fig. 27(A+D) shows such damage.

At Flagstones House, Dorchester, excavations in 1987 revealed a chalk block with inscribed markings of Neolithic Age, making it the oldest mural in England (see Fig. 28). Meaden sees the lines to represent, again, the sacred consummation of the sun and earth deity.

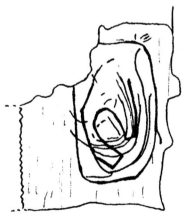

Fig. 28. Inscribed Neolithic chalk block at Flagstones, Dorchester.

Martin Greene of Down Farm, Sixpenny Handley, has recently been excavating newly discovered small henges on land close to the Cursus. Objects found were more chalk balls and phallic-shaped flints. He also uncovered a river boulder shaped like an animal's head, with eye and nose holes. The flints and the boulder are natural objects but were clearly recognised and selected by Neolithic Man, who saw symbolism and magic in inanimate objects. To them the land itself was alive and filled with signs of the presence of the Earth Goddess.

Ancient Phallic Megaliths

It has long been recognised that many megalithic stones may have been selected for their phallic shapes. At Avebury, alternating tall and lozenge stones at the henge and the adjacent avenue are thought to represent male and female principle. Britain's tallest megalith, the 28ft tall Rudston monolith, in Humberside, is phallic shaped. In Brittany dozens more huge stones seem to mimic the male member.

In Dorset, too, I believe prehistoric stones were often selected because of their phallic shape. Fig. 29 shows a selection of these, all of which can still be seen today (For details and grid references see *"Ancient Stones of Dorset"*).

The Cross-in-Hand stone, at Batcombe is similar to several in Ethiopia and, nearer home, the Lanholm market cross, Dumfrieshire, has an almost identical bulbous top. The tallest megalith at the Nine Stones, near Dorchester, is 7ft high and is phallic (Plate 4), as too is the Tark's Hill stone, Yetminster (grid ref:593102).

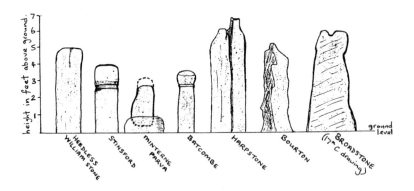

Fig. 29. Dorset megaliths displaying phallic symbolism. The Broadstone is John Aubrey's impression of the now recumbent stone; the Minterne Parva cross is thought to be a Christianised megalith.

74

In 1994 I was surveying the surviving stones at the Littlemayne Stone Circle, in the vicinity of Littlemayne Farm (grid ref:723870), south east of Dorchester. In the woods immediately south of the farmhouse I located the largest stone found to date at the site. It lies prone and covered in moss and ivy but measures over 8ft long by 3ft wide. This would clearly have been a phallic representative at the circle when it was standing.

Another phallic symbol is the obelisk and several modern examples of this ancient design have been erected around Dorset. A prominent one stands on a barrow at the west end of Ballard Down (grid ref:023814) and is shown on O.S. maps just north of Ulwell. Another is an 18th century example hidden away in woods at Weatherby Castle, near Milborne St Andrew. The shaft is some 60ft high, capped by a metal sphere.

A genuine ancient obelisk is the Philae Stone standing in the grounds of Kingston Lacy House, near Wimborne. It is inscribed with hieroglyphics and originally stood in the Isis temple on the Egyptian Isle of Philae, on the Nile. These shafts of stone adorned many Egyptian temples, such as at Karnac, where two are on show.

Yet the veneration of phallic stones is not restricted to extinct cultures of distant ages. In modern India, for instance, phallic stones are still regarded as sacred, seen to represent the world axis under it's fertility aspect.

This links us agreeably to Christian crosses. The obelisk is also taken to be a symbol for the world axis, the Axis Mundi, the shaft connecting the heavens and earth, the Tree of Life in fact. Megaliths replaced trees as totem objects with the widespread clearance of the forests in the Neolithic, and the megalith culture evolved. I have cited many examples in my previous book of my belief that many of Dorset's crosses are replacements or modifications of earlier ancient stones. These often

Plate 29. The Obelisk at Kingston Lacy House.

Plate 30. The village cross at Child Okeford, retaining a memory of phallic megaliths and obelisks. The cross replaced a previously recorded stone.

stood on ley lines, a subject we will look at later. By Celtic times tall pillars and crosses had lost the phallic meanings of their predecessors, but the shape is still there (see Plate 30). Female deities, (as research by my wife has revealed) often had male as well as female attributes, such as the bearded Ishtar of Babylonia. This suggests that apparently male images, such as the phallus, could actually be a reminder of a time when the Earth Goddess, not a Heavenly Father, was worshipped.

Phallicism of the Celts and Romans

The veneration of phallic objects continued unabashed into Celtic and Roman cultures, which spread across the Channel to colonise these lands. In Dorset we find many examples of fertility objects passed down to us from around 2,000-1,600 years ago.

We have already discussed how stone heads have been give phallic noses (see Fig. 12, 13 and 18). In Fig. 30(A) can be seen another, more obvious, example. It shows

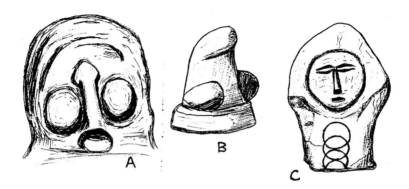

Fig. 30. Phallic symbolism in Celtic and Roman-British objects found in Dorset. See text for details. Objects are not to the same scale. All are on display in the County Museum, Dorchester.

the facial detail from a figurine of dark pottery. It dates from the 1st century AD and was found at the Colliton Park Townhouse, Dorchester (grid ref:690910 - site open to the public). Note the phallic nose and ball-like eyes. Even on an object described as a "Mother Goddess" on the accompanying museum label, both male and female find representation, a balance of the male/female principle being achieved.

Fig 30(B) is the central detail to a fragment of carved red deer antler. It comes from excavations of Romano-British date at South Street, Dorchester. The museum description states it comes from a "fertility cult".

Fig. 30(C) is perhaps the most intriguing object of the three. It is about 6" high, made from local greensand and is thought to be Celtic. It was found in 1935 in a garden at Eype, SW of Bridport. The stone is clearly glans-shaped with a face on one side. This face, too, has a phallic nose. The head may have originally been mounted on a post or pillar, or stood on an altar. Of interest are the interlocking circles on the lower half of the stone. We have seen this symbol before, in the Buddhist mana and the Christian vesica piscis (see Plate 28). Is there a parallel here, or perhaps something more? Do the circles represent the orbits of the planets, or solar, lunar and planetary discs, or even eclipses? Or do they even depict the chakra energy centres of the human body? Food for thought!

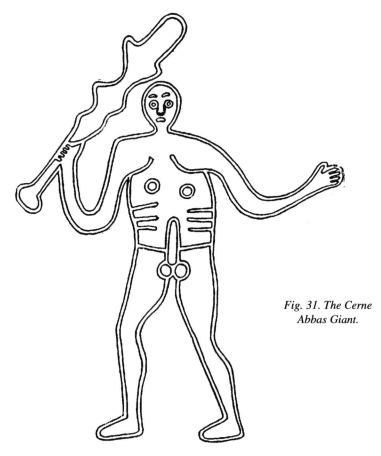

*Fig. 31. The Cerne
Abbas Giant.*

Britain's best known, and certainly largest, phallic figure is the Cerne Abbas Giant. Arguments still rage as to his age, but a Celtic or Romano-British origin cannot be ruled out. His proud 30ft penis scoured into the chalk hillside still attracts thousands of onlookers every year.

Controversy still surrounds the Giant's identity. Some regard him as the Saxon God Heil, whilst others see him as the Celtic deity Helith. Wielding as he does a club, Hercules is a contender, as almost all depiction's of this masculine deity show a club in his hand.

A strong candidate must be the Celtic God Cernunnos. Cerne village was a major spiritual centre for the local Celtic tribe, the Durotriges. It therefore seems probable that the origin of the village's name was "kern", from the original spelling of Cernunnos as "Kernunnos". When Augustine visited the village in 603 AD he found "pagan idol-worshippers" and took the measure of founding a Christian mission there, so strong was the local veneration of the old god.

In 1842 John Sydenham, in "*Baal Durotrigensis*", first suggests that the Giant was a huge fertility prop. In 1888 it is recorded that couples were visiting the Giant in hope of fertility miracles, a practice still observed today. A maypole once stood either on the hill or else in the village centre. This is an ancient spring fertility symbol. This link to old spring festivals is shown by the Giant himself. In early May, around the time of the Beltaine festival, the sun rises directly in line with the Giant's penis.

"This monstrous figure viewed from the
opposite hill appears almost erect.....
just going to strike a blow which seems
sufficient, as it were, to overturn a mountain" .
Gentleman's magazine, 1764.

Christian Phallicism

It may come as a surprise to many that phallic symbols were still being incorporated into Christian architecture right through Medieval times. Despite strict doctrines on sex and sin, local masons still found ways to depict fertility symbolism. Incredibly, Prof. G. Webb, of Cambridge, discovered that around 90% of all pre-Reformation churches erected before the start of the 15th century incorporated altars (often hollow) with concealed phallic and other fertility symbols.

In the Medieval church at Whittlesford, Cambridgeshire, is a carving depicting a penis and a vulva. At Margam, in Wales, a corbel carving exhibits the male genitalia. Many more of this period were carved in non religious places, such as the phallus on a carved window at Ballynagown Castle, Co Clare, and two carvings formerly seen to flank the entrance to a Kennixton farmhouse, in South Wales.

In Dorset, perhaps more may reveal themselves if we look close enough. I believe that two such phallic symbols have been depicted in stone at Witchampton church, north of Wimborne. Two corbel sculptures can be seen just inside as one enters the church (Plate 31). Four dragon-winged balls are visible. The long, bearded Celtic-style heads with phallic noses rise up from between these spheres. Note also the "third eye" orb above the noses. Although a predominantly Eastern symbol, we shall encounter it again in this chapter.

Plate 31. Two phallic carvings in Witchampton church.

The Horned Fertility Cults

It was for a long time believed by archaeologists that the countless antlers dug up at prehistoric sacred sites were merely used as construction tools. It is now realised that many have ritual significance. Unbroken antlers were placed in a circular wreath around a cremation in a Bronze Age barrow in Wiltshire (Hunter's Barrow). Other barrows contain corpses with antlers placed at the head and feet. In Dorset, antlers were found ritually placed at Mount Pleasant henge, and several have been found in the neighbourhood of the Neolithic Dorset Cursus.

Fig. 32. The 'Sorcerer of Trois Freres'. France.

On a hill overlooking Chaldon Herring, NW of Lulworth, a Bronze Age barrow covered two adult skeletons with antlers resting on their shoulders. Another barrow close by had a single skeleton laid out in an identical fashion. Clearly the antlers were considered to be a symbol of growth and re-birth and were to aid the deceased on their journey to the spirit world.

Across the ancient world, horned deities abound such as Pan, Mars, the Roman Satyrs, Silvanus and, of interest here, the Celtic god Cernunnos. Bulls, oxen, stags and rams were all beasts used in rituals, either in the form of amulets and statues, or as actual sacrifices to the gods.

Prehistoric cave paintings in France show stags and bison, whilst rock drawings of horned faces have been found near Santa Fe, New Mexico. One of the most famous examples is that of the "Sorcerer of Trois Freres", a cave painting found in France in 1914 (see Fig. 32). This is thought to represent a shaman/priest figure doing sympathetic magic ritual using stag antlers and skins.

The Bull

The bull, due to his strength and sexual virility, was almost universally adopted in ancient times as a symbol of masculine fertility, and the creative forces of the Earth as a whole. The Egyptians, Greeks, Romans and Celts all held the bull in high regard. The ancient Catal Huyuk culture of Anatolia named the Taurus Mountains after their veneration of the bull, and many of their paintings depict the horned beast. Druids used to be wrapped within a bull's hide as part of seership rituals, a similar practice to that of some North American Indians. Statues of the Ephesian Goddess Artemis show here accompanied by small bulls.

In Dorset, Bull worship has left it's relics. Bull horns were found in the Neolithic bank barrow on Maiden Castle, and several others from Dorset are housed in the County Museum. Fig. 33 shows a "Taurus Trigaramus", a bronze bull found at the Roman temple on Maiden Castle. Similar bulls fashioned in bronze have been found at Romano-British sites at Stoke Abbot and Lychett Minster. These are on display in the County Museum.

Fig. 33. A bronze bull found at the Roman temple on Maiden Castle.

Perhaps surprisingly, bull symbolism continued into the Christian Era. Clearly the Church used the symbology of the bull's fertility attributes to further it's own ends, endowing many saints with bull motifs and emblems. St Luke is symbolised by a bull, of which a winged variety can be seen on the frontispiece of his gospel in the Book Of Cerne. This was written in the late 10th century at Cerne Abbas Abbey. Inside Wimborne Minster, directly behind the gift shop, a bull can be seen at the bottom of a window dedicated to St Luke (see Plate 32).

On the pulpit in the church at Cattistock is a beautiful carved winged bull, shown in Plate 33. On the same pulpit a dragon can also be found. A similar bull can be seen on the font at Turnworth, west of Blandford.

A connection between the bull's fertility status and the Earth Goddess is shown in Fig. 59, where the Goddess is suckling a bull and a serpent. We will look into survivals of bull rituals later in this chapter. On the landscape today we can see bull

82

Top: Plate 32 . The bull on the stained glass window in Wimborne Minster.
Lower: Plate 33. The winged bull on the pulpit at Cattistock.

Plate 34. The ram on the outside of Chideock church

cult sites that have survived the ravages of time. There are two "Bulbarrows" in Dorset, and these probably owe their names to bull fertility rites.

The Ram

In many ancient cultures throughout the world, the ram has been a revered symbol of virility and fertility. For instance, the Auritae tribe of ancient Egypt adopted the ram as a symbol of the generative forces of Nature. At the Egyptian temple at Karnac, I remember seeing rows of ram-headed sphinxes, associated with the god Amon. Nearer home, in the Devon village of Holne, a ram-roast used to take place every May Day, the time of the Old Beltain fertility festival. The festivities were held at an ancient standing stone.

We have already seen the ram's head on the font at Toller Porcorum, in Fig. 18(B). At Chideock a carved ram hangs from the outer walls of the church (Plate 34). Another ram gargoyle can be seen on the north side of Maiden Newton church. Others can be seen scattered around Dorset's churches: I''ll leave you to spot them!

The Stag

We have already discussed the stag antlers found in Dorset Bronze Age barrows. This veneration of the stag, and in particular it's antlers, continued into Celtic and later ages. The stag appears in many of the legends of Merlin, and Medieval heraldry employed the stag extensively.

A 13-14th century floor tile on show in the County Museum has a depiction of a stag.

At Melbury Bubb, the Saxon font, dated c1000, shows a beautifully carved stag. This is now inverted, as is the whole Saxon feature, but Fig. 34 shows the stag the right-way-up.

Fig. 34. The stag on the Saxon font at Melbury Bubb.

We will meet the stag again, as he links us to a most important Celtic horned deity, Cernunnos. This figure is well represented in Dorset and we shall now take a look at him in detail.

Cernunnos - Lord of the Animals

"Pan, Oh great Pan, to thee
Thus do we sing,
Thou that keep'st us chaste and free,
As the young spring" .
From *"Great God Pan"*, John Fletcher, 1609

Plate 35. Pan in the grounds of Portman Lodge, Durweston.

Cernunnos was the Celtic counterpart of the classical god Pan, the pasture and woodland deity, who had the legs, horns and hooves of a goat and played his "pan-pipes". He was the shepherd's god, protecting them and their flocks. He made goats and ewes prolific, hence the portrayal of him seen in the grounds of Portman Lodge, at Durweston, near Blandford. Plate 35 shows him standing under a tree, pan-pipes in hand.

As the Roman Empire spread into the Celtic lands of northern Europe and Britain, it recognised the similar attributes of the classical deity Pan to the Celtic god Cernunnos. The latter was integrated into the Roman pantheon. On a Gallo-Roman relief at Rheims, Cernunnos is sitting between Mercury and Apollo. Below him are a bull and a stag. Fig. 35 shows his association with a serpent. In fact, Cernunnos

Fig. 35. Cernunnos
on the Gundestrup
Cauldron.

himself is depicted serpent-legged on carvings in the museum at Edinburgh and Cirencester.

On the Gundestrup Cauldron, a beautifully decorated Celtic vessel from Denmark, Cernunnos is shown accompanied by a stag, which has identical antlers (Fig. 35). He sits in a cross-legged, almost meditative position and holds a torc and a serpent. The torc is a symbol of his authority, whilst the serpent represents the fire, energies and vitality of the earth. He is surrounded by other beasts and sits regally as the "Lord of the Animals", or the "Horned One".

The attributes of Cernunnos range from self-gratification, virility and sexual extremes, to an overseer of crop growth, hunting and culling. He is described in the Medieval *Mabinogion*:

"and he took his club and struck a stag, which loudly brayed, and all the animals came together serpents, dragons and all sorts of animals.He bade them go and eat and they bowed their heads and did homage as vassals to their lord" .

The sole written record of the name Cernunnos is a Celtic carving found under the choir of Notre Dame, Paris, in 1711. It dates from AD 17 and once formed part of a pillar of an earlier shrine. This is shown in Fig. 36 and again he carries the torc on each antler. He also has two sets of ears, one animal, the other human.

Fig. 36. Cernunnos, found under Notre Dame Cathedral in 1711, but of Celtic age.

"And the Nymphs of the woods
And the waves,
To the edge of the moist river-lawns,
And the brink of the dewy caves,
And all that then did attend and follow,
Were silent with love as you now, Apollo,
With envy of my sweet pipings" .
From *"Hymn of Pan"*, Shelley

In Dorset, the local Celtic tribe, the Durotriges, would have venerated Cernunnos. We have already seen fertility and phallic symbols from the county and it seems probable that Cernunnos was a central fertility deity. The Cerne Giant may yet be proven to be him, and it is possible that his antlers or horns were removed by the church.

Fig. 16(B) may be a Romano-British carving of Cernunnos, with antlers. Of similar age are five Romano-British roof antifixes, 6" high, found during excavations in High East St, Dorchester. They are made of red tile clay and date from 1st century AD. Fig. 37 shows one of them and a short horn can be seen.

Fig. 37. Romana-British horned head from Dorchester.

Cernunnos and the Devil

The obsession of the Church with stamping out phallic and fertility worship and festivals showed total ignorance of the vital place of Nature worship in sociological evolution. It also displayed an irreverence to the land and indeed the Earth as a whole. This set a trend that has continued to modern times, and only now are we trying to redress the balance.

To the early missionary Christians, all Nature spirits and deities were servants of the Devil. In Fact, Cernunnos became the Devil. From being a god of fecundity and fertility, propaganda turned him into something seductive, sinful and evil. The threat of the Devil, who was a political invention, enabled the Church to stamp out fertility cults and rituals in the name of God.

It is somewhat ironic that the appearance of the Devil in paintings, carvings and so forth in fact ensured the *survival* of the image of Cernunnos! It is a fallacy that church gargoyles of dragons, demons and the Devil were on show to alert congregations of the sins of the flesh and Satan. Would a meeting of Chocoholics be held in a sweet shop? Would Alcoholics Anonymous be conducted in a pub? Why flaunt that which one is trying to stamp out? Why not have carvings of the saints, kings, queens, beautiful animals, etc. on waterspouts, instead of overtly Pagan images? How do we come to have carvings on churches of male and female genitalia, and other explicit exhibitionism?

Late-Medieval masons were still carving Pagan images, even in the more sophisticated towns and cities. It is a mystery how this tradition was maintained considering the prohibitions of the Church. A tenacity existed in the Medieval mind that ensured the survival of Paganism, especially in rural areas as was most of Dorset. Of relevance, perhaps, is the fact that hardly any Medieval heraldry occurs outside of churches. It could be that the stone masons retained the right to design their gargoyles, immune from the structures of the Church.

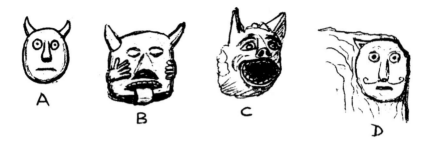

Fig. 38. Examples of horned heads on Dorset stonework. A & B: Studland; C: Pulham; D: Shaftesbury Abbey, 11th century.

There are numerous churches across Dorset displaying gargoyles and other carved stonework with horned creatures and Fig. 38 shows four examples. The heads from Studland are two of four horned ones on the south-facing corbel table (where the sloping roof meets the vertical walls). These are Norman in age and others include animals and a sheela-na-gig (see Fig. 60).

On the outside of the church at Mappowder, 5 miles NW of Milton Abbas, is a small creature, complete with spiny back, a long tail and small horns. A similar one can be found on Piddletrenthide church.

Two horned gargoyles adorn the outside of Stinsford church, just east of Dorchester. One of these is a "tongue-puller", similar to that seen elsewhere and are thought by some researchers to have phallic significance. The displaying of the tongue as a phallic symbol is widespread across Europe. (Three English examples are shown in Janet and Colin Bord's "*Earthrites*", pages 82-3).

An example of a horned "frightener" is shown in Fig. 38(C), at Pulham, midway between Sherborne and Milton Abbas. His gaping mouth and teeth stare down at onlookers. Others can be seen at Osmington and on the outside of St Mary's, Cerne Abbas. At Hilton, just west of Milton Abbey, we have perhaps the best example of the corruption of the old god Cernunnos. One of the worn gargoyles depicts, according to the church booklet, "a devil flying out of the mouth of a child after Baptism". A sad debasement of a once-proud Celtic god.

More gargoyles will be encountered later in this book. But in the meantime, try and look at church architecture with new eyes, and I guarantee that sooner or later you will find relics of Pagan belief.

Plate 36. The horned creature at Mappowder church.

Two ancient horned heads have been reset into the walls of the church at Maiden Newton (see Plate 37). The first one (A) is in the porch, to the left as one approaches the door. The other (B) is set into the wall near the altar, close to where the piano usually stands. They appear to be of different stone, and also vary in the style of their eyes, horns and hair. They may be of different age, or perhaps the work of two different masons.

At Cranborne, two large Medieval wall paintings can still be discerned, though they are very faded. The figure on the left appears to be a two legged horned creature. To the right of it is a scene depicting the Tree of Life, issuing forth from a woman's head (Fig. 58). Climbing up the tree are, amongst other figures, a bull and a horned "demon".

We have already seen a horned head in the church of St Mary, Charminster, north of Dorchester (see Fig. 7 and Plate 13). Another can be seen on the outside of the

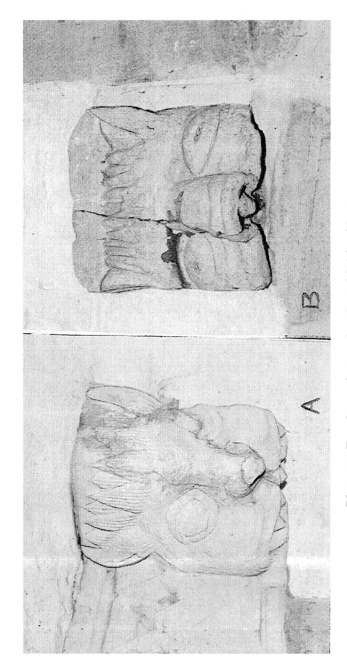

Plate 37. Two horned stone heads at Maiden Newton.

92

Plate 38. The horned head on the outside of Charminster church.

church, as a 15th century head stop on the east window of the north aisle. It's features could be either gender and looks far from "evil" or devil like (Plate 38).

The last horned example here is that of a Medieval head at Loders, near Bridport. After one enters the churchyard a long wall is to your right. A green door is soon encountered, above which the head can be found (see Fig. 39). It is very worn, lichen-covered and not very photogenic. I have attempted an impression of it as shown, based on photographs I have taken. Note the "third eye" above the nose. It is a feature we encountered previously at Witchampton (plate 31), and which we will encounter again as we take a look at survivals of the old fertility cults and, in particular, the famous Dorset Ooser.

Fig. 39. The horned head on the wall in Loders churchyard.

"Watch out or the Ooser"ll get "ee."
(Old Dorset Saying).

Survivals of Fertility Rites and Superstitions

Despite anti-pagan Church dogma, fertility rites and festivals continued to be practised through Medieval into modern times by a people determined to hang onto their roots. They saw the importance of upholding fertility and Earth Goddess festivals at key times of the year.

The Romans had a feast day for Terminus, the god of fields. From this evolved the Pagan festival of Robilgalia, which involved a procession through the crop fields to honour the earth and the fertility deities. It is this ceremony that probably developed into the Rogation, or Beating-the-Bounds, processions. These latter ceremonies are recorded from the 8th century in England and persist to the present day.

An old cure for a headache was to wear a snake skin in one's hat. We have seen how the serpent was thought to have the power of fire and vitality and no doubt it was hoped that the serpent's power would be transferred into the head of the sufferer. In Dorset, it was a custom to place a bull's heart up the chimney to ward off evil spirits. Several old ones have been found, such as at Shipton Gorge and Hawkchurch.

In 1583 puritan Philip Stubbs recorded his revulsion of overtly Pagan practices still being practised in rural areas:

"hundreds of men, women and children go off to the woods and spend all night in pastimes and they bring home with great veneration the Mai-pole, their stinking idol and they leaped and danced about it, as all heathen people did".

In 1635 the Cerne Abbas maypole was pulled down, as were others around this time. Bridport, Cattistock and Shillingstone all had maypoles. By Victorian times only Shillingstone was still upholding the ancient spring Celtic festival, as William Barnes observed:

And Shillingstone, that on her height,
Shows up her tower to opening day,
And high-shot maypole, yearly dight,
With flowery wreaths of merry May".

It appears that Dorset was one of the last strongholds of the old Pagan ways and superstitions. Folklorist John Udel wrote:

Fig. 40. The Dorset Ooser, drawn by the author from an old photograph.

There is no part of England more prone to belief in the supernatural than that of the West; and of the Western counties, none more so than Dorsetshire".

At Burton Bradstock, plays with a Pagan origin were performed by the Bradstock Mummers, which involved the figure of "Beelzebub", which puffed smoke, had four legs and a reptilian tail (our old friend the dragon, perhaps?) Other Dorset mummers donned masks around the Winter Solstice. At Symondsbury, near Bridport, as late as 1857 villagers would proceed up a neighbouring hill and enact earth fertility ceremonies, which involved standing and kneeling in a circle.

The Dorset Ooser is a famous relic of by-gone fertility festivals. Even into Victorian days the hollow mask, which had a hinged jaw, was paraded around Melbury Osmond, a village south of Yetminster. The mask had a pair of Bullock's horns and a "third eye" is again in evidence (Fig. 40: compare to Plate 31 and Fig. 39). It is told that the appearance of the Ooser would frighten adults as well as children. The old god was truly "devilised" with the addition of smoke coming from his nostrils to accompany the hideous facial design.

"It is not difficult to trace the evolution of a god of an early cult, or a fertility spirit with attendant ritual, to the Devil of a succeeding religion" .
From *"The Dorset Ooser"*, H S L Dewar.

The mask was last seen in 1897 and it's present whereabouts, if it indeed survives at all, are unknown. A replica mask was made in 1973 by the Weymouth Morris Dancers and is periodically used by them. Morris dancing itself probably originated from old spring ceremonies carried out to ensure the crops were blessed with rain, the white handkerchiefs representing clouds.

Parallels can be drawn between the Melbury Osmond Ooser and both the Abbots Bromley Horn Dance, of Staffordshire, and the Padstow 'Obby 'Oss, of Cornwall. These festivals thrive today, remnants of hundreds of similar ones that once took place to pay homage to fertility gods and the Earth Mother.

With great irony, one of the finest carvings of Cernunnos is in St George's Chapel, Windsor, home of the Queen, who is of course head of the Church of England. His fearsome appearance on the carving is perhaps justified. He now looks down on the head of the Church, and perhaps reflects how her predecessors relegated him from Celtic god to being of evil.

96

It is said that Herne the Hunter (another name for Cernunnos), with stag antlers on his brow, still haunts Windsor Great Park. Cernunnos, it seems, will not lie down and perhaps, for our sakes, it is just as well.

"Unite, unite, let us all unite,
For Summer is a-come unto day,
And whither we are going we will unite
On the merry morning of May".
Padstow May Day Song (Anon).

Chapter Six

Waters of Purification

> *"The wells, rivers and lakes used by priests were, as holy places, invested with curative properties"* .
> Antiquarian Sir Norman Lockyer.

Evidence for water cults is found from around 6000 BC in Europe. Greeks, Romans and Egyptians alike all saw water as possessing magical powers, as do the Australian Aborigines and North American Indians of today. In Chinese folklore it is said that baby dragons are hatched from eggs which are usually laid on hillsides near running water.

A Mayan tribe, the Chorti, reported dragon-like serpents residing in streams, lakes and springs. The Celts called sea and river mists the "dragon's breath".

Natural water supplies have always been venerated. Water is essential for our survival and this life-giving elixir was seen to issue forth from the womb of the Earth Goddess.

Water welling up from the earth was often held as having great potency, especially when occurring in the vicinity of sacred sites, examples of which we will

Fig. 41. A Romano-British sea or river god from a mosaic found in a Dorset villa. Now on display in the County Museum.

Plate 39. Devil's Brook, at Dewlish

Plate 40. Egbert's Stone at Bourton, standing next to a river.

see in Dorset below. Our ancestors saw water as a living entity, with the power to instill life, health and vigour.

There are many Celtic water cults, with countless legends associated with rivers and lakes. Water spirits and goddesses were seen to be responsible for curative waters and any miracles that took place. Many Norse and Anglo-Saxon tales involve bodies of water. Dragons, serpents and fairies were seen to inhabit or guard watery places. Consecrated or holy water is used in rituals and healing today and to pass through water, as in Baptism, is symbolic of death and rebirth. Baptism derived from earlier purification ceremonies, used to cleanse body, mind and spirit. The Greeks would wash the statues of their goddesses annually. The Saudi king ritually washes the Ka'ba Stone, focal point of the Muslims, at Mecca every year.

Let us now take a look at the various kinds of bodies of water, the folklore that has grown up around them, and the numerous Dorset examples of sacred water localities.

Rivers and Streams

"The wise take pleasure in the rivers and lakes"
Confucius

The river is an ancient metaphor for human life. From birth (at it's source) to death (where it meets the sea), the river reminds us of the eternal cycles of Nature and Man. In folklore and legend, rivers often form a boundary, a crossing point between life and death. Many sacred rivers exist across the world, the Nile and the Ganges being good examples of how two cultures believe still that the rivers are not just physical life sustainers but are in fact spiritual arteries too.

Many sacred sites occur in the proximity of rivers and streams. The Nile and the Ganges are accompanied for much of their routes by numerous temples and shrines. In Britain, many Roman temples are close to rivers, the waters no doubt used for rituals as well as drinking (such as Witchampton). Folklore and legends associated with rivers abound. For instance, a dragon is said to live at the bottom of a whirlpool in the River Taff, at Cardiff. The Christchurch dragon manifested where two large rivers meet the sea. The tale of the Bisterne dragon is located near the River Avon.

Clues to the ancient reverence of rivers can be found in Dorset in the form of the naming of rivers and streams. At Dewlish (which means "dark stream"), we find Devil's Brook. When ever we find the Devil in a place name it is fair to bet that the locality was used for Pagan worship and that the bestowing of the name was due to Church propaganda to stop such practices. It is perhaps relevant that Devil's Brook has it's source just below Bulbarrow to the north. We have already seen how this barrow may have derived it's name from bull worship fertility rites. Another example of a revered stream in Dorset is Holy Stream, at Hethfelton, near Wool. This is still named on 1:25 000 sheets and flows from Stoke Heath, south past "Monkey World", to join the River Frome near Bindon Abbey. Many ancient sites around Dorset are located close to streams and dowsing would suggest a link between the two. Underground springs are frequently dowsed below stone circles. The Nine Stones circle, at Winterbourne Abbas, is situated within feet of an ancient stream (see *"Ancient Stone of Dorset"*, Fig. 103). Egbert's Stone, standing at Bourton, is quite literally in the river when the adjacent stream swells after rain (see Plate 40).

At Brockhampton Green, 5 miles NE of Cerne Abbas, a large ley markstone lies next to a bridge over a stream (grid ref:718062).

The Harpstone, near Kimmeridge, stands on gently sloping ground that descends to a nearby river to the north. Martin Driscoll informs me of an ancient pavement that links the stone and the river. This has parallels at Stonehenge, where and earthen avenue joins the monument to the River Avon.

The ley markstone at Muckleford (grid ref:643937) is only yards north of a bridge going over the River Frome. The ancient chapel of St Luke's, in secluded woods south of Long Bredy, was built yards from a stream which meanders through this atmospheric locality. We shall encounter more ancient stones in close proximity to water later.

The Romans, in particular, seem to have venerated rivers and the spirits therein. They built a villa, for instance, close to the River Divelish (which probably derived from "devilish) at Fifehead Neville, SW of Sturminster Newton. At Horton, north of Wimborne, excavations in 1875 uncovered gravel from a former stream bed. In it was uncovered a hoard of Roman coins, amber beads and pottery. The finds were considered to be a "votive deposit" by Royal Commission archaeologists. The site is not far from the Witchampton Temple.

There can be little doubt that rivers were seen as the abode of god and goddesses. For example, the River Seine, France, derives it's name from the goddess Sequana, whilst the River Marne comes from Matrona, the "Divine Mother". Here in Britain, the River Dee comes from Deva, a "goddess or holy one". Scotland's River Clyde evolved from Clota, the "divine washer". The River Thames is feminine, originating from Tamesa, a river goddess. Finally, here in Dorset, the River Bride derive from the Celtic goddess Bridget/Brighid. Even today, the flow, eddies and dark depths of rivers capture our imagination and, indeed, our participation. Bathing in rivers is perhaps a subconscious re-enactment of ancient purification rituals long since gone. "The sensation of weightlessness could be emotionally returning to us to the blissful amniotic state in our own mother's womb", is how my wife, Ghermaine, sees this analogy of Mother Earth's life-giving waters.

"Pure stream, in whose transparent wave
My youthful limbs I wont to lave;
Devolving from thy parent lake
a charming maze thy waters make" .
From *"To Leven Water"*, Tobias Smollet, 18th century

Lakes and Ponds

In legends and myths lakes are often places of mystery and the abode, especially in Arthurian tales, of a female enchantress or a dragon. The Lady of the Lake was the giver of Arthur's sword Excalibur, and the guardian of "Lancelot of the Lake". She can be compared to the Greek goddess Aphrodite, who likewise rose from water. In Greek legends lakes and pools harboured nymphs. Hylas went ashore from the ship of the Argonauts in search of fresh water. He came to a fountain feeding a pool in which nymphs swam. They were so enchanted by his beauty that they carried him to the depths of the pool.

We have already see how Merlin ordered a pool to be drained, revealing two opposing dragons at the bottom. The Lyminster Knucker, a Sussex dragon, dwelt in a deep pond by the village church. The Padstow Hobby Horse procession used to stop at Treator Pool, where the "Os sprinkled water over onlookers for good luck. The most famous lake creature is of course the illusive Nessie of Loch Ness, but is in fact typical of many lake monsters all around the world.

In Dorset several folklore stories involve lakes and ponds. A pool in the River Stour at Durweston is thought to be bottomless and a vehicle is supposed to have disappeared into it! The valley dominated by the Poundbury earthworks, Dorchester, is that of the River Frome. Although now an area of watery meadows, tradition speaks of a lake there, inhabited by an unspecified monster.

Plate 41. The Blue Pool, near Corfe Castle, said to be the home of an illusive creature.

103

There is a pond next to the A354 Dorchester to Weymouth road at Winterborne Monkton (grid ref:681880). Tales survive to spectral Roman soldiers close by, as well as a phantom coach and horses. This pond is shown in Fig 98 of *"Ancient Stones of Dorset"* (incorrectly described as being next to the A35). It is directly on a ley alignment running from Langton Herring to the Roman stone at Brockhampton. Alfred Watkins, in his book *"The Old Straight Track"*, saw ponds as useful ley markers to travellers walking a ley. The sky's reflection in a pool would be visible up to a mile away, he deduced.

Another pond at Parkwood (grid ref:854828) similarly lies on a long ley going from three tumuli east of Rempstone stone circle to Chalbury.

The Blue Pool, a well frequented tourist beauty spot near Corfe Castle, is said to be visited by the Devil, who pushes people in! In recent years there has been a resurgence in sightings of an illusive creature said to inhabit the pond, named Norman, despite the fact the pond is in fact an old water-filled clay pit, and probably no more than 100 years old. The pond is said to have some medicinal properties, possibly due to the high Kaolin content of the pool.

Heedless William's Pond (Plate 42) is situated south of Hardy's Birthplace, east of Dorchester (grid ref:732913). Folklore exists of a reckless coachman named William who one night drove his coach off the road and into the pond. Coach, horses and passengers were all lost. Nearby is Heedless William's Stone (Fig. 29), a megalith at least Roman in age. We have already discussed how many sacred sites occur in the vicinity of bodies of water. Perhaps the stone marked a drinking or ritual site long before William's mishap. The pond is fed by a spring from the north side. The Celts thought these were entrances to the Underworld.

Another link between water, coaches and ancient sites is found at Trent Barrow. Close to the barrow is another pond, this time associated with a phantom coach. Does water have some mystical quality that attracts ghosts, or is it that the waters are, in truth, inhabited by spirits beckoning people in, as illustrated by the legend of Hylas and the Nymphs?

Wells and Springs

"Drink of this and take thy fill,
for the water falls by the wizard's will" .
Carved above well at Alderley Edge, Cheshire.

Plate 42. Heedless William's Pond, as seen from the megalith to the south.

Wells and springs represent the exit from the womb of the Earth Goddess and for thousands of years the issuing waters have been regarded as magical, curative and even possessing divination attributes. The practice of throwing offerings into wells and springs dates back to the Neolithic and Bronze Ages. The modern ritual of tossing coins into a wishing well for good luck has an ancient, spiritual origin. Our distant ancestors made sacrificial offerings, such as bones, shells and weapons, to placate their gods and goddesses. It was this practice that was developed by the Romans into our present day ritual of throwing coins. In Dorset, a Roman well west of Winterborne Kingston was found with such offered coins and other objects (see Fig. 49, *"Ancient Stone of Dorset"*). Another example is a 24ft deep Bronze Age well shaft at Swanwick, Hampshire, also containing votive offerings.

Place names give us a clue to associations between wells and deities. Wanswell, in Gloucestershire, was named after Woden, whilst in North Yorkshire there is a Thor's Well. Both of these were major Norse gods. The Norse myth Prose Edda, from the 12th century, tells us:

"....the third root of the Ash [the World Tree] stands in heaven and beneath it is a spring, exceeding sacred, named the well of Urdr. That is where the gods have their judgement seat".

Throughout British history wells and springs have been venerated. The Roman baths at Bath developed from a local spring sacred to the Celts as the abode of Sulis Minerva. In Scotland, a shaman/priest would be wrapped in an animal skin and spend all night by a waterfall or sacred well in order to experience visions.

At Brinsop, in Herefordshire, a dragon lived in a well in Duck's Pool Meadow. It was slain by none other than St George himself. Many other wells had either stone heads, or in some cases actual skulls, associated with them. These remind us of the head cults discussed in Chapter Four. One such example is at Holywell, in Flint. Several Scottish wells are called the Well of Head(s). The Cerne Giant, near St Augustine's Well, may have once held a severed head.

In Arthurian legend. The shaman Merlin was cured of his madness by taking the waters from a magical spring, which suddenly appeared from beneath the earth.

The tradition of well dressing is very old. Wells are "dressed" usually around Pagan festivals of Beltaine and Lammas. These festivals dates were kept up by the Church, who took over sacred wells and springs for baptism. This ritual is seen to transpose the mortal soul from that of a sinner to one who is saved. Wells were Christianised by reconsecrating them in the name of, usually female, saints. The most frequently used was Mary herself, who filled the gap left vacant by the vanquished Goddess.

Medieval holy well yielded revenue for local religious foundations as pilgrims come to partake of the sacred waters. Where a holy well was absent, baptism moved into the church, in the form of the font. The word font in fact comes from the OE "*functa*", which derived from the Latin "*fontis*", literally meaning "a spring".

There have probably been in excess of 2000 holy wells in England alone. Estimates suggest that over 8000 may have existed in Britain and Eire, of which only a small fraction remain today. The lowering of water tables led to many wells drying up and being abandoned.

Dorset abounds with well and spring folklore. One tale is associated with an actual historical event, however, and this will serve well to commence our survey.

In 978 Edward King of Wessex was murdered at Corfe Castle, following a sinister plot. His body was thrown down a local well. A year later the body was found uncorrupted following the apparition of a pillar of fire at the well. Thereafter, the well water was said to have cured people of many diseases.

"A city may be moved - but not a well".
The I Ching.

Of Golden Tables and Coffins

A repetitive element of folklore of Dorset's wells and springs is that of golden tables. Dungeon Hill rises from the north of Buckland Newton (grid ref:690074) and has on it's summit the remains of Iron Age occupation. Folklore tells us of a golden table that lies in a well on the hill. Locals once tried to retrieve it but apparently the earth shook, rocking the foundations of a nearby cottage. The attempt was abandoned!

At Rhyme Intrinseca, near Yetminster, a similar golden table is reported in a well on Court's Hill. At Sturminster Newton Castle, a hillfort with Medieval modifications, another golden table is reported from the 19th century. This time it is accompanied

Plate 43. Dungeon Hill, looking up it's slope from the east. A golden table is said to lie in a well on the hill.

107

by "valuable silver articles". Anchoret's Well, on Woodbury Hill, Bere Regis (Plate 44) reportedly had a golden table or coffin buried in it. The origins of these tales of golden tables is debatable. The stories could, of course, refer to actual burial treasure, but why nearly always a table? Folklore concerning barrows is given in Chapter Ten, where it will be seen that these earthen tombs contain all manner of "treasure", from golden coffins to daggers.

Tales of golden tables could simply refer to the water table. The availability of well water would often have been a matter of life or death to many communities in the past, especially during the summer droughts. Perhaps a well that never dried up was seen to be "golden" in every sense of the word. Or, just maybe, the "golden" folklore originated from actual earth energies witnessed at wells, such as we saw at Corfe Castle. Fairy lights are frequently reported at wells and these may have connections with well booty tales.

Holy and Curative Wells and Springs

The number of past and present holy wells in Dorset probably exceeds forty. Several villages bear the name Holywell or Holwell. Let us take a look at those known to have derived their names from holy waters.

Plate 44. Woodbury Hill, from the south. Folklore of a golden table down the well on the hill have persisted to this day.

Plate 45. Inscribed stone at Holwell.

Holwell, north of Cerne Abbas, is named from an old well north of the church. A bridge over the River Caundle takes one to some overgrown stones. Excavated in 1968, seven stone steps were found. It's close proximity to the adjacent river caused the well to constantly silt up, yet it was used for baptisms and curing eye disorders. The well is on a ley alignment running up from Bridport, via Shaftesbury up to Stonehenge itself. More instances of Holy wells on Stonehenge leys will be seen later. Is it coincidence?

Holwell Farm, near Broadwey, (grid ref:654833) is in the *Doomsday Book* as "Halegewelle". This is from OE meaning "holy well or spring". We have already uncovered a "Holy Stream" at Hethfelton, near Wool. The stream was apparently fed by "Holy Well". There are tales that a spectral coach drives along the stream at midnight. Ulwell, on the outskirts of Swanage, was originally spelt Holewell in records dating from 1236. This may have been the reference to a holy well in the vicinity. Of interest, perhaps, is that another ley line going right up to Stonehenge passes through Ulwell, passing close to an interesting tree with reptilian images (Plate 93).

Just east of Cranborne the name Holwell appears again. Approximately one mile along the lane from Cranborne to Alderholt, Roman remains were found and thought to be associated with a nearby pond "in which rises a never-failing stream of the purest water, which flows into the neighbouring stream" (Wake Smart, 1887). The well is thought to have been within the present water cress farm, according to the owner. She showed me an inscribed stone in her garden next to the cress beds, and this is shown in plate 45. The Ebenezer Chapel at nearby Cripplestyle (grid ref:090121) dates from 1807 and marks a resting place for pilgrims going to the holy well. The chapel had an annual spring clean and a Whit-Tuesday festival which was attended by over 1000 people. The tradition died out in the last century and the commemorative stone is dated 1929.

It is a sad testament to Man and his transient ways that a sacred spring, revered from Roman times right through to the 19th century, is now only marked by a small stone in a cottage garden.

What might bring this stone out of relative obscurity is that, once again, it marks a holy well situated on a ley line going up to Stonehenge. The line goes through Ulwell, the site of the former holy well, north via Staplehill and Holt Heath, passes through the Holwell site before continuing north via a hillfort at Blackheath Down to Stonehenge. We will look further into leys in Chapter Twelve.

St Augustine's Well, or the Silver Well, at Cerne Abbas is a surviving holy well dating back to at least Saxon times. The well lies at the end of an ancient cobbled path, nestling under tall limes. The locality is both sacred and atmospheric. The water flows from a spring that was formerly located in the centre of the Abbey churchyard. A record of 1620 speaks of a chapel at the well dedicated to St Augustine. Some of it's walls can still be seen close by today. Legend has it that Augustine, one of several missionary monks sent to England by Pope Gregory in 596, miraculously produced the spring when he struck the ground with his staff. This act was said to have converted many of the hitherto Pagan villagers, who had in fact just kicked him out of the village!

Edwold, brother of Edmund the Saxon king of East Anglia, lived as a hermit here at the 'Silver Well, Cerne". The village was certainly a Pagan stronghold in Saxon times. The stone Catherine Wheel found at the well (Fig. 24) probably indicates a former Goddess sanctuary.

A tradition exists that new-born infants were dipped in the well for health and good fortune, a ritual associated with many sacred wells. Apparently care was taken to insure that the child faced the sun and was immersed just as the sun was rising. Young girls drank the waters whilst touching the wishing stone and prayed for a husband.

"From thy forehead thus I take
These herbs, and charge thee not awake
Till in yonder holy well" .
From *"The Holy Well"*, John Fletcher (1579-1625).

Plate 46. St Augustine's Well, Cerne Abbas, a sacred locality since at least Saxon times.

On the top of Woodbury Hill is the site of Anchoret's Well (grid ref:c.856947). Antiquarian John Hutchins noted that crowds would visit the well annually on September 21st, around the autumn Equinox, to drink the waters, which had "many virtues attributed to it". A well of never-failing water still survives on the hill, but is thought not to be Anchoret's Well. A chapel was built near the well, confirming the importance of the locality as a sacred site.

A tradition exists that girls at Milton Abbas would meet annually at St Catherine's Well, on the feast day of the saint, and make their way to St Catherine's Chapel, on the hill-top. This has similarities to old processions elsewhere at Pagan festival times.

The well that gave the village of St Andrew's Well, Bridport, its name once had a chapel nearby, echoing the wells at Cerne and Woodbury. This would suggest that this well too may have been regarded as "holy".

A spring at Walditch, SE of Bridport, was said to have curative properties, being especially beneficial for sore eyes. A well at Symondsbury Farm, west of Bridport, is also said to have waters that cure eye complaints. Here, the waters must be taken as the sun rises, just as the sun's rays hit the well. This is similar to the child dipping at Cerne Abbas and probably has a Pagan purification ceremony origin. Young children were dipped in the Symondsbury Well also, a tradition that is very widespread.

The Wishing Well at Upwey is marked on OS maps and locally signposted. This beautiful site is maintained by English Heritage (check opening times prior to visit). The Saxons founded a chantry here and St Laurence's Church, next to the well, probably evolved from it. This would indicate that the well is not only ancient but has been regarded as a holy well. The well has a long tradition as a wishing well, the former railway station at Upwey being named Wishing Well Halt. One is supposed to stand with one's back to the well (shown in Fig. 42), sip the water from a glass and wish. The remaining water is then thrown over the shoulder back into the well. This locality is worth a visit, standing as it does amidst peaceful gardens next to the River Wey.

Warmwell is the site of another curative spring. The name "Warmwelle" appears in the Doomsday Book (1086) literally meaning "the warm well or spring". There was a warm spring at Fifehead Neville. The Romans built a villa near to it (see *Ancient Stones of Dorset*, page 188). We will discuss possible connections between warm water wells, faults and earth energies in Chapter Thirteen.

Another surviving holy well is that of St Wite's, Morecombelake. From the pub one proceeds up Ship Knapp Lane until one sees a signpost to the well. The well is on open ground overlooking the village (grid ref:399938). It is in fact a natural spring

112

issuing from the ground. A plaque (Plate 47) tells us of a possible association between the well and St Wite, the 13th century martyr of Whitechurch Canonicorum, a mile to the north. The well is recorded from the 17th century and the waters are considered, as with some other Dorset wells, to have curative properties for eye disorders. The water today is still clear and swift and is received into a small basin (see Plate 48). Access to the waters is via a small gate.

Tutton's Well, at Stanpit in Christchurch, was the only source of freshwater in the immediate area. The Canons of the Priory held its waters in high regard as a cure for blindness. The well's water was sold inland by hawkers for its properties, especially for treating eye complaints. The well was capped in World War Two. Nearby Purewell derived its name from a small rivulet that flowed alongside Purewell Road.

Tales of the curative properties of wells and springs could derive from three possible origins. Firstly, it is possible that the waters do contain qualities which affect the

Fig. 42. The Wishing Well at Upwey

body. This could be some mineral, such as iron. The curative properties could also be due to earth energies present at sites. After all, dowsers can detect the presence of water underground: what is it they are detecting?

Lastly, it could be that the participant's own healing abilities are simulated by the visit to a holy well. A pilgrim would have expectations during his journey to a well, and presumably would have faith in the divine properties of the waters, which would be ritually drunk. He would thus be in a susceptible frame of mind for healing. This mental and spiritual process takes place every year by millions of pilgrims visiting countless sacred places.

Holy wells still attract pilgrims today, of all cultures and religions. A well at Little Walsingham, Norfolk, still has 100,000 visitors annually. Well dressing ceremonies, notably in Derbyshire, attract large numbers eager to venerate the powers of sacred wells and springs.

Plate 47. St Wite's Well plaque.

Plate 48. The waters of St Wite's Well

Other Wells and Springs of Note

Many wells and springs dedicated to Christian saints, etc. are undoubtedly the result of the Christianisation of existing Pagan sacred places. On the hillside north of Abbotsbury, 1:25 0000 maps show Lady's Well. We have already seen how Mary took over the role of the Goddess at wells and springs. Another Lady's Well, at Hermitage, is also associated with the Virgin Mary cult. Over 70 Scottish wells are dedicated to her. This well, as with others in Dorset, is on a ley line. It was plotted by myself (*"Ancient Stones of Dorset"*, Fig. 127) and runs from Clarkham Cross to Bulbarrow.

At Powerstock, the well water occasionally runs red and no doubt this gave rise to folklore associated with the Devil at the well. The red waters may have been regarded as the blood of the Earth Goddess issuing from Her body. Iron-rich waters at the Chalice Well, Glastonbury, turn the adjacent rocks and stones red.

At Stoke Abbot, near Beaminster, spring water pours from the mouth of a lion's head (Plate 49), as seen again at the Chalice Well. Nearby the waters are received into a small pool, flowing from deep within the earth. One can look into the dark interior of the Goddess, the pure waters bubbling (Plate 78). An old tree shelters the spot and the village nestles quietly under Gerrard's Hill.

At Witchampton, north of Wimborne, a spring is received into a small, flint-lined shrine (Plate 50). A small altar-like ledge is present and a short flight of steps enables one to access the waters.

Of interest is the fact that St John's Well, at Evershot, is very close to the intersection of two leys, one of which goes all the way to Stonehenge (see *Ancient Stones of Dorset*, Figs 118 and 119). In *The Sun and the Serpent*, it is described how many holy wells lie on the 'Mary line'.

Thousands of modern pilgrims still continue the ancient tradition of visiting and venerating sacred wells and springs. At many places people leave pieces of cloth, flowers, crystals and other offerings. A myriad of articles have been left at Madron Well, Cornwall, and the White Well, in the lane next to the Chalice Well gardens, Glastonbury. This tradition is thought to have originated way back in prehistoric times, when votive objects were offered to the deities and spirits of a locality. From this beginning evolved the practice of rubbing a piece of rag onto a wound or diseased area of the body and leaving it in a sacred well or spring. It was hoped that as the rag rotted the ailment would depart the body. Things seem to have gone full circle now, with people once again leaving personal offerings in recognition of the sacredness of the Goddess waters.

All of the above is not simply superstitious nonsense. Indeed miracles, it seems, are still manifesting today. Issue 19 (Summer 1997) of *Celtic Connections* carries an

Plate 49. The Lions head spring at Stoke Abbot. (See also plate 78).

Plate 50. The spring shrine at Witchampton. The spring dries up during dry spells, as shown here. A Roman temple site lies in a field to the north.

article about the healing waters of two ancient wells on the site of the abbey at Minster, on the Isle of Sheppey. In 1991 a small statuette of the triple Goddess was found in one of the well shafts. Since then all sorts of wondrous events have taken place, such as barren women becoming pregnant and women with previous histories of miscarriages coming to term. Other "miracles" are cited, such as a man being cured of a serious foot complaint after taking the well waters. The Earth still gives, it seems, despite all we have done to Her.

---

*"Water never rests, neither by day
nor night. When flowing above, it
causes rain and dew. When flowing
below, it forms streams and rivers.
Water is outstanding in doing good".*
Lao-Tse.

Chapter Seven

Heights of Aspiration

> *"The Mother has told us to look after all mountains.... they are all alive."*
> The Kogi, Columbia.

The Kogi, quoted above, are an ancient tribe still living on a high and isolated mountain top, which they say is sacred. High places have always been sources of inspiration and aspiration. They quite literally inspire us to greater heights, both physically and spiritually. Perhaps it is the height itself of a hill, tor or mountain, and the effort needed to climb it, that gives it a magical quality. The earth reaches up to the skies, towards the heavens.

High places are metaphors for transcendental states of being, places to not only look down on the landscape below, but also into the landscape of our heart and soul. Hills are the dwelling places of sacred energies and beings in cultures across the world. Some say the word hill comes from *"kel"*, of Indo-European root, meaning "concealed sacred place". Another possible derivative is *"halig"*, meaning "holy". Many sacred traditions certainly centre around hills.

In the Bible, Moses went up Mount Sinai to receive the Ten Commandments, probably during meditation or trance. Mount Olympus is the legendary home of the Greek gods. Mount Fuji is Japan's most sacred place. In Australia we find Ayre's Rock, sacred to the Aborigines since prehistory.

In northern European folklore mountains and hills are the home to dwarfs and elves, experts in metalwork and the forging of magical swords and rings. Ancient people saw the shapes of hills and ridges as being the Earth Goddess, or at least parts of Her anatomy. We will look into local examples of this in Chapter Nine.

In our search for the dragon, the underlying theme of this book, it is not surprising that many high places were their abode. For instance, a dragon is supposed to haunt the two Iron Age hillforts of Dolbury Hill and Cadbury Hill, in Devon's Exe valley,

120

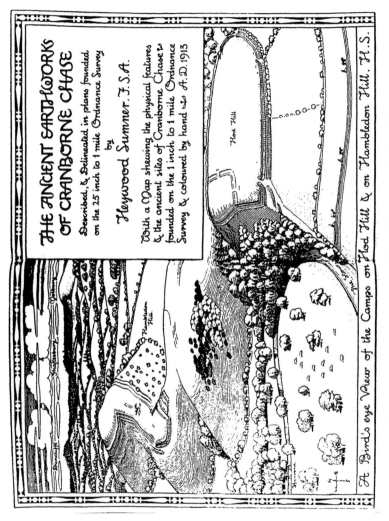

Fig. 43. An old picturesque drawing of Hod Hill and Hambledon Hill.

121

and in fact flies between the two. Another dragon had it's home in the hillfort above Norton Fitzwarren, Somerset. At Kilve, also in Somerset, a dragon named Blue Ben lived inside Outsham Hill, periodically going down to the sea to cool himself. A dragon at Sexhow, in Yorkshire, lived inside a rounded hill there. The famous White Horse of Uffington is cut into the chalk on Dragon's Hill. St Michael, the dragon-slayer, is frequently associated with hills. The erection of numerous hilltop chapels dedicated to him were means of stamping out pagan practices on hilltops. The tower on top of Glastonbury Tor is all that remains of St Michael's Chapel, which was destroyed by an earthquake! The Tor is the legendary home of Gwyn-up-Nudd, God of the Underworld in Celtic myth.

Cadbury Castle, a hillfort near Yeovil, is one of the possible locations of Camelot, Arthur's castle. According to tradition, the hill is hollow and every seven years the hillside opens and Arthur and his gallant knights ride down to the spring at Sutton Montis to water their horses. Also in Arthurian legend is the hilltop "fort" of Dinas Emrys, in Wales. This site is associated with two dragons, Druids and none other than Merlin himself. King Sil is reputably residing inside Silbury Hill, the sacred man-made mound at Avebury. It is said that on moonlit nights he rides his horse around the base of the hill.

"Within them [hillforts] lie hidden all
the secrets of time before history begins...."
Hadrian Allcroft.

High places, and the hillforts often found on their summits, certainly have an air of mystery and have attracted folklore. Let us turn to Dorset with this in mind.

Dorset High Places

"Deep within the sacred hollow hill a crystal spring,
Naiad guarded, bubbles and sparkles through cavern after cavern.
Yin and Yang, male hill and female spring,
the eternal balanced whole which is the only sure foundation"
From *"Outpourings"*, by Ken Bailey

Many Dorset hills have folklore and legendary associations. The so called "hillforts" are likewise embellished with magical tales. Even today, we can

Plate 51. Looking up the steep southern slopes of Hambledon Hill, showing earthworks and barrows on the skyline.

123

experience some of the magical atmosphere of far-gone days, times when hills were empowered and sacred places. Let us take a look at some of these "heights of aspiration".

There is a tradition that the hillforts on Hod Hill and Hambledon Hill, NW of Blandford, protect the villages of Durweston and Stourpaine by supernatural forces. The Romans built a fort on Hod Hill and it is said that a Roman centurion haunts both hills. A golden coffin is also supposedly buried beneath Hod Hill. A dense yew forest on Hambledon Hill is said to have been planted by Druids as groves in which to worship. It is said to be an unlucky place, a story no doubt spread by the local Church, eager to stop the locals visiting what sounds like a sacred wood. The views from the tops of the twin hills are worth the climb, and Neolithic barrows survive to remind us of the ancient sacredness of the place (see Plate 51 and Fig. 43).

A hill possessing particular magic and timelessness is Lambert's Castle, close to the Dorset-Devon border. Modern bard Ken Bailey describes the hill in his poem "Re-awakening":

> "....At the top of the hill no recognisable physical home
> just a long, wide roughly hedged enclosure
> but a spiritual home of almost unbelievable peace and calm,
> hiding, almost afraid of being re-discovered
> lest once again this sacred place now marked "hill fort"
> should become a new site of battle and bloodshed...."

Ken captures the mood of the place perfectly. Plate 52 is a photo taken by him looking into the tree-encircled enclosure. Here the spirit of the place reaches out into our very being. One tree has branches in the form of antlers, as if Cernunnos himself were holding court (see Plate 101).

In 1630 Gerard spoke of Lambert's Castle having "a hole in the top of the hill", and speaks of "the spirits haunting the place". Three hillocks on the hill are called the Devil's Three Jumps, a sure sign of an old pagan sacred place. On Thorncombe Beacon, on the coast to the south, there is a Devil's Jump Mound. Folklore tells us that the Devil was kicked out by the Abbot of Forde and bounced all the way to the sea!

> "The mountains skipped like rams,
> and the little hills like lambs."
> Psalm 114

Plate 52. The enclosure on Lambert's Castle. (photograph by Ken Bailey, used with kind permission.)

Eggardon Hill is another high place with intriguing folklore. Occupation of the hill commenced back in the Neolithic and culminated in an Iron Age defensive enclosure, built to withstand the invading Romans. From the 1950's there is an account of a man being chased across the hill by the Devil. Another tale speaks of voices being heard on a misty day up on the hill. The hill is also said to be haunted by Diana and her hounds, collecting the souls of the dead. Eggardon appears to come from the Celtic "Egawr", meaning "to open-expand". This could bear witness to the former use of the hill as a sacred place.

Badbury Rings is a popular recreation spot near Wimborne. The Iron Age ramparts are topped by modern plantations (Plate53). The hill has never been excavated but was probably taken by the Romans in AD43. Numerous Roman roads radiate from the base of the hillfort across Dorset. It is claimed by many that Badbury Rings is by tradition in fact Mount Badon, where Arthur defeated the Saxons in AD 518. Prior to 1978 archaeological students camping on the summit one night heard the clashing of metal, sounds of marching men and shouting in a strange tongue. They are reported to have left in panic!

More spectral happenings have been witnessed at Dudsbury, an Iron Age hillfort on the northern outskirts of Bournemouth. Here, a Roman ghost is in residence. Flower's Barrow hillfort, between Lulworth and Tyneham, is thought to have been constructed by Belgic invaders, who landed at Lulworth and established a beach head. The cliff top location is breathtaking and offers quiet relaxation and meditation. Portland rises in one direction, whilst eastwards the Purbecks rise out of chalk cliffs. In 1678 it is recorded that a phantom army was sighted, "a vast number of men, several thousands, marching from Flower's Barrow, over Grange Hill". There are also reports of "queer unidentifiable noises" at Flower's Barrow, as well as "strange music" and "strange calling voices". Greyish phantoms have also been seen thereabouts. Clearly, the place is alive with the memory of events that have gone before, events left impressed on the locality; every now and then, when conditions are right, things "flicker" in and out of our reality.

"O ancestors, powerful spirits, who live amongst us, your tombs are the mountains."
Sumatran incantation.

The list of Dorset's high places worthy of mention is a long one. But I do not intend to attempt further coverage of them here. Places such as Pilsden Pen, Bulbarrow, Swyre Head and the Purbeck Hills alone inspire us all to investigate and visit others. Anyone studying ancient stone sites of Dorset will notice that several sites are on hill tops, such as Kingston Russell stone circle, Hampton Hill circle, Poxwell Cairn

Plate 53. Badbury Rings, as seen from one of the tumuli alongside the access road.

stones, Devil's Stone (at Bere Regis) and the Hellstone Cromlech (see "Ancient Stone of Dorset" for details of these and others).

What I aim to do here is to concentrate on Dorset's largest and finest hillfort, Maiden Castle, a sacred place of the highest order.

Maîðen Castle

> *"The profile of the whole stupendous ruin, as seen*
> *from a distance a mile eastwards, is clearly cut as*
> *that of a marble inlay. It may indeed be likened*
> *to an enormous many-limbed organism, lying lifeless" .*
> From *"A Tryst at an Ancient Earthwork"*, Thomas Hardy.

I am not going to describe in detail the archaeology and topography of Maiden Castle, that has been accomplished many times before. It is the magical essence of the place I wish to capture. I am also going to use the locality as a model to demonstrate that many of our so-called "hillforts" have a more ancient and sacred origin.

Maiden Castle is a truly huge earthwork, SW of Dorchester, running around a high hill which rises out of the surrounding cultivated landscape. It has a length of 3,000ft, an inner circumference of about $1^{1}/_{2}$ miles, and covers 120 acres. The name Maiden Castle crops up elsewhere in Britain. For instance, it is recorded in 1587 that Cumberland folk took their cattle....at Beltan times....to Maidencastle". There are around 40 hillforts listed with the name, as well as numerous Maiden wells.

The Maiden in question could of course be the Virgin Mary. But it must be remembered that the Virgin Mary Cult derived from that of Brighid, the Celtic maiden-spring goddess. St Bride derives from Brighid and her river still flows into the sea at Burton Bradstock. If Maiden Castle is a hill sacred to the goddess Brighid then its use as a spiritual centre predates the use of the hill as a defensive enclosure, possibly by centuries.

The name "Mai-Daan" occurs in eastern cities, and means a "place of assembly", which the hill certainly has been, be it spiritual or tribal. The veneration of the place goes back to the Neolithic and continued right up to the Romans, who built a temple on the top (Plate 56).

Plate 54. Maiden Castle on the skyline from the north. To the right hand side undulations mark out the huge ramparts at the west entrance.

Plate 55. Maiden Castle.

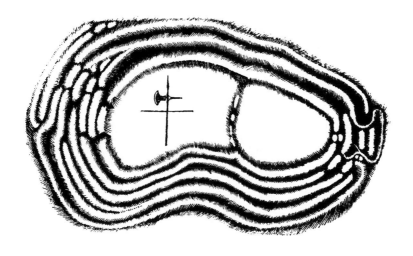

Fig. 44. An 1833 engraving of Maiden Castle, showing the labyrinthine banks and ditches.

It is my opinion, and the view of several others, that the huge earthen ramparts of Maiden Castle are the result of modifications of earlier, more ancient structures. In its heyday the defences, capped by wooden stockades, would have been an awesome sight to any visitor of the hill. The complicated labyrinthine entrances would remind the ancient traveller of Troy itself. Yet these huge features may have had a more sacred origin. It has been estimated that 250, 000 would have been needed to defend the hillfort from attack. Across the country, many hillforts did not have wells, nor were they close to running water supplies, essential for any community under siege. It must be concluded that these places were originally utilised as spiritual centres, places where ancient sacred rituals were carried out.

There is a tradition that Maiden Castle was built by giants, and indeed the ramparts are of gigantic proportions. Forbes, in *The Unchronicled Past* suggests that the fortifications at the west end were primarily processional, only later being altered for defence. These labyrinth-like earthern structures (Fig. 44) remind us of mazes, discussed earlier. One can envisage processions, in the Neolithic Age, proceeding through these multiple entrances as part of festival rituals. The labyrinth is a

131

Plate 56. The remains of the Roman-British temple on Maiden Castle.

metaphor for our own personal journey towards spiritual attainment. Whenever I wend my way slowly up through these earthern banks, time seems to stand still. The high earthern walls restrict my view, they close around me. Then, quite suddenly, I am at the top. This is an area of openness, a vast emptiness, and my mind is set free from its subconscious confines. Birds of prey ride the thermals above my head and I feel as if I could fly.

Here on this height, holiness, purity and blessing comes welling out of the earth.
Grace and Ivan Cooke, speaking of Maiden Castle, in *The Light In Britain.*

In 1926 H J Massingham wrote, in *Downland Man*, Maiden Castle has a solitude that frightened one a little because it was so vast and calm. Although it is a high, isolated hill, one cannot see all the surrounding countryside from a single spot. One has to discover each corner of the hill if one wishes to look to distant skylines. Even in the vastness of the enclosure, one is still enclosed, separate from the outside world.

The hill is certainly one where unusual phenomena have been witnessed. There is a, quite modern, tradition that fairy lights are seen on the castle ramparts. Light phenomena such as these are dealt with further in Chapter Thirteen. In the 1970s, a group of people were parked below Maiden Castle, one November moonlit night. As they sat in the vehicle, it mysteriously started moving up and down. It also tilted to and fro at the front and back along its long axis. The occupants looked out of the windows but no one was to be seen. They drove off in a frightened state.

Within recent memory, probably the early 1980s. a woman walking on the hill one night witnessed a group of Roman soldiers marching across the enclosure. She was very shaken by the experience.

There are tales of a hollow cave beneath the hill. Some believe it to be the outcrop of conglomerate rock at grid ref: 668883, below the southern ramparts, half way along. There is a slight overhang and a hollow underneath, vaguely arch-shaped. Hubbard and Hubbard, in 1907, tell us local tradition has it that beneath this stone lintel was a stairway, and that after so much was discovered, the staircase was filled up with earth. Modern records speak of a World War II tunnel, linking the hill to Dorchester, but no proof of this exists. The legendary view that some hills are hollow, such as at Silbury, Glastonbury and Cadbury, invites comparisons to the cave and tunnel folklore of Maiden Castle.

The whole area around Maiden Castle is peppered with Neolithic long barrows and Bronze Age round barrows. The long barrow at grid ref: 665887 aligns with the western end of the Neolithic bank barrow that crosses the enclosure. More alignments with the hill will be looked at in Chapter twelve, regarding ley lines. Perhaps it is enough for now to note that the hillforts of Maiden Castle, Eggardon and Pilsden Pen lie in a straight line.

The idea of energy leys is quite a recent one and is a controversial subject indeed. But landscape sculpturing is an archaeological fact. At many hillforts the shape of the land was altered and one wonders if this was done to enhance earth energies. Ceremonies and rituals long ago were carried out to ensure the harmony and enhancement of the earths life forces. Perhaps once again, we should head for the hills and experience those heights of aspiration that is our spiritual heritage.

Hills will always be the haunts
of him who seeks to cultivate
his original nature.
Kuo Hsi.

Chapter Eight

Brother Sun - Sister Moon

If the sun and moon should doubt,
They'd immediately go out.
William Blake.

The sun and the moon have been venerated and indeed deified since early prehistoric times. Cave paintings depicting both heavenly bodies have been found right across the world.. Early Man would have held in awe these two luminous bodies that illuminated his way, ripened his crops and brought about the seasons. Life on earth is dependant on the sun as our primary source of warmth and vitality.

With the dawning of the megalithic age, our ancestors had acquired the technology, and the spiritual incentive, to mark out the monthly and yearly lunar and solar cycles with standing stones, circles and chambered tombs. And they did so with great accuracy, dramatically seen at Stonehenge and Newgrange, for instance. Stone sites of similar purpose to these occur across Europe and we shall look at some Dorset examples later. In *Ancient Stones of Dorset* I describe many astronomical events visible from sacred sites in the county. In this chapter I will describe some additional examples, plus present illustrations to elaborate on previously described ones not before illustrated.

Some examples of sun and moon worship from around the world may serve to illustrate the universal extent of the practice. In the New Hebrides, in the Pacific Ocean, the sun and moon were regarded as the divine husband and wife. In China, the Emperor gave annual sacrifices to both heavenly bodies. In Norse/Viking myths, the sun and moon were constantly chased across the skies by two wolves, Skoll and Hati.

Into historical times both the sun and moon continued to be regarded as deities. Solar and lunar gods are carved on an ancient Persian stone dated 2nd century AD. More examples of solar and lunar gods will be found below, under their respective headings.

As the human population steadily increased it became more important to ensure the fecundity of the land and the vitality of crops. A Celtic calendar found at Coligny, near Lyons, seems to have been used to synchronise solar and lunar events, probably for agricultural purposes. The primary Celtic cycle seems to have been lunar and night orientated, rather than counted by solar events and days.

Brother Sun

"Round-a, round-a, keep your ring:
To the glorious sun we sing,
He that wears the flaming rays,
And the imperial crown of bays,
Him with shouts and songs we praise..."
from *The Satyr's Dance*, Thomas Ravenscroft, 1614.

Ancient relics of solar significance have been widely found, as too myths and legends associated with the sun. A Bronze Age Sun-Chariot found at Trundholm, Denmark, consists of a horse pulling a chariot carrying a solar disc. In Greek and Roman mythology sun gods were often depicted as being carried across the heavens by a horse-drawn chariot.

In the Old Testament of the Bible we find that the Israelites were avid sun worshippers, as indicated by the oft-mentioned denunciation of the practice. For instance, in 1 Kings, XI, 7, we read that Solomon built a high place "...called Chemosh, for the worship of the sun." The kings of Judah dedicated their horses to the solar god (2 Kings, XXIII, 11).

Bacchus was the phallic Roman sun god, described as a saviour and a liberator. He was born on December 25th, to a virgin mother. Sound familiar? The contrived birth date of Jesus the Christ was the Church's attempt to take-over pagan festivals.

The Hindus have the sun god Indra, Lord of the Gods and destroyer of their enemies. At the Inca city of Macchu Picchu is a stone called the Solar Stone, thought to be a locality for either sacrifices or astronomical observations. The Aztecs venerated the solar god Tezcatliopoca, who doubled as deity of the moon and evenings. The Egyptians were avid sun worshippers, the gods Hathor and Ra being depicted with the solar disc above their heads. On our trip to Egypt in 1995, Ghermaine and I saw the sun's orb painted or carved in every temple we visited (see plate 57). Both the Egyptians and the Babylonians wore amulets of gold or bronze discs. (Fig. 23 (A)

Plate 57. The sun god Ra Horakhete, with solar disc above his head, at the Egyptian temple of Abu Simbel.

shows an example of gold discs found at Clandon Barrow, in Dorset). In the Egyptian temple of Karnak I was impressed with the alignment of the towering buildings, columns and corridors with the midwinter sunrise.

...vessels marked with the image of the sun, the moon, or Dagon, which were accounted symbols of Divinity among the heathens.
Thomas Lewis, *Origines Hebrae*, 1734.

The Pawness Indians of North America had the sun god Shakuru, whilst the Slavonic tribes venerated Dazhbog. The Serbs saw the sun as a handsome king.

Although I have used Brother Sun to head this section, I readily accept that the worshipping of the sun as a male deity is not necessarily universal. Many Australian Aborigine tribes regard the sun as feminine. The Japanese worshipped the sun goddess Ameterasu, whilst the Arab solar goddess was Atthar. In Norse mythology the sun was likewise feminine, named Sunna.

The Celts thought the sun to be the goddess Sul or Sol. Brigit, or Brighid, was a solar goddess, her attributes being light and inspiration. Bel or Belenos likewise had many solar associations and was the Celtic equivalent of the classical god Apollo. She is said to have hung her cloak on the rays of the sun. In modern German, the sun is feminine, *die sonne*.

To the Celts it seems to have been the *cycles* of the sun and moon that interested them, rather than individual solar and lunar gods and goddesses. The so called fire festivals of the pagan calendar can be traced back to prehistoric times, as we find today many megalithic sites aligned to sun rises and sunsets around these dates. These festivals have solar myths and superstitions associated with them. May Day festivals evolved from Beltain, the festival of Belenos, the Shining One. The growing sun was releasing the earth from the grips of winter, and the fairy folk revelled. The festival of Samhain is now Halloween, marking the cooling of the sun as the winter nears. It was a time when the veil between mortals and the spirit world was thin, a time for divination and storytelling.

Although the summer solstice hits the headlines every year, as modern pagans try to enter Stonehenge, it is the winter solstice that appears to have been more important to our prehistoric ancestors. My own studies of Dorset long barrow, bank barrow and other alignments suggest that the shortest day of the year was very sacred to prehistoric people. We will look at some of these alignments later.

Plate 58. A beautiful sunset seen from the top of Hengistbury Head during spring 1997.

Into Medieval times solar ceremonies and superstitions were still common. Great fires were lit on midsummer's eve and Maypole dancing, a phallic solar ritual, was still very popular. In Medieval dancing it was important to move around the circle in the same direction as the sun, for good fortune. We have already seen how many sacred wells and springs in Dorset have solar rituals connected with them. It was often important to ritually bathe or dip as the dawn sun hit the waters.

Eastwards I stand, for favours I pray,
I pray the great Lord, I pray the mighty prince,
I pray the Holy Warden of the heavenly kingdom,
To earth I pray and to up-heaven.
Anglo-Saxon sunrise charm.

Some Dorset Solar Alignments

Much excellent work has been published in recent years on the solar and lunar alignments of barrows and stone sites in Wessex. Two worthy of particular praise are *Stonehenge: The Secret of the Solstice* by George Terence Meaden, and the authoritative *Stonehenge* by John North (see Bibliography). Both works describe the Dorset Cursus alignments in great detail with new material and interpretations. Norths book is noteworthy for his stellar and solar alignments of the wooden henge at Mount Pleasant.

In my previous book, *Ancient Stones of Dorset* I gave a chart of compass directions for the various solar festivals, as well as details of sunrise and sunset events to be seen from sites around the county. I do not intend to duplicate that material here, except when necessary to either demonstrate particularly fine examples, or to illustrate in figure or plate photograph some alignments described, but not illustrated, previously.

On numerous occasions I have found myself, sometimes accompanied by Ghermaine, at an ancient site on a particular solstice or festival dawn, awaiting the appearance of the Sky God on the skyline. At such times I get a profound feeling of participation in something sacred, moments in time when I glimpse what has been before. My feelings during a sunrise at a stone circle, or any other ancient site for that matter, are different than I experience during other times of the day. There is a hushed expectancy, a magical alchemy that allows a change of awareness. For sacred sites also possess sacred time, those occasions when they literally come alive.

Due to the wealth of material now available, it was a problem to know what to include and what to exclude from this section. In the end I decided to describe astronomical alignments that the reader can easily check out, as well as some I have observed myself at the relevant sunrises and sunsets. It is hoped the reader will be inspired to experience them, as well as look for new ones as yet undiscovered.

The Dorset Cursus

You are she who restores day and puts the darkness to flight...you send forth the glad daylight...
from a 12th century herbal treatise (referring to a female sun!).

No survey of Dorset solar alignments, no matter how brief, would be complete without reference to the Dorset Cursus. This mammoth Neolithic earthwork weaves its way across the landscape for about six miles. Two banks of earth ran parallel to each other, with ditches on the outside. The banks are now largely levelled, but at one time would have stood up to 6¹/₂ft high, comprising of earth and chalk.

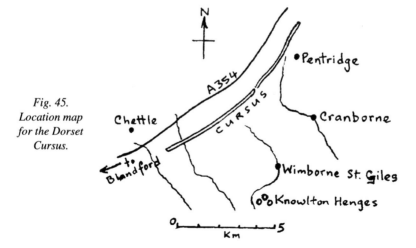

Fig. 45. Location map for the Dorset Cursus.

The cursus is actually two cursuses, joined around the midway point. John North in fact suggests that curves and kinks seen elsewhere in the course of the cursus imply different stages of construction, spanning perhaps long periods of time. The cursus evolved, in line perhaps with the construction of the many long barrows associated with it. The cursus traverses river valleys and high ridges, and the positioning of long barrows on the latter is one of the keys to unravelling the meaning and use of the structure.

It has been assessed that creation of the cursus involved the moving of some six and a half million tons of earth and chalk, nearly twice as much as needed to erect the Avebury monument. The efforts of 450,000 worker-hours would have been necessary, a major enterprise for any culture. These estimates exclude the 12 long barrows within a mile of the cursus, which were an integral part of its ritual activities.

George Terence Meaden suggests that the curving and jumpy course of the cursus is the result of Neolithic Man commemorating the actual path of a tornado across the landscape. He convincingly cites several long barrow self-alignments as indicating the date of the event. He also cites other cursuses that do not run dead straight across the land, a feature apparently of tornado paths. He argues that our Neolithic ancestors would have seen this violent natural event as the coming together, a sacred marriage no less, of the Sky God and the Earth Goddess.

The best surviving section of the cursus, which is fortunately also very accessible, is at the southern extremity, the Thickthorn Terminal (A in Fig. 46). Here we get some idea of the enormity of the construction, the terminal banks of earth rising out of the field, next to the road (grid ref: 969125). Plate 59 shows the cursus bank on the left hand side, with the Thickthorn Long Barrow to the right. To the south east another long barrow, in the same field. When this barrow was excavated it was found to be devoid of burial or cremation remains, making it a purely ritual structure. However, three post holes were found at the east end. The axis of these post holes, and indeed both barrows, is aligned with the midwinter solstice sunrise. Plate 60 shows the two barrows. Clearly, these mounds were positioned for use by the living, not the dead. Further to this, the actual end bank of the cursus is not 90^0 to the banks structure, but is skewed in the direction, again, of the solstice. Fig. 47 expands the area, with the barrows and cursus end aligned with the midwinter sun rising on the skyline.

Meaden has pointed out that at the few moments after the midwinter sunrise, both barrows cast shadows behind them which fall on the Thickthorn Barrow and the cursus itself. In other words, all three earthworks are connected by a visual phenomena, Meadens sacred marriage being played out in dramatic fashion. Fig. 47 shows the shadows in my interpretation of the scene.

142

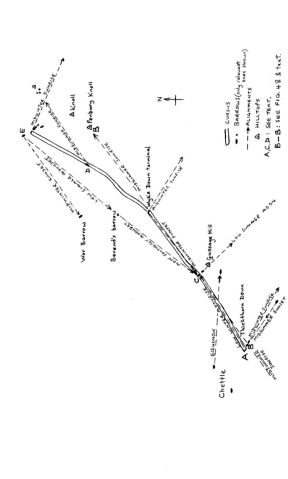

Fig. 46. The Dorset Cursus, showing relevant barrows, solar and lunar alignments and features in the text.

143

Fig. 46 also shows a more distant long barrow to the south east of the two just discussed. This very denuded barrow lies west of Gussage St Michael church at grid ref: 982113. Viewed from this barrow, the summer solstice sunset occurs in the direction of the cursus terminal and the long barrows next to it. A low ridge rises in between, however, but it is just possible that all three barrows and the cursus may have been intervisible prior to barrow erosion and hedge plantation. Plate 60 looks along the axis of the midsummer sunset towards the cursus bank. The sun goes down into the distant skyline above the barrow marked with an arrow in the photograph. I actually observed this on June 19, 1997 (the position of solstice sunrises and sunsets does not alter radically for a few days either side of the official solstice date). The sun appears to set at 21.19 BST, slightly earlier than one might expect due to the height of the skyline.

It was a magical evening and just as the sun set on the horizon two small deer sprang out of the nearby hedgerow and darted across the field between the sun and myself. As I turned away from the scene I was surprised by a beautiful full moon rising in the south-east, icing on the cake indeed!

Midway between the Thickthorn and Wyke Down terminals, a large long barrow lies actually within the course of the former cursus banks, its axis being approximately 90^{0} to them (C in Fig. 46, grid ref: 993138). The barrow is accessible via bridlepaths along Gussage Hill. It is still 10 ft high and 155 ft long and stands on a prominent ridge at 360 ft OD. Its location was chosen with care to enable it to be visible on the skyline along the cursus from both the north and south.

This barrow is a vital hub of several astronomical observations. From the region of the south terminal, and its accompanying long barrows, barrow C is visible on the ridge, and aligned with it on the skyline is Penbury Knoll. At midsummer solstice the sun rises above these two aligned features, viewed from the Thickthorn Barrow (see Fig. 48). This is a beautiful example of the harmony that can be achieved between Man and Nature when the inspiration is present. When standing on the cursus bank at the south terminal, or within its former parallel banks for that matter, barrow C also marks out the rising of the moon at its most southerly winter full moon. This line is also almost coincidental with Beltaine and Lammas sunrises.

Barrow C is again important at another key time of the year. At the Wyke Down Terminal there is a break in the cursus banks. Some believe this may have been for the procession access to the interior of the cursus. From the low remaining banks south of the break (next to the B3081 on Bottlebush Down) we can look south and again see barrow C, but from the opposite direction from which we viewed it before. The barrow now marks out the midwinter sunset. Studies by John North (*Stonehenge*) and John Edwin Wood (*Sun, Moon and Standing Stones*) has shown that around c.3750 the last glint of the setting sun would have been at the entrance of the barrow (see Fig. 49). By 2500 BC the sun was setting below the highest point of

144

the barrow. The later in time we go, the further to the right along the barrow the sunsets. By 600 AD the last glint was in mid-barrow. Today, the sunset is at the western, right extremity.

I was fortunate and privileged to witness the winter solstice sunset of 1996 from the Wyke Down terminal. The sun sank into the long barrow on the skyline on a clear, cold dusk. It was a breathtaking spectacle and one that transported me back thousands of years in time (see Plate 61).

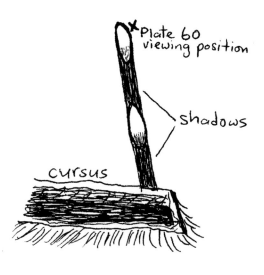

Fig. 47. The moment of the midwinter sunrise at the south terminal of the cursus, showing how the long barrows and cursus are linked by the shadows cast by the sun. (see Plate 6-0.)

Barrow D in Fig. 46 is set into the west bank of the cursus, in woodland south west of Pentridge (grid ref: 025169). It is self-aligned with the midsummer sunrise, and some barrows and a hilltop in that direction may have relevance.

At the northern terminal of the cursus we find that the closing bank is again askew to the right angle, as is the case at the Thickthorn and Wyke Down termini. The alignment is again towards the midwinter sunrise, an alignment that just clips the northern edge of a long barrow next to the cursus, at grid ref: 042191. This barrow is easily viewed from adjacent bridle paths.

More solar and lunar alignments are shown on fig. 46 and there are several others in the vicinity not shown. The lunar associations with the cursus will be looked at later in this chapter. The positions of the long barrows around the cursus, and their self-alignments, would suggest that rituals were held at certain times of the year. The barrows continued to be used by the living, long after their use, if at all, as tombs for the dead.

As I have pointed out before, sunrises and sunsets enable daily contact between the Sky God and the Earth Mother. The sacred marriage duly takes place, the Earth Goddess being fertilised in sacred consummation by the solar god. It may well be worth visualising what events may have taken place here in the Neolithic, over 5000

Plate 59. The south terminal of the Dorset Cursus.

Plate 60. The line of the midsummer solstice sunset, as seen from the point indicated in Fig. 47.

146

Fig. 48. The alignment of the long barrow on Gussage Hill and Penbury Knoll, seen from the east side of thickthorn Barrow. This is the direction of the midsummer sunrise, axis B-B in Fig. 46.

years ago. Ritual bonfires, chants and processions must have been evocative sights. Meaden suggests that perhaps priests, or priestesses, would have observed the midwinter sunset sinking into the Gussage Hill barrow from the Wyke Down terminal to the north. During the night they may have then proceeded in torchlit processions to the southern terminal, to view the sunrise coming up over the long barrows the following morning.

Martin Greene, of Down Farm, and Meaden have both found natural flints resembling animal heads, especially that of bulls, in the neighbourhood of the cursus. Phallic stones have also been found during barrow excavations, as seen in Fig. 27(D). The Dorset Cursus and Knowlton Henges, nearby, were major spiritual and cultural centres during the Neolithic and, judging from the number and location of round barrows in the vicinity, the area was still held in high reverence by Bronze Age people.

The Cursus was an extraordinary solar temple, one that could only have been truly utilised and appreciated when one was within its banks. Only from within the cursus was the design apparent, where one was cut off from the external world. From within the banks just the long barrows set into the cursus would have been visible.

The cursus appears to have been built to be part of Nature itself, not separate from it. It has been described as a processional avenue of the dead, by Devereux and others,

Fig. 49. The changing path of the midwinter solstice sunset seen from the Wyke Down terminal looking towards the Gussage Hill long barrow. (After North and Wood, with Amendments.)

147

Plate 61. The setting of the 1996 midwinter sun into the long barrow on Gussage Hill, seen from the Wyke Down terminal.

a route both funerary rituals and a path for the spirits. The dead were seen, here at least, to be connected to the unchanging world of the landscape.

The Grey Mare and Her Colt is a long barrow near Portesham (grid ref: 584871). As with many long barrows it is aligned with the midwinter sunset. Standing at the barrow at midsummer solstice one can see the sun set between two hills on the skyline (see Fig. 64) thought to represent the breasts of the Goddess. In the opposite direction, on midwinter morning around dec. 20-22, the sun rises from between the two remaining standing stones at the barrow (see plate 62). The point of sunrise is actually slightly south of the theoretical position, due to the closeness of the skyline.

Plate 62. The Grey Mare and Her Colts Long Barrow. This view looks south-east towards the midwinter sunrise, which occurs between the two standing stones.

Another very instructive sacred site for viewing solar and lunar events is the Nine Stones, near Winterbourne Abbas (grid ref: 611904: see Ancient Stones of Dorset for detailed site plan and other illustrations). The stone circle is in fact an ellipse of nine stones. Fig. 50 shows some of the alignments found at the site. The Beltaine/Lammas sunrise line is noteworthy as it extends to two barrows on the skyline. Likewise, seen from stone E the equinox sunset grazes the tallest stone (A) and sets amongst more barrows on the horizon (this is now obscured due to trees next to the circle and woodland around the skyline barrows).

One of my fondest memories is of the autumn equinox morning of September 1996. Ghermaine, our daughter Leela, and myself had travelled out from Bournemouth to Knowlton Henge, a sacred site north of Wimborne (grid ref: 024103, see *Ancient Stones of Dorset* pages 48-53). We had come to see the sun rise out of the belly of the Goddess, whose form was the Great Barrow in the field due east of the henge. The sky was clear as the sun rose, it seemed, from the very womb of the Earth Mother (see Plate 63). It evoked all sorts of ancient primeval feelings within us and I can recommend the reader to attempt to witness either of the twice-yearly equinox sunrises from the henge.

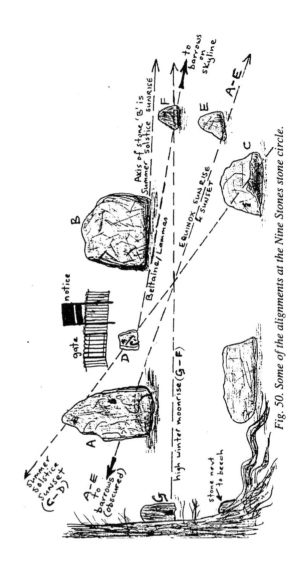

Fig. 50. Some of the alignments at the Nine Stones stone circle.

Summer solstice sunset (C–D)

A–E to barrows (obscured)

high winter moonrise (G–F)

stone next to beech

Summer solstice sunset

to barrows on skyline

A–E

Axis of stone 'B' is Summer solstice sunrise

Beltaine/Lammas

EQUINOX SUNRISE & SUNSET

A–E

notice

gate

A

B

C

D

E

F

G

Plate 63. The September 1996 equinox sunrise over the Great Barrow, seen from the ruined church in the centre of Knowlton Henge. (Photograph: Ghermaine Knight: her copyright.)

One thing I impressed on readers of my previous book, and still indeed try to get across to the audiences of my lectures, is that our distant ancestors did not only rely on man-made structures to mark out astronomical events on the landscape. They recognised that the land itself displayed these calendical happenings. On countless occasions across Dorset I have stood on a hill or at a sacred site and seen some distant natural feature denoting sunrises and sunsets of solstices or festivals. For instance, if one stands at the Hampton Hill stone circle, near Portisham (grid ref: 596868) we can look to the south east and see the cliffs of White Nothe cascade into the sea. This is the precise point where the sun rises on the morning of the Imbolc (early February) and Samhain (early November) festivals. Fig. 51 (A) shows the view on those days as the sun rises. From St Alban's Head we can look east and see the Isle of Portland in profile. At around the equinoxes the sun sets into the body of

Fig. 51. A: The Imbolc and Samhain sunrise from the Hampton Hill stone circle; B: The view from the St Alban's Head around equinox dates, with the sun setting behind Portland.

the Goddess, when viewed from the chapel on the summit of the Head, as shown in Fig. 51 (B).

From the earthworks on top of Shipton Hill, some interesting astronomical events are laid out before us by other natural features. Looking east we can see equinox sunrises over Chilcombe Hill. Turning our attention to the north-east we see the towering heights of Eggardon Hill with prehistoric tumuli and Iron Age earthworks crowning it. Seen from Shipton Hill, the sun rises from out of Eggardon Hill around the summer solstice. Looking west from Shipton Hill we see the cliffs of Golden Cap rising out of the sea. This marks the equinox sunsets in March and September.

Plate 65. Looking towards the Cerne Abbas Giant, from the viewing layby. The arrow denotes the sunrise point during early May and aligns with the giant's penis.

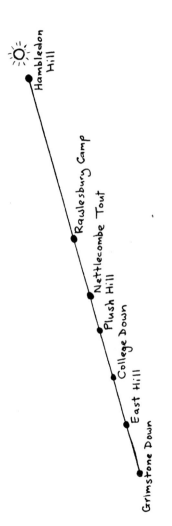

Fig. 52. The midsummer sunrise alignment between Grimstone Down and Hambledon Hill.

Plate 64. The earthworks of Rawlsbury Camp, high on a ridge near Bulbarrow. From this vantage point one can look both NE and SW along the midsummer sunrise alignment, shown in Fig. 52.

Some solar alignments go for long distances across the landscape, using both natural and man-made features. Fig. 52 shows one such alignment, over 15 miles in length, linking hills along the line of the summer solstice sunrise. Is this coincidence, or did our distant ancestors utilise aligned high points to enact midsummer sunrise rituals? Working down the line from Hambledon Hill, the sun would rise over the preceding site, right down to Grimstone Down, where the sun rises over East Hill on solstice morning.

The Cerne Abbas Giant has already been described in Chapter Five. It will be remembered that his huge phallus aligns with the May Day sunrise. From the viewing lay-by west of the Giant, grid ref: 663016 on the A352, one is almost in alignment with the penis and the rising of the sun on the May (formerly Beltaine) festival (Plate 65).

Bank barrows are very elongated Neolithic long barrows. Several have astronomical alignments, including some Dorset examples. One such example runs for about 600 ft in a NE direction from the triangulation pillar on Martins Down (grid ref: 571911). Access is via public foot paths from the A35 or Long Bredy church. The axis of the earthwork is along the line of the midsummer sunrise, which rises over the Roman road south of Compton Valence. Two other bank barrows to the SE are aligned with lunar events (see below).

This links us nicely into the next section, which looks at the Goddess of the Night.

Sister Moon

Luna, every woman's friend,
To me thy goodness condescend,
Let this night in visions see
Emblems of my destiny.
Prayer to Moon Goddess, (Trad).

The belief that the moon has influence over our lives has been a prominent one for thousands of years. Cultures all over the world have revered the Goddess of the night, even unto today. Prehistoric cave paintings and reliefs show lunar symbols. The Venus of Laussel, found in France, dates back to 15,000 BC. The bas relief incredibly shows her holding a crescent shaped bison's horn, inscribed with thirteen notches. This is the number of lunar cycles every year! (Fig. 53)

The ancient Hebrews had a lunar cult. In Jeremiah vii, 18 we read:

"The children gather wood, and the fathers kindle the fire, and the women knead their dough, to make cakes for the queen of heaven".

Moses went up Mount Sinai to receive the commandments. The name of the place means mountain of the moon. Also in the middle east, pre-Islamic Arabs worshipped a moon goddess, revealed today by the crescent moon appearing on many Arab flags. It is the waxing moon that is shown, symbolising increasing power and vitality.

To today's Wiccans and pagans, the Moon Goddess is often seen in a triple aspect. Kali, Hecate and Heli is the Crone Goddess of the waning or dark moon. At new moon she is Artemis, the virgin goddess. At full moon the goddess is revered as Anu,

Fig. 53. The 'Venus of Laussel' holding a bison's horn marked with thirteen notches.

Isis or Cybele. In Egypt I saw many lunar goddesses and gods with moon head-dresses (Fig. 54), demon-strating the long lineage of lunar worship.

At the Romano-Celtic temple in the centre of Bath, we find a huge stone carving of the Goddess Luna. The Celts, however, were primarily concerned with the *cycles* of the solar and lunar events, rather than veneration of the sun and moon per se. They counted time by nights, not days, using the moon, not the sun, to create their calendars. The term fortnight may have derived from such practices, two weeks being around half a lunar cycle. Month comes from the moon, and the word honeymoon is likewise still with us today.

All hail to thee, Moon! All hail to thee!
I pray thee, good Moon, declare to me
This night, who my husband shall be.
Traditional New Year incantation.

156

The Druids thought the first quarter moon was particularly potent. In AD 77 the Roman Pliny wrote: *"They [the Druids] chose the sixth day because the moon, which though not yet in the middle of her course, has already considerable influence..."*

Fig. 54. The god Thoth in an Egyptian temple. (Drawn from a photo by the author.)

This could be because the moon is half light, half dark, symbolic of balance, of yin and yang in equal proportions. With the incoming of Christianity the old pagan ways come under attack by Church dogma and moon reverence did not escape. They saw Diana the Moon Goddess as evil. A 9th century church record speaks of:

"...deluded women who believe that in the dead of night they ride upon certain beasts with Diana and fly through the sky."

Interestingly, the Devil is sometimes called Lucifer who, in early mythology, was Diana's twin brother. It is perhaps a little puzzling and ironic that the crescent moon appears at the feet of many Catholic icons of the Virgin Mary.

The chariot of the Moon shall disorder the zodiac, and the Pleiades break forth into weeping.
from the *Prophesies of Merlin*, Monmouth.

In modern times superstitions and folklore associated with the moon have survived. The growing moon is one of increasing energies. Farmers and gardeners still sow with the waxing moon. There is an old saying the seed will grow with the moon. People bury coins under a young tree at the New Moon nearest the winter solstice. It is hoped that as the moon, year and the tree grows, then ones income will increase also. I have carried out this particular ritual in a park in Bournemouth.

A traditional remedy for the removal of warts was to go out into a full moon night, face the moon and recite three times "moony, moony, take my warts away". In Orkney and Shetland, maidens would dance six times around a standing stone when the first new moon of winter appeared. It is said that a vision of their future husband would appear. It was also thought unlucky to get married when the moon was waning.

The power of the moon was recently brought home to me on a trip to the New Forest. We camped out overnight in an isolated spot, next to a dark wood and a trickling stream. The full moon rose resplendent over distant trees, the stars shone in attendance and a blanket of illuminated mist filled the meadows. The whole forest was at peace and peace welled up from my own inner being.

Modern wicca covens continue the long tradition of reverence to the moon goddess. In a ritual called drawing down the moon they induce the lunar energies into the members of the coven. One of the most lucid and enlightening experiences I have ever had was on a cold winter full moon night. The vivid image of a wizard-like priest came into my minds eye. He was turning the pages of a huge ancient book, the pages of which were glowing with a gentle light. He told me that all the ancient knowledge of the old ways would be mine if I continued diligently on my path. I was then shown the way to my guardian tree, silhouetted against an illuminated sky. I have sat under that tree many times since.

Frail crescent moon, seven times I bow my head,
Since of the night you are the mystic queen.
from *Benighted*, Walter de la Mare (1873-1936).

Some Dorset Lunar Alignments

We have already seen how some of the long barrows in the vicinity of the Dorset Cursus align with lunar events. We saw how the line from the southern terminal to the long barrow on Gussage Hill marks out the most southerly winter moon rise. Another glance at Fig. 46 reveals two more alignments. Viewed from long barrow E one sees the most southerly summer moon set behind Berend's Barrow. This line in fact continues through this barrow to the one on Gussage Hill (C). When standing on the latter barrow, within the cursus itself, we can look south east and see another long barrow and the high point of Gussage Hill beyond. All three align with the lowest summer moonrise.

High on the top of Maiden Castle is the low mound of an extremely long Neolithic bank barrow. It originally ran for 1,790 ft approximately E-W, yet bending sharply south near the east end. The main course of the mound aligns with the most southerly equinox moonrise and, in the opposite direction, the northernmost equinox moonset. The change in direction of the mound points towards the east entrance of the Iron Age fortifications. This may indicate that the entrance was in the same position back in the Neolithic.

On high ground NE of Bincombe is another Neolithic bank barrow, east of Came Wood (grid ref: 703853). It can be seen from the adjacent road (Plate 66). Views to the south are superb, with barrows visible on Bincombe Hill and Portland rising from the sea beyond. The bank barrow is accompanied by several Bronze Age round barrows, indicating site continuity over a long period. The axis of the 600 ft earthen mound is aligned with the northernmost position that the moon can rise in summer. The line is only slightly off that of the Samhain/Imbolc sunrise.

A bank barrow on Martins Down, north of Long Bredy (grid ref: 573912) is again aligned with he southernmost rising of the moon at the equinoxes, like the long mound at Maiden Castle. The barrow stands close to another I described earlier, which is aligned to the midsummer sunrise.

All these examples serve to illustrate the reverence placed on the moon by our prehistoric ancestors. The precision with which long barrows were placed on the landscape is to be admired, especially considering the complicated 18.61 year cycle of the moon as it weaves its wobbly path across the heavens. Observations over many years would have been required before a structure aligned with a lunar

Plate 66. The Bincombe Bank Barrow, aligned with the northernmost summer moonrise.

standstill (its most northerly or southerly rising or setting) could be erected with any accuracy.

Dorset Solar and Lunar Monuments

Two post-prehistoric monuments show solar and lunar symbols which are worthy of inspection. They both display the concept of the sun and moon representing balance, both in the cosmos and here on earth.

In the church at Shillingstone, NW of Blandford, is an inscribed stone set into the chancel walls, near the bell ropes. Discovered in 1888, it is generally thought to be a coffin lid. It is dated by the Royal Commission as 14th century, which I find a bit curious. The style of the sun and moon symbols, and that of the head (see Fig. 55) are more in keeping with the period from Celtic to Saxon times, rather than Medieval. As was noticed by my wife, Ghermaine, the moon is depicted to the mans left side, thought to be the intuitive, feminine side of a person. The sun is on the right, masculine side.

The second monument is a modern one. At Studland, north of Swanage, the new village cross stands south of the church. Erected in 1976, it was placed on top of the original Saxon cross base (see *Ancient Stones of* *Fig. 55. The solar and lunar symbols on the stone in Shillingstone church.*
Dorset, Plate 45). On the arms of the cross the mason has carved the sun and moon in balance, on the underside of each arm (Plate 67). It is reassuring to see some of the old symbology being kept alive for future generations.

End Word

Thus we conclude our brief survey of solar and lunar aligned sites and folklore from around Dorset and elsewhere. I can but encourage the reader to seek out solar and lunar symbology in churches, crosses and such like, for more are likely to be found. It may be recalled that in Chapter Four we saw how the wheel of the Celtic cross was originally a solar symbol. We also looked at how the circle has been revered as a magical symbol, originating from the visible discs of the sun and moon.

160

Plate 67. The solar and lunar symbols on the underside of the cross head at Studland. (Photo by Ghermaine Knight.)

Try also, if possible, to observe some of the solar and lunar rises and settings. the atmosphere and sense of anticipation on these sacred occasions is wonderful and truly magical. Do not be put off if a particular solstice sunrise or sunset is clouded out. For a couple of days either side of these dates the sun still rises in almost identical positions on the skyline. Perhaps I could do no better than to leave the last example in this chapter to poet and mystic William Blake. In his *Jerusalem* (Fig. 56) he portrays not just the glory of former times but also paints a picture of magical times to come. The sun and moon, divine balance in the heavens, are seen to shine down on megalithic avenues and circles. He shows us that a time may yet arrive when order is returned tot he earth.

161

"...Queen of heaven, the true wife of the sky god.
For she, too, loved the solitude of the woods and the
lonely hills, and sailing overhead on clear nights
in the likeness of the silver moon looked down with
pleasure on her own fair image reflected on the calm,
the burnished surface of the lake, Diana's Mirror".
from *The Golden Bough*, Sir James Frazer, 19th C.

Fig. 56. From 'Jerusalem', by William Blake. Note the solar and lunar symbols
above the megalithic avenues and circles.

Chapter Nine

The Goddess in the Landscape

The valley spirit never dies;
It is the woman, primal mother.
Her gateway is the root of
heaven and earth.
Lao Tzu, *Tao Te Ching*, c. 525 BC.

In ancient times it was the Earth Goddess who was the primary deity, the spiritual and cultural driving force of most early peoples. We have seen how spirals, tombs, mazes, wells and springs were associated with the Earth Mother. The very dragon itself was seen to represent the beneficial properties and power of the Earth.

In this chapter we shall seek out the Earth Goddess in the landscape, in standing stones and, perhaps surprising of all, in churches. We do not have to step outside Dorset to do this, such is the wealth of examples within the county. The Goddess is never far away for those who have eyes to see Her.

For most human prehistory few signs portraying any spiritual beliefs appear to have been undertaken. However, around 35,000-40,000 BC Cro-Magnon Man underwent something of a creative explosion, probably indicative of a leap in his spiritual evolution. At around this time we have the appearance of incised bones, cave paintings and reliefs, and carved figurines. These people lived within caves, the womb body of the Earth Goddess, environments which saw the birth of mankind.

Europe is rich in such cave relics. At the cave at La Bastide, stones with vulva engravings were found inside a subterranean stone circle. The famous Venus of Willendorf figurine is around 30,000 years old, whilst the Venus of Laussel dates from around 15,000 BC (see Fig. 53). Archaeologists have found nearly 1,000 of these Stone Age figurines and almost all portray female images. Although most have large breasts, tummies and thighs, most are not pregnant. They represent the power of the goddess, the power of the feminine, a sort of prehistoric girl power!

163

Vulva symbols abound in caves and on stones. The link between the menstrual and lunar cycles makes the vulva a symbol of the cosmos, not just that of physiology.

Visit the interior of the earth and
by purifying you will find the secret.
The Kabalah.

The Earth Goddess cult had at least a 20,000 year old pedigree when it arrived in Britain in earnest in the early Neolithic. Despite the objections of the old breed of archaeologists, there is little doubt now, due to the brilliant work of Meaden and other contemporaries, that Avebury and Newgrange, as well as many other Neolithic sites, were Goddess temples. In Dorset, too, these ancient people saw the Goddess in the land and erected their own sacred sites in veneration. They saw the body of the Goddess everywhere, in everything they touched, smelt, drank or ate. As with todays aboriginal tribes, they saw themselves as part of the Earth Mother, physical extensions of Her body.

We shall look at some topographical features from around Britain and Dorset in this chapter which I believe early Man may have interpreted as the body of the Goddess. Some are well established Goddess sites, but most of the Dorset examples have not been seen for what they are.

It was the Earth Goddess which people of the Neolithic and Bronze ages primarily worshipped and turned to for help with crops, weather, hunting, animal stock welfare, etc. She was seen to have unending productiveness, the soil and earth being the very skin of Her body. It was indeed the Goddess that stirred their hearts and souls to erect many of the stone and earthern monuments of the Megalithic Age. She was the cycle of life, death and rebirth. She was not only nature symbolised, she *was* nature.

For centuries archaeologists have rigidly adhered to the idea that most megaliths, stone circles and such like were erected by some patriarchal, Druid-type, sun worshipping cult. But ideas are changed as new evidence (presented, I might add, by many amateurs as well as professionals) is amassed. The Earth Goddess is gradually being recognised as the powerful spiritual drive that She was, rocking the academic world out of its self-indulgent slumber.

The signs were always there but, as Terence Meaden puts it, all the time most observers were not observing well enough. Maybe they just did not want to. Recognition of a Goddess culture, prehistoric and present day, raises all sorts of theological arguments. But, once again, we can dip into the Bible and see evidence

164

of the Goddess. In fact the God of Moses, almighty Yahweh, was originally a goddess, according to researcher Monica Sjoo. Her derivative name Ichu anat, came from the Sumerian goddess Inanna.

Many Muslims, too, might be surprised to learn that the sacred Kaaba stone at Mecca is imprinted with a vulva, and is sheltered within a cover called The Skirt of Kaaba. The male priests of the shrine are called Ben Shaybah, Sons of the Old Woman. Clearly both these examples indicate survivals of former Goddess veneration.

The Celts and Romans worshipped the Earth Goddess and brought their beliefs to Dorset. Images of the Goddesses Diana and Minerva have been found at Maiden Castle. We have already seen the head of the goddess figurine from Colliton Park, Dorchester (see Fig. 30). As discussed previously, the oncoming of Christianity saw the eventual demise of the Earth Goddess. She had to go underground to survive, so to speak. She became female saints, especially those associated with wells and springs (see Chapter Six). Her images are still to be found even in Dorset churches, if we look with new eyes. For now, however, this Dorset survey of the Goddess will digress slightly, as we leave the historical period behind, continuing with a search for Goddess signs on the ancient megaliths of Dorset.

The Goddess of the Megaliths

Around Dorset it is possible to see many examples of prehistoric stones that were selected, at least in part I believe, due to holes and crevices present in them. Many of the huge stones at Avebury have similar vulva-like holes, whilst others display faces (see Plate 68).

Many of the stones detailed below are sarsen stones. It could be argued that these stones naturally display holes, which is true. But it is also true that many completely smooth ones weather out in fields, whilst others are of the conglomeratic type, composed of countless pebbles. The ancients had plenty of choice of rock types in Dorset, and I believe that those erected with holes were selected for, amongst other things, Goddess symbology (*Stonehenge - The Secret of the Solstice*, by Terence Meaden, has more examples).

I was prompted to look for symbolism in megaliths firstly in the light of Terence Meaden's books (see Bibliography) and in conversation with him. This was followed by visits to Avebury, where my wife and I saw vulvic shapes in many of the stones. Meaden has recently discovered vulvic markings at West Kennet long barrow, just south of Avebury.

At Nine Stones circle, near Dorchester (see Fig. 50 and plate 69) the tallest stone (A) has several fissures and holes in it, some of which could be deemed vulvic. The best is on the east side, facing the inside of the circle. Plate 69 shows the deep cavity, with a floral offering within.

At Corscombe, 8 miles NW of Sturminster Newton, there are several megaliths, thought to be the remains of a chambered barrow. The northernmost stone (stone C in Fig. 117 in Ancient Stones of Dorset) is domed on its north side, resembling a belly. Low down on this side, often obscured by nettles, is a deep vulva hole (Plate 70).

Behind nature, throughout nature,
Spirit is present.
Ralph W Emerson, *Nature*, 1836

Plate 68. The face of the Goddess in one of the stones of the West Kennet Avenue in Avebury.

166

Plate 69. The Goddess vulva hole in a megalith at the Nine Stones, with votive flower. Perhaps significantly, the hole faces the centre of the circle, as does the one at Rempstone (see text).

Old records speak of former stones that had Goddess healing holes. A record of 1833 tells us of a 5 ft long stone at Wraxall, NW of Cattistock. It was thought to be the capstone of a chambered long barrow (Grinsell, 1952). The stone apparently had a hollow place in the middle, 1 ft in diameter, which locals called The Crack. The stone was venerated by people as a beneficial good-luck or healing stone.

Another holed stone was seen at Littlemayne, south east of Dorchester, on a 1909 field trip. The hole was 12 in diameter and may have gone right through the stone. One of the surviving sarsens of the former stone circle at Littlemayne lies to the south of the farm, in the open field (stone 1 in Fig. 90, Ancient Stones of Dorset). The stone is prone and around 6 ft long, and displays several craters and holes (see Plate 71). I believe this stone may have also been selected as a Goddess stone.

At Parkstone, Poole, a 4 ft long stone was found in 1909 near the top of Constitutional Hill. It now rests in the rear garden of Branksome Library (grid ref: 050922). The stone is not a sarsen, and may be a quartz-rich glacial erratic. There are two deep depressions on the surface, perfect for votive offerings.

On the north side of the Helstone megalith (grid ref: 573915) is a large depression about 1 ft in diameter. The stone also has a ledge to enable seating.

At Pamphill, Wimborne, a small stone stands by the roadside, at the foot of Vine Hill. Plate 17 of *Ancient Stones of Dorset* shows a small, deep hole near the foot of the stone. At the Rempstone stone circle, near Corfe Castle (grid ref: 995821) it is the stone nearest the road, the one in front of you as you cross over the break in the fence, that is of interest here (stone E of previous accounts). On the south side of the 4 ft high stone another vulva-like cavity will be seen, similar to the one illustrated at the Nine Stones. The hole is still used for offerings of flowers and candles by modern pagans, as is a hole/ledge on the Harpstone (Plate 72).

In *Stonehenge - Secret of the Solstice*, Terence Meaden gives examples in Brittany and the Isle of Man of partly tooled megaliths with necks and shoulders. Other stones displaying these features are found accompanied by carved breasts, so we can be sure, argues Meaden, that the neck and shoulder stones are Goddess stones. Fig. 57 (A) shows a megalith at Medreac, Brittany. Several lozenge stones can be seen at Avebury (Fig. 57 (B)).

I believe at least one excellent example of this type of Goddess image has survived in Dorset. In Ancient Stones of Dorset (page 116 and Figs. 76 &77) I describe a large (6 ft.) stone, not described previously, lying prone between Kingston Russell stone circle and the Grey Mare and Her Colts long barrow. It lies in the ditch which is the ancient Ridgeway track, just east of a hedge boundary (grid ref: 583873). The stone is situated at the intersection of two ley line alignments, one of which goes all the way to Stonehenge, a major Goddess temple. In February 1998 I cleared the

168

Top: Plate 70. The Corscombe Stones, showing the rounded Goddess stone and the position (arrowed) of the hole.
Bottom: Plate 71. Deep holes in a sarsen at Littlemayne, site of a former stone circle.

169

Plate 72. Vulvic hole and votive ledge on the Harpstone, near Kimmeridge.

stone of years of vegetation cover and was amazed at the shape of the megalith. Fig. 57 (C) shows the outline, drawn accurately from a photograph. The neck and shoulder Goddess symbolism is here beautifully evident.

On clearing the stone I found six coins on the upper surface of the stone, bearing various dates between 1971 and 1990. It would appear that someone prior to my visit had left offerings at this Goddess stone, over 3,000 years after it was probably erected.

Similarly, the Helstone megalith also shows a hint of neck and shoulder symbolism, as do some of the supporting stones of the Hellstone Cromlech (both sites near Dorchester). One of the two stones still standing at the Grey Mare and Her Colts chambered long barrow shows similar shoulders, this time either side of a very thick-set neck (see *Ancient Stones of Dorset*, Plates 62 and 64).

I would suggest that the reader takes a new look at Dorset's megaliths, as I have, and this may reveal more vulva-like holes. Early Man had thousands of smooth, featureless sarsens to choose from in Dorset, as elsewhere, yet repeatedly selected stones with suggestive holes and crevices. The Goddess was symbolically represented in these long lasting epitaphs.

170

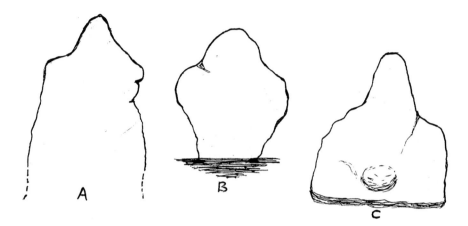

Fig. 57. Goddess Stones. A: Brittany. B: Avebury. C. Fallen megalith between Grey Mare & Her Colts and Kingston Russell Stone Circle. Note 'vulvic depression' near base. (Note: these figures are not drawn to scale)

Stone Faceð

Many people have previously noted the apparent facial and head images in megaliths notably at Avebury. The Heel Stone at Stonehenge has a well known face on the side of the henge. Plate 68 shows a stone clearly selected by the ancients for its similarity to a head, complete with frowning features. In Dorset we have two examples of stones resembling figures. Returning to Littlemayne, there are old records of a former stone shaped like children petrified in stone.

The second example still survives to this day. Stone B at the Rempstone stone circle stands on the eastern side. Around 5 ft of stone protrudes out of the ground and the whole simulacrum is the shape of a head. Plate 73 shows two views of this amazing stone. The most immediate feature is the large nose. Above this can be made out two eyes with prominent eye brows. Beneath the nose are cracks in the rock resembling the lines of the mouth. As at Stonehenge the face is looking toward the centre of the monument.

171

Plate 73. The anthromorphic stone at Rempstone, showing facial features.

John Edmunds, of Bournemouth, brought to my attention a head-shaped depression, with horns/ears, on one of the southern stones of the Nine Stones (Fig. 50).

I think it is unrealistic to suppose that the builders of the above two circles did not also recognise these stone features, some may argue that they are the effects of thousands of years of weathering. But the features are so integral to the shape of the stones that they must always have been evident. Furthermore, the weathering argument is not convincing, for the facial features of the stone would surely have been more obvious prior to being softened by the elements over the aeons of time. The stones may not have necessarily been fashioned by human effort, but they were recognised by the human spirit. The link between the mundane world and the magical landscape of the Goddess need be no more than our imagination.

Plate 74. The Hellstone Dolmen, near Portisham.

Into the Womb of the Goddess

*The dolmen symbolises a stone grave, the
cave through which the dead must pass on
their journey to the otherworld, and the
womb through which the living may achieve rebirth.*
Joseph Campbell.

My initial pilgrimages to West Kennet Long Barrow changed forever my way of interacting and experiencing ancient sites. Todays pilgrims are still allowed into the barrows interior, with its stone-clad passage and mysterious dark anti-chambers.. The place is atmospheric, damp and primeval. I enter this Goddess womb with humility and expectation.

Plate 75. Looking east from the Hellstone. The Ridgeway is on the horizon and numerous barrows pepper the skyline. Many ancient cultures saw long ridges as the recumbent Goddess, so the view from the Hellstone may be relevant.

174

In Dorset, the Hellstone is the best surviving chambered dolmen. It stands on an isolated ridge, north of Portisham (grid ref: 606867). After thousands of years of decay the dolmen was restored in 1866, if somewhat inaccurately.

The Hellstone is Neolithic in age, consisting of a huge 20 ton, 10 ft x 8 ft capstone, supported by nine megaliths (Plate 74). Sitting inside the stone chamber, beneath the giant capstone roof, I always get a feeling of the sacred nature of the place. One can now peer outwards through the gaps between the stones, but at one time a mound of earth probably covered most of the stones.

One can but imagine what rituals were played out here thousands of years ago, perhaps under full moon skies and at solstice sunrises. I can recommend the reader to visit the Hellstone and enter this Goddess shrine. The surrounding landscape is isolated and frequently windswept and one readily feels transported back in time.

Meðieual Legacy of the Goððess

Hail to thee, Earth, Mother of Men!
Be fruitful in Gods embrace,
Filled with food for the use of men.
Anglo-Saxon Charm.

As I have already pointed out, the conversion of Britain's population to Christianity did not go smoothly. Well into Middle Ages papal proclamations were still being issued, and missionaries still being dispatched, to combat the tenacity of Goddess worship. In the end it was the policy of Christianising existing sacred sites that prevailed. Churches were erected on Goddess sites, and wells and springs were rededicated to saints. Propaganda even turned many sites into the abode of the Devil.

Some aspects of the Goddess culture did persist, however, to be integrated into Christian rituals, art and architecture. It is clear that many local masons working on Norman and Medieval churches were still pagan. They found ways to incorporate Goddess images into Church paintings and stonework. This was usually accomplished in the guise that work was of female saints, the Virgin Mary, or else so-called grotesque gargoyles.

The 16th century horned head inside Charminster church (see Fig. 7 and Plate 13) can easily be seen to be female. On the outside of the same church, is a horned head on the east window of the north aisle. It is 15th century and could again be a

175

feminine image (Plate 38). Fig. 14 shows some details from the 12th century font at Toller Fratrum. Around the font can also be seen standing women, supporting the top of the scenes.

At Cranborne church there is a much-faded, yet illuminating, 14th century wall painting. The work is said to represent the seven deadly sins, which indeed appears to be true. Several demons and naked sinners can be seen by a tree. However, this tree, in my opinion, represents the Tree of Life, an ancient symbol, representing a unifying structure, linking the Underworld, Man and the heavens. It was a conduit for the flow of divine energies.

Fig, 58, The Goddess on the 14th century wall painting at Cranbourne.

Incredibly, the whole tree on the Cranborne painting rises from the head of a woman, richly clad and of some authority. I believe this is the Goddess, the Earth Mother surviving, in disguise, into Medieval times. Interestingly, the tree is holly, whose berries led to it being regarded as a Goddess tree. A bull and a dragon are also depicted, more pagan symbology.

The Cranborne painting has direct parallels with other Medieval works of art throughout Europe. For instance, Fig. 59 shows an interesting manuscript illumination from the Abbey of Monte Cassino, Italy, dated 1070 - 1100. The Mother Goddess is seen rising from the earth, which is in fact her very body. She is suckling a bull and a serpent, both pagan symbols of fertility and life-force. It is quite amazing that images such as these were undertaken in an age when patriarchy ruled ruthlessly and women were generally downtrodden.

Not surprisingly, anti-Goddess Medieval art and architecture was also created. In Dorset we are fortunate to have a strong image of this type of work. In Cheselbourne church, midway between Blandford and Dorchester, is a curious piece

176

Fig. 59. The Earth Goddess in an 11th century Italian manuscript.

of 15th century stonework, set into the wall next to the font. The work is of a woman in a prone position under a wall support (Plate 76). She is depicted as grotesque and disfigured. I interpret this image to be representative of the subdued Goddess and, perhaps, of all women for that matter.

Sheela-na-gigs are images of naked female figures, exhibiting and emphasising their genitalia. Hundreds are known and they are particularly widespread in Ireland. The name derives from the Irish Sighle nag Cioch, meaning old hag of the breasts. They became popular in the 12th century and hundreds were carved over the next few centuries, adorning churches, castles and town walls. They appear to crop up where the Gaelic language was spoken, as well as Gallic and Ancient British strongholds. These were areas where veneration of the Earth Goddess persisted long after the coming of Christianity.

Plate 76. Stonework of a woman in Cheselbourne church. symbolic of the subduing of the Goddess?

Sheela-na-gigs began life as symbols of the Earth Goddess, I believe, and continued to appear throughout the middle Ages because of the medieval preoccupation with lust. The Church took them on as a reminder to its flock of the sinful ways of the flesh! There is evidence that sheela-na-gigs were once regarded as having beneficial powers, assisting fertility and bringing good luck. Many have been rubbed smooth around the vulva area by generations of people seeking health, fertility and good fortune. At St Michael's in Oxford all brides would look upon the sheela-na-gig on the way to their wedding. As late as 1795 comes a report from the Isle of Wight regards another one at the parish church at Binstead. The record states that the idol was taken down during church repairs but was returned to its original position after being productive of displeasure of the inhabitants.

Fig. 60. The sheela-na-gig at Studland; B: At Kilpeck, Herefordshire.

Whilst on a visit to the beautiful Saxon-Norman church at Studland a few years ago, I noticed a sheela-na-gig amongst other corbel table gargoyles, on the south side of the church, near the porch. She is shown in Fig. 60, along with a famous sheela from Kilpeck, Herefordshire. I wonder how many people walk into Studland church every year unaware that an ancient symbol of the Earth Mother is just feet above their heads.

Unless any more turn up in Dorset, the nearest other sheela-na-gigs are at Romsey Abbey, Fiddington, Somerset and, as mentioned above, at Binstead on the Isle of Wight. But I would urge the reader to keep a look out for others around Dorset. I would be interested to hear of any others.

The Triple Goddess

Chapter Six ended with the modern day story of how a well on the Isle of Sheppey started manifesting miracles following the unearthing of an image of the Triple Goddess.

The concept of a Triple Goddess goes back some 12,000 years. A stone relief in a cave at Angles-sul-Anglin, France, shows three female images, with exposed vulvas. Later, around 3,200 BC carvings of triple spirals were made on the stones of the

Fig. 61. A: Three 'Matres' from Cirencester. B: A primitive relief from near Bath, showing the triple aspect of the Goddess.

Neolithic passage mound at Newgrange, in Ireland. Goddess effigies often depict three female figures, the Deae Martrones, demonstrating the fundamental Celtic belief in a threefold divinity. Fig. 61(A) shows these Matres, or Earth Mothers, holding fruit or other food, of Romano-British age found near a spring in Cirencester, Gloucestershire. Note the serpents between each of their legs. The whole scene symbolises the fertility and vitality of the earth.

A typical interpretation of the threefold Goddess is that each one is a different aspect of the cycles of Nature. The first is the Maiden. She represents birth and beginnings. She is the virgin goddess, Rhiannon, Athena, Minerva and Brighid. The Virgin Mary and St Bride took over this role with the incoming of Christianity.

The second aspect is that of the Mother. She represents increasing, reproduction, fertile power and sexuality. She is the Celtic Blodeuwedd and Epona and the classical Decima and Venus. She is often depicted carrying an infant, as in Fig. 61(B).

The third aspect is that of the Crone Goddess. She is the destroyer, the Goddess of life and death. She is Morrigan, Morta, Hecate and Ana. In Arthurian myth she is Morgan le Fey or Morgana. Mary Magdalene took on the role of the Crone Goddess, as too Sophia of the Gnostics.

180

*Fig. 62. The triple
Goddess or Wyrd
Sisters from a
woodcut in
Holished's
'Chronicles'.*

The triple Goddess tradition continued into Anglo-Saxon times with the Wyrd Sisters, made famous by *The Way of Wyrd* by Brian Bates, and of course the books of Terry Pratchett. Shakespeare wrote of them in *Macbeth*, for his three witches are indeed the aspects of the triple Goddess. In Holished's 1577 *Chronicles*, the three Goddesses appear in a tale, "....in strange and wild apparel, resembling creatures of elder wood [the Otherworld]...." goddesses of destiny. Fig. 62 shows these figures in a woodcut from the Chronicles, showing them in Elizabethan garb! Significantly, the Tree of Life stands next to them, an association we have seen previously.

In Greek, Roman, Norse and Anglo-Saxon myth the three Wyrd Sisters were supposed to weave the destiny of people on giant looms, spinning out their fate in the form of webs. In Norse legend they are said to dwell within the roots of Yggdrasil, the World Tree. A corruption of the triple Goddess could in fact be the holy Trinity. Many Christian icons and stonework occur in triplicate. In Dorset I believe we have such a survival. Three female saints are depicted on the south side of the chapel within Charminster Cemetery, in Bournemouth (Plate 77). Although dated as late as 1877, I stand below them and see the Triple Goddess returning my gaze. On the same building are two carvings of the Green Man, another pagan character, whom we shall meet again later (see Plate 104).

181

Goᶁᶁess Lanᶁscapes - Minᶁshift anᶁ Perception

There was an old woman lived under a hill,
And if she's not gone, she lives there still.
Traditional Rhyme.

But where is the Goddess, this Earth Mother of which our ancestors spoke of and venerated? Some of our forebears knew the answer. Gustav Fechner, the 19th century German poet and psychologist, had a change in perception that enabled him to see the Goddess in the land. He wrote in 1861:

Plate 77. Statues on the chapel in Charminster Cemetery, in Bournemouth. Is this a Christian depiction of the triple Goddess?

"...as my look embraced Her more and more it seemed to me not only so beautiful an idea, but so true and clear a fact, that she is an angel....but an experience such as this will be deemed fantastic".

In 1932 mystic and poet George William Russell wrote of his changes in consciousness:

"Earth revealed itself to me as a living being, and rock and clay were made transparent so that I saw lovelier and lordier beings than I had known before".

I believe that the way to such a state of awareness of Nature is to look at hills, rivers and stones not just with the eyes, but with the imagination. This is how the ancients viewed the earth, as indeed do the Aborigine and tribal cultures surviving to this day. We must inhabit the landscape, but we must do it not only outwards, but inwardly too. Once we regard the earth as a living entity, we can ask ourselves if the solar system is alive. And what of the whole Universe?

Plate 70. The waters of the Goddess flowing from within Her womb, Stoke Abbot, near Beaminster.

Living organisms self-regulate and self-generate their bodies, which is exactly what the earth achieves. We come to question then of what is organic and what is inorganic. For instance, in a large tree over 90% of its bulk is made up of dead wood, yet the tree is alive. This can be extended out into the landscape where we begin to question what is alive and what is dead. If the earth is a living being, the belief of many ancient cultures and todays pagans, then does anything exist that is not instilled with life, on some level? Perhaps there is only one inhabitant of this planet, life itself. If the earth is a living entity, then everything of it is likewise infused with life-force.

*In fertility and generation, woman does
not set an example to the earth, but the
earth sets and example to woman.*
Plato, *Menexenus*.

Following many visits to ancient sites and sacred places around the world, I have come to the conclusion that the Goddess is not only still in residence at these places, but is in fact all around us. A change in perception has enabled me to see Her breasts on the skyline or Her body rising from the land as hills and tors. Her bodily fluids rise from the earth in wells and springs, and shower down on us from the skies. She sings to us via birdsong and in the very wind that blows. We walk on the skin of the Earth Mother and we are nourished with food from Her body. Her canopy of air shields us from the fierce rays of the sun. I see faces in rocks, trees and on the landscape. Her vulva is imprinted on megaliths. I sense the power of Her spirit when I dowse.

The time has come to look at some British landforms, including some from Dorset, that exhibit Goddess features symbolically on the landscape. I use the word symbolically reservedly, as our distant ancestors would not have perceived landscape features as symbolic at all. To them, they were the Goddess incarnate. Such perceptions transform the land into a magical, living place.

Journeying With the Goddess

*There is a spirit in the valley of a mountain...we can
know it as the life-giving mother of all things.*
Lao Tzu, *Tao The Ching*, (c.525 BC).

Fig. 63. Symbolic landscapes of the Goddess. A: Mount Hymettos, as seen from the Acropolis, Athens. The temple of the Goddess Athena is orientated towards these twins peaks.

B: The Breasts of Anu, Killarney in Ireland. Named after the Celtic earth Goddess Anu, who is the local fairy queen. Every Lammas people still gather on this powerful Goddess symbol.

C: The view of a mountain range seen form Poros in Greece. The image is of a woman lying down. The head and breasts are on the right side.

D: Silbury Hill, Avebury. This is Europe's tallest Neolithic man-made mound. Although breast shaped, some see it as the womb of the pregnant Mother Goddess.

185

Plate 79. Glastonbury Tor.

All around the world we find evidence of sacred sites that were built within view of breast-shaped hills, cleft-topped mountains and ranges of hills resembling prone female figures. Topographical features have their stories to tell, possessing their own myths and legends. These myths belong as much to the land as they do to Man. Let us first see a selection of symbolic landscapes from outside Dorset, to set the scene and expand the theme.

Fig. 63 shows a selection of Goddess simulacrums in the landscape. Many more are known from around the world and, significantly, many of them can be viewed from ancient sacred sites. Many Goddess temples are aligned to skyline features, an example of which is shown in Fig. 63(A). In Glastonbury Tor we have one of the most famous Goddess symbols, long regarded as the breast or tummy of the Earth Mother (see Plate 79). It is somewhat of an irony that the chapel on top of the tor, built by the Church to Christianise the Goddess site, enhances the breast shape by the addition of a nipple! This leads us into Dorset's symbolic landscape. St Catherine's Hill, Abbotsbury, is likewise enhanced by the chapel on its summit. The Abbotsbury area has many prehistoric and Christian sites and it seems probable that the hill was sacred prior to the erection of the chapel.

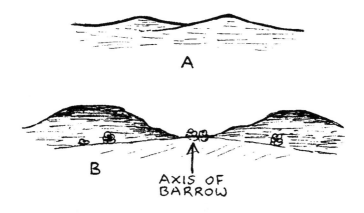

A

B   AXIS OF
     BARROW

*Fig. 64.A: The breast shaped hills seen from the former stone site at Litton Cheney.
B: The view north-west from the Grey mare & Her Colts long barrow, showing two
more symbolic skyline features. Both views are in the direction of the midsummer
sunset.*

On a trip to a former chambered tomb site near Litton Cheney in 1995, I perceived a
beautiful example of the breasts of the Earth Goddess. From the site (grid ref:
552918, north of the A35) the summer solstice sunset is marked out in the landscape
by two distant skyline features, shown in Fig. 64(A). These symbolic hills are many
miles away and are in fact only visible from the site because of a dip in the nearer
hill line. Another example of Goddess paps in Dorset can be seen from the Grey
Mare and Her Colts chambered long barrow, near Portesham (grid ref: 584871, see
Plate 62, and *Ancient Stones of Dorset*, pages 33 and 114-117 for details). Looking
towards the midsummer solstice sunset we see that the sun goes down between two
more breast-shaped hills on the skyline, as shown in Fig. 64(B). The axis of the
barrow points towards these two hills (See Plate 26 also).

----

*....our Sister, mother Earth,
who sustains and governs us.*
St Francis of Assisi.

Hengistbury Head rises out of the sea and marshes south of Christchurch. Seen from
the latter it appears as a prone figure, the summit being the head. Viewed from the

Plate 80. Hengistbury Head, from the west. I see this as symbolic of the Goddess lying with her back to us, with her head on the right hand side.

west, as shown in Plate 80, the summit forms the shoulders and arms of the Earth Mother, with Her head lying on the earth towards the right. The Head is peppered with tumuli and the 360^0 distant skylines would make it an ideal ritual site. From the summit the Isle of Wight looms out of the sea, like the Goddess arising from the waters.

Whilst I was on the summit of Hengistbury Head to view the sunset on a beautiful May evening in 1996, I was surveying the distant skylines and saw, in the direction of Corfe Castle and Creechbarrow, the features shown in Fig. 65(A). Two distinct breast-shaped hills rise from the background skyline of the Purbecks. To the left, eastwards, of these the Purbecks gently undulate towards Old Harry, the Goddess stretching out before me like some sleeping beauty.

South of Wareham is the prominent Creechbarrow Hill (grid ref: 922824). When viewed from Wareham, an ancient Saxon town, Creechbarrow resembles a human head looking skywards. Fig. 65(B) is drawn from a photograph taken by the author just south of South Bridge. I have taken great care not to use any artistic license on the drawing and the hill really does appear like this. For the best effect, turn this page clockwise until the features appear vertical. The eyebrow, nose and lips are

188

Fig. 65. A: Two hills seen from Hengistbury Head looking towards Corfe. B: Creechbarrow seen from the bridge at Wareham. The skyward gazing face can be appreciated by turing this page clockwise until the features are vertical.

clearly defined. Creechbarrow was held sacred by our distant ancestors who built barrows, hence the name, on the hill.

In issue No. 123 of *The Ley Hunter*, Jill Smith gives an illustration of a similar feature at South Harris, known as Hag Mountain. Here too a woman's head is seen in profile, in addition to her upper torso.

Two more examples of Goddess breasts or tummies on the landscape are shown in Fig. 66. The first is Colmers Hill, at Symondsbury near Bridport. I am always struck by its breast-shaped form, summit trees adding to the symbology. Interestingly, the hill is known by tradition as Witches Hill, indicative of former pagan ceremonies (see Fig. 66A). The drawing in Fig. 66B is a view from Preston church (grid ref: 706829). This unnamed hill, along with Chalbury Hill, towers over

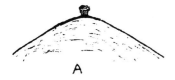

Fig. 66. A: Colmer's Hill, west of Bridport. B: Hill north-west of Preston as seen from the church. Both hills have 'nipple'-like features due to vegetation.

Fig. 67. An old woodcut of the Agglestone, before its collapse.

Preston village like the breasts of the Goddess. Incredibly, the effect is enhanced by a clump of vegetation on the skyline.

The last illustrated examples of Goddess features rising out of the land are at the Agglestone, near Studland (grid ref: 024828). This huge natural monolith has Druidic associations and folklore says it was thrown from the Isle of Wight by the Devil. The latter is a sure sign of a former pagan sacred site. At present the huge block of sandstone sits solidly on a small knoll. But old accounts speak of it being a logan stone, capable of being rocked as it pivoted on a much-denuded base. Unfortunately, the whole structure collapsed, but we have an old woodcut of its former glory, shown in Fig. 67. I believe that in this former state the Agglestone was a Goddess site, and the illustration shows a face in profile, on the right hand side. The whole outcrop rises from the heathland like the craggy Crone Goddess.

190

Deep peace of the quiet earth to you,
Deep peace of the sleeping stones to you.
Celtic blessing, from *Under the Dark Star*,
Fiona Macleod, 1912.

A close inspection of the Agglestone reveals Goddess images again. The rock is craggy, full of pits and hollows and several faces can be made out, if one has the eyes and the imagination to perceive them. In Plate 81 huge eyes and a nose with nostrils can be made out. The large crack below forms the mouth and the Goddess seems to be yawning or groaning. Out of neglect perhaps?

In her book *Cathedrals of the Spirit* (Thorsons, 1996) T C Mcluhan gives many incredible photographic examples of rocks and trees that resemble animal and

Plate 81. The Agglestone, near Studland. Can you see the face in the rock? Due to their large size, the features are best appreciated from a distance.

191

Plate 82. Culpeper's Dish. A place of quiet contemplation.

human features. I can recommend this work to the reader wholeheartedly. Earlier in this book I showed the reader a face in a stone at Rempstone (see Plate 73). On page 199 of *Re-Visioning the Earth*, Paul Devereux shows a photo of a remarkable simulacrum of a head, complete with eyes, cheeks bones and lips, in a rock outcrop at Carn Brae, in Cornwall. Many other faces can be seen in stones at Avebury (see *Symbolic Landscapes*, Devereux).

If you would know the earth for what it really is, learn it through its sacred places.
N Scott Momaday, Kiowa Indian.

Ranges of hills, such as the Purbecks and the Ridgeway, were sacred high places to prehistoric people, who festooned them with countless barrows and stone sites. These heights were the body of the Goddess rising skywards. Fig. 51 shows two more landscape features that resemble the prone body of the earth Mother. Plate 63 shows the equinox sunrise over the huge barrow at Knowlton. Here we have the Sky God being reborn out of the very womb of the Goddess. Plates 54 and 55 show Maiden Castle lying majestically within the land. Perhaps the whole hill was regarded as the Maiden aspect of the Triple Goddess, which was discussed earlier.

We have looked at megaliths standing on the land, and hills rising from the land, as elements of the symbolic landscape of the Goddess. But depressions in the earth can be likewise sacred, not to mention caves and underground passages. In Dorset, Culpepper's Dish is one such example. This large hole in the ground is 2 miles SW of Bere Regis (grid ref: 815925). It is a conical pit some 50 yards deep and 150 yards wide. It is a natural formation caused by geological agencies and many smaller ones are known throughout Dorset's heathlands. Plate 82 looks down into its depths from above.

At the bottom of this natural amphitheatre, silence and peace are found. The sky is but a small blue bowl above ones head, enclosed by the trees and steep banks. I would not accept the idea that early Man did not know of and utilise such places as this. The chasm is ideal for meditation, quiet reflection and experiencing solitude. Here we go down into the body of the Earth Mother, to find rest and solace on beds of brown leaves and pine needles.

Many other culture use sacred canyons, pits or even meteor craters to carry out rituals, or weave such places into their myths. For instance, , in 1865 a report by the Ethnological Society of London recorded a spring festival undertaken by Australian Aborigines. Singing and dancing took place around a large pit, which was surrounded by bushes, so as to imitate the female private parts (of the Earth Goddess, no doubt).

I hope this chapter has helped the reader to perceive the landscape differently than perhaps had been possible before. A land of enchantment and magic is everywhere, all for the want of seeing it and sensing it. The best way to experience the Earth Goddess, Gaia herself, is on foot. A walk in the countryside can be transformed into a walking meditation, partaking in what the Aborigines called the Dreamtime. How else can one feel the earth except by reaching out with all your senses, and letting the earth reach into your inner being. She is the teacher. Let today be the first day at school.

As we walk about the earth, or indeed enter a sacred place, we are obliged, it seems to me, to pay attention to what we are being taught, rather than ask questions. We must appreciate the land as we would a beloved, opening up a two way dialogue.

The earth is more complex than any language, and more wise than any sage, so give Her credit. Perhaps we need to approach the earth with humility, and look at the landscape through the soul, rather than the level of our bodies.

Man does not have the only memory. The stones remember, the earth remembers.
Hopi spiritual leader.

Chapter Ten

Graves of the Giants

There were giants in the earth in those days.
Genesis, 6:4.

We have already discussed barrows in this book on several occasions. We have looked at fairy folklore associated with them, astronomical events aligned with them, as well as introducing the concept of chambered barrows as wombs of the Earth Goddess. Numerous folklore and other material, however, did not fit into previously covered sections. Such was the wealth of barrow-related Dorset material that I was prompted to devote a whole chapter to them.

Neolithic long barrows and Bronze Age round barrows festoon Britain in their thousands. Many have colourful folklore associated with them, as well as numerous unexplained phenomena. A common element linking every chapter of this book is the dragon, and barrows too were often regarded as the abode of this mystical beast.

A dragon is said to guard hidden treasure in a barrow called Wormelow Tump, Herefordshire. A winged Welsh dragon guards a tumulus at Treelech ar Betwis, Dyfed. On Exmoor, dragons at Challacombe lived in a group of Bronze Age barrows, whilst another guards more treasure at Gunnarton Fell, just north of Hadrian's Wall. As if to go one better, a long barrow at Walmsgate, Lincolnshire, is reputed to have the body of a dragon actually buried within. Nearer to Dorset, it may be recalled that the Bisterne Dragon dwelt on Burley Beacon (see Chapter Three). Interestingly, there are several barrows in the vicinity of the hill.

All these tales, and numerous others from across the world, echo the close association of dragons and barrows. The Anglo-Saxon tale of Beowulf contains the following line:

> *Draca sceal on hlaew, frod, fruetum wlanc.*
> (The dragon shall be in the tumuli, old, rich in treasures).

Fig. 68. William Stukeley's 1724 drawing of the Oakley Down barrow Group, near the Dorset Cursus. He shows a Roman road cutting through a disk barrow.

Buried Treasure

The connection between barrows and tales of buried treasure is well documented. Prior to 1890, a tradition is recorded of a golden coffin that lies within a barrow between Badbury Rings and Shapwick. Another coffin of gold is said to be buried within barrows on Cowleaze, near Milborne St Andrew. These are shown on 1:25 000 OS maps at c. 811967. Just east of Bere Regis is a group of barrows on Bloxworth Down, NE of Bere Wood (grid ref: 877963). Buried treasure folklore is associated with these also.

When the Thickthorn Barrow, at the southern terminal of the Dorset Cursus, was opened up in 1933, Prof Piggott and his excavators were frequently asked by locals if they were searching for the silver or gold coffin said to be interred there. No such coffin was found.

One wonders what the tales of buried riches really refer to, considering that very few barrows have actually yielded major finds of gold or silver. Perhaps a buried treasure tale is a memory of the sacredness and sanctity of the place. The treasure spoken of could be the spirits of ancestors or even earth energies phenomena experienced or witnessed. In *Needles of Stone Revisited*, Tom Graves suggests that barrows are important to the well-being of the land and may even be vital to our weather processes. Master dowser Guy Underwood found that every barrow he dowsed was a foci for earth energies.

Perhaps the treasure of these ancient tales is Mother Earth herself.

Of Giants and Gods

As the title of this chapter suggests, giants have long been associated with prehistoric burial mounds, as well as other ancient earthworks. Countless tales of giants abound around Britain and the West Country is no exception. For instance, the Lanyon Cromlech, in Cornwall, is also thought to be a giants quoit. A tumuli near Combe St Nicholas, Somerset, is known as Giants Grave.

In Dorset, too, we find giant folklore associated with tumuli and other earthern structures. From Preston, north of Weymouth, comes a 13th century record which

Plate 83. The sarsen at Giant's Grave, near Melcombe Bingham.

speaks of Thursdyche, meaning a ditch haunted by a thyrs or ogre. In the Anglo-Saxon tale of Beowulf a giant called thyrs is mentioned.

Grim's Ditch is another name for Bokerley Dyke, a huge earthwork near the northern terminal of the Dorset Cursus, near Cranborne. It was first named in 1280 as The Dyke of Grimr. Grim is a pseudonym for the giant shaman Odin, who was later elevated to the god Woden.

Giants Grave, near the village of Melcombe Bingham, has interesting folklore attached to it. A sarsen stone lies at one end of a mound possibly representing a long barrow. Two giants were having a stone throwing contest between here and Nordon Hill nearby. Apparently the loser was so mortified that he dropped down dead, and the mound is his earthern grave. I have shown previously (see Ancient Stones of Dorset, Fig. 14) that Giant's Grave and Nordon Hill are linked by a ley line. Is the stone throwing contest a distorted memory of the ley?

On Godlingston Hill, near Swanage, there are barrows known as the Giants Grave and Giant s Trencher on OS maps (grid ref: 012811). Further information on the origin of these namings are not available.

From Brockhampton Green, 5 miles NE of Cerne Abbas, comes a tale of how villagers tried to haul a large stone up a hill in order to kill a giant. The author has in fact located a stone near the village (see Ancient Stones of Dorset, page 183 and Plate 125), but it is uncertain if this is the one in question.

It was only natural for the Medieval mind to regard barrows as graves of a race of large people, the giants of myth. But perhaps many giant legends originated from respect for prehistoric shamans and priests, the Merlin-like practitioners of the Old Ways, were seen as literally giants amongst men. Perhaps we too could be searching for the 'giant' within ourselves.

Musical Mounds

*...Truely as thou sayest, a Fairy King
And Fairy Queens have built the city, son;
They came from out of a sacred mountain-cleft
Toward the sunrise, each with harp in hand,
And built it to the music of their harps.*
Tennyson.

Plate 84. Culliford Tree Barrow, NE of Bincombe. Mysterious music and voices are reported to issue from within.

As Tennyson suggests, ancient sites have long been seen as the abode of supernatural races, who seem nearly always to be musically inclined. From around Dorset various barrows are associated with musical renditions.

In 1866 the antiquarian Charles Warne wrote:

"On Bincombe Down there is a music barrow, of which rustics say that if the ear be laid close to the apex at midday the sweetest melody will be heard within".

The Bincombe area is a high one, with glorious views south to the Fleet and Portland. Dozens of barrows form skyline features in the vicinity of Bincombe Hill, Came Wood and White Horse Hill. The two musical barrows are reportedly those at grid refs 679857 and 680857, west of Came Wood. In the Readers Digest *Folklore, Myths and Legends of Britain*, we read on page 151 that a few years ago a woman hired a taxi in Dorchester to take her up to the Bincombe barrows by midday to check out the legend. It is not recorded if she was successful or otherwise.

Just a mile to the east stands Culliford Tree Barrow, at the eastern extremity of Came Wood (grid ref: 698854). Plate 84 shows the large, tree-covered barrow from the lane that passes to the east of it. Charles Warne states that the music tradition is also associated with this barrow. On the other side of the north-south lane can be seen another tumuli (grid ref: 699854) and this one, too, shares the mysterious musical folklore. In the 1970s two people heard sounds like traditional music emanating from within. They heard humming and whining noises. The barrow is now known as the Singing Barrow.

Baꞧꞧows of the Mysteꞧious

In addition to musical folklore, many barrows are associated with other unexplained phenomena, and Dorset has its fair share.

A former barrow at Ashmore was described by E W Watson, in 1890. He recites that within living memory strange sounds had been heard in the vicinity of the barrow. They were said to be made by creatures called Gappergennies. A spectral woman in white has also been seen near the barrow.

Returning to Bincombe Down our interest turns to a barrow just east of the A354 (grid ref: 673858). The barrow is approached via some rusty farm implements from the lane. Look for the hawthorns that grow on the barrow. This is the famed Burning Barrow of modern lore. In the early 1980s a man and a woman on a motorbike were passing the barrow one night. They saw an orange glow around the top and flames shooting up. They felt ill-at-ease and did not stop to investigate. Jeremy Harte notes the similarity between this tale and Norse myths, which speak of fires which emanate from barrows said to contain treasure. Several stones lie on the

Plate 25. A close-up view of the Burning Barrow, Bincombe, looking west. Some stones and a hawthorn can be seen on the mound.

barrow, and another mound on an adjacent hill marks out Beltaine and Lammas sunsets (see *Ancient Stones of Dorset*, Fig. 72). Plate 85 shows the Burning Barrow, looking west.

In addition to musical phenomena, the Culliford Tree Barrow is also connected with a strange happening prior to 1977. A woman visited the adjacent land on two separate occasions, to make up her mind about a possibly building a house there. On both occasions she heard the voice of an invisible person, warning her not to go ahead with her plans. She indeed changed her mind. She stated that no one knew of her visits beforehand.

Surely many noble bones and ashes have been
contented with such hilly tombs, which may, if
earthquakes spare them, out last all other
monuments.
Sir Thomas Browne, 1658.

A small barrow lies at the northern end of Came Down golf course, west of Downwood Lodge (grid ref: 688869). In the late summer of 1918 a woman wondering over the downs sat on the barrow to take in the extensive views. She sat day dreaming looking over the downs. After a while she became aware of distant singing, which she thought to be soldiers singing whilst on the march. The singing gradually became louder and nearer, consisting of rhythmical chanting. The voices were accompanied by crashes of metal against metal. She then realised that they were singing Latin. As she exclaimed aloud all went instantly silent. She was alone, with not a soldier in sight. Quite independently, prior to my knowledge of the above tale, I had plotted a ley line running from Herringston Barrow, south via several tumuli, to the Roman temple at Jordan Hill. The barrow where the woman heard the singing Roman soldiers is exactly on the ley! There are many other documented cases of unusual phenomena on ley lines, and the subject will be dealt with later on in this book.

On Bottlebush Down, west of Cranborne, the Dorset Cursus crosses the B3081, just west of some barrows next to the road (the same ones shown in Plate 12). In the winter of 1924 a Dr R Clay was driving past the spot in the direction of Handley. He spotted a rider on horseback going in the same direction on the downs. The rider came closer at one point and appeared to be a prehistoric man, with a long coat and bare legs. The horse had neither bridle or stirrups. The rider appeared to threaten Clay with some kind of implement. After travelling parallel with the car around 100 yards the rider and horse suddenly vanished. He noted the spot, which next day turned out to be a low round barrow.

Fig. 69. The 'wild rider' of Norse legend rides past burial mounds in C J Billmark's 19th century painting. Thunder and lightning complete the atmospheric scene.

The above tale has parallels in Anglo-Saxon and Norse legends. The Wild Hunt is a myth in which Herne, Odin or Thor variously ride across the land on a speeding horse, often accompanied by thunder and lightening. In his 19th century painting, C J Billmark depicts Odin charging past the ancient royal barrows at Old Upsala. In AD 1127 the Anglo-Saxon Chronicle tells of another spectral rider apparition at Peterborough, on February 6th, close to Beltaine.

We have already discussed the reported treasure beneath barrows at Milborne St Andrew. Tradition also has it that every time there is an attempt to dig it up thunder and lightening ensues. Is this the wrath of Odin perhaps?

Barrows of the Dead and the Living

The earth under which men are buried is
the mother of the dead. The tomb builder
would have tried to make the tomb as much
like the body of a Mother as he was able.
Archaeologist T Cyriax, 1921.

Most barrows are places where tribal ancestors were buried, sacred places where the spirits of the deceased departed for the Otherworld. Perhaps they were also somewhere these spirits could be contacted, for help and advice.

In 1976 Desmond Bonney discussed the fact that many pagan Saxon barrows occur on parish boundaries. He saw a possibility that people hoped spirits of the dead would afford protection to the land within. Medieval and later parish boundaries made much use of barrows of all ages to mark out the land. For instance, the Burning Barrow (Plate 85) lies on a parish boundary, as does the prominent Conquer Barrow at Mount Pleasant (grid ref: 707899).

The builders of barrows saw them as a threshold, a crossing place where the deceased started their journey to the Otherworld. In Celtic mythology, these spirits of the dead were carried to the afterlife on horseback. The remains of horses have been found in countless excavated barrows, accompanying their masters. In Dorset two such interments were found, for instance, at Fordington.

Barrows are often grouped into so-called cemeteries, where often dozens were built in an area of just a few acres. Good Dorset examples are to be found along the Ridgeway, where many stand out in close succession on the skyline. The Poor Lot group, on Black Down (see Plate 86) is easily viewed from the A35, circa grid ref:

Plate 86. The Poor Lot barrow group, next to the A35 at Kingston Russell.

Plate 87. The Grey Mare and Her Colts, showing megaliths and collapsed chamber.

588907. At Oakley Down, near the Dorset Cursus, many fine barrows can be seen grouped together from the A354 (see Fig. 68 for an old drawing).

Countless barrows stand out on skylines on hill tops and ridges. It is as if the departed were already elevated half way up to the heavens. Perhaps the mounds were meant to be viewed by the living, not only as reminders of ancestors, but also of the cycles of birth and death. Round barrows are shaped like breasts and tummies, no doubt symbolic of the Earth Goddess. The dead were returning to their Mother.

There can be little doubt that barrows were not only intended for the dead, but were on occasions used by the living. Post holes, representing wooden posts positioned to enable astronomical observations, have been found at many barrows, such as the

Fig. 70. A 17th century sketch by Johan Picardt, depicting the popular view that barrows were built by giants.

Thickthorn Barrow. At the Pimperne Long Barrow a berm or platform on the side of the mound was probably used for ritual or astronomical purposes. It has already been discussed how chambered barrows were used as meditation and ritual chambers. Plate 87 shows one such collapsed chamber at the Grey Mare and Her Colts long barrow (see also Plate 62).

The Great Barrow, at Knowlton, would have been the only place one could have seen the interior of all three henges (through their entrances), inviting comparison with Silbury Hill as a ritual viewing site.

Throughout Medieval times barrows continued to evoke mystery, and much barrow-related folklore originated during these times. In the 14th century tale of Gawain and the Green Knight, the hero Gawain is searching for a Green Chapel and is disappointed when he finds it to be an overgrown long barrow. The Medieval Welsh legends of the *Mabinogion* frequently refer to burial mounds as the abode of spirits, fairies and otherworldly races.

Nearer modern times, local parish or hundreds moots would often be held at barrows, where whole villages would meet for formal affairs and festivities. The

Chettle Long Barrow, the Hundred barrow (Bere Regis) and the Hasler Barrow (Steeple) are Dorset examples.

A procession used to take place up to the 19th century from the chapel at Cripplestyle, east of Cranborne, up to King Barrow (grid ref: 094123) to open the Whit Week proceedings.

It is a sad testament to Man and his transient ways that we have lost thousands of barrows due to building work, road projects and agricultural activities. It is vital that no more be lost. Barrows are part of our heritage both archaeologically and spiritually. Barrows represent continuity, they are places of burial and initiation. they can be likened to churches, which are used for both baptism but also house the departed. There is, after all, no discontinuity, we are born, we perish, to be reborn again. Barrows are the graves of our distant ancestors, but they are more than this. They are places the living can also visit, to connect with the past, the Earth and ourselves.

We started this chapter with the biblical quote there were giants in the earth in those days. There can be no denying that we are the giants of the earth at the moment, with the well-being of all life in our hands. But perhaps we should approach life like Roald Dahl's *Big Friendly Giant*. I believe we should use our power to heal, not to kill, to mend and not to damage the earth. Then we may just be able to stand as tall and proud as the giants of old.

The fairies usually took up their abode during
the day underground in the bosom of isolated round
green hills...indeed almost every circular mound
must once have been used thus, if all tales be true.
Folklorist William Brockie, 1886.

Chapter Eleven

Sacred Trees - The Spirit of the Green Man

I sit in your realm, Oh companions of my soul,
In silent supplication your arms reach for the heavens.
Your skin is craggy, your branches dancing and gyrating
as in some beautiful ballet.
Your spirit reaches out to mine - I feel it.
What is it you are saying?
In silence, you feel, enjoy, cry, are born and die.
You are sentinels of Mans conscience,
Yielding, submissive, yet wise and eternal.
Will you be here after Man is spent,
And say where are you, our departed friends?
Peter Knight, Sitting in Delph Wood, 21-4-97.

We have already discussed the concept of the Earth as a living entity. We have likewise dealt with various animals, mythical and real, that are part of Mans' folklore, or subject to his veneration. In this chapter I will expand the theme to explore another group of beings that inhabit the earth, namely Trees. We shall also look at two pagan characters, the Wodehouse and the Green Man, who came to represent the trees, woodland creatures and the spirit of the wood itself. We will see examples of them in stonework and wood from around Dorset and compare these to ones elsewhere.

Trees in Folklore and Myth

When the trees were enchanted,
there was hope for the trees.
Old Welsh Triad.

Forests held special significance to ancient races, and the veneration of trees is almost universal. The longevity of trees gave them the distinctions of wisdom and vitality. The tree was often seen as the earth phallus, the male principle growing out of the Earth Goddess. The Egyptians considered the sycamore to be the living body of the Goddess Hathor. The god Osiris was enclosed in a sycamore after his murder. We discussed the World Tree, the Tree of Life, in Chapter Nine and how Wyrd Sisters dwelt within the roots of Yggdrasil, the World Ash. Also of Norse myth is the tale of the god Odin, who hung on the same tree until receiving knowledge of the runes. Greek and Roman myths have stories of nymphs and gods associated with trees. Laurel trees symbolised immortality to the Romans, and their emperors wore wreaths of laurel leaves on their heads.

Fig. 71. 'Flower Deva' by
Ghermaine Knight.

The Druids were closely associated with woods and sacred groves, usually of oak or yew. Fig. 2 captures the atmosphere of the wise Druid amidst trees, next to a megalithic henge. The Roman Pliny described the Druids thus:

They seek the oak tree for their sacred groves, and no ceremony is complete without its branches.

Another Roman, the poet Lucan, wrote in the 1st century AD:

"You, ye Druids...you dwell in deep woods in sequestered groves".

210

Plate 88. Ashley Wood, near Blandford, the scene of spooky happenings.

The Druids are reported to have planted a Yew forest on the slopes of Hambledon Hill, NW of Blandford. Gog and Magog are two ancient oaks on the slopes of Glastonbury Tor, and are thought to be the last remains of an avenue of oaks planted by the Druids.

Trees and flowers were the home of spirits and dryads according to Classical and Celtic beliefs. The spirits of plants, called Devas, would be contacted for divination and for seeking plentiful harvests. In some cultures the unnecessary felling of trees carried the death penalty, such was the reverence placed on them. The poet Wordsworth felt something of the sacredness of all living things when he wrote "Nature always speaks of spirit". Of all the plants and trees of the woods, mistletoe seems to have been particularly favoured. In Norse mythology mistletoe was said to be the home for woodland spirits until the trees were in leaf again. The Druid association with the plant is well known and they took great care to cut down pieces of it with a golden sickle, so as not to touch it with human hands. The oak tree was called the King of Trees by the Druids and to find mistletoe growing on one was particularly magical.

I have no other masters than
the beeches and the oaks.
St Bernard of Clairvaux (1091-1153).

When Ghermaine and I moved into a new home in Bournemouth in 1996, it was with great delight that we found mistletoe growing in a great clump on one of our trees in our garden.

There is an ancient affinity between Man and trees. The association between the Earth Goddess and trees is likewise well-established. We see in Fig. 58 an image in Cranborne church, which I interpreted to be the Tree of Life rising from the head of the Goddess. The connection between the earth, trees and women is exemplified by a tradition from India, whereby all women had to be married to a tree.

Trees were, and still are, regarded by many as possessing healing and magical attributes. Traditionally, hawthorn, elder and rowan are sacred to the Goddess. The apple is associated with Venus and love, hence its appearance in the Garden of Eden myth as the means of Adams temptation. The hazel was venerated by the Celts as a symbol of wisdom and fecundity, and is still used today for making ceremonial wands. Hazel twigs have long since been a favoured tool of dowsers for water divining. The list of tree attributes is long and other works deal with this aspect, such as those by Marian Green.

212

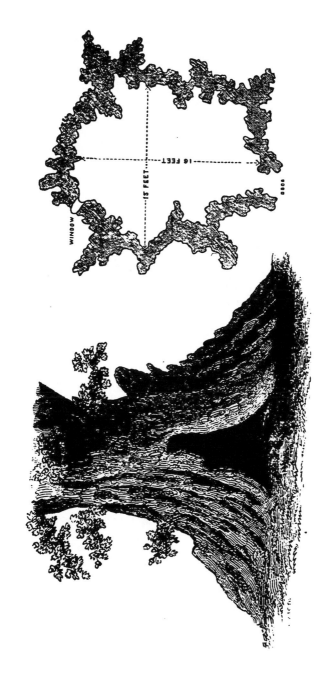

Fig. 72 The Damory Oak, a huge old oak tree which once housed a makeshift inn. It was uprooted in 1755. The site is just north of the Damory Oak Inn, Blandford.

213

Folklore and superstitions regarding trees is widespread and the South has its share, including some from Dorset. Some, in fact, are universal, such as the touch wood superstition for good luck, whilst others are more local. In Hampshire, people would gather at the Cadham Oak, Copythorn, to see the first winter buds open. The held festivities in honour of the event. There is a cure for toothache in Dorset tradition. One is supposed to make a slit in a young oak, cut a piece of hair off and put it in the slit. With hand on tree, one then recites this I bequeath to the oak tree.

Another Dorset tradition says one should not be in a beech grove at dusk. It is said that the disruptions in the smooth bark, representing former growth, were the evil eye. On the summit of Crichel Down, a beech and a pine grow together. They are called the Two Lovers and locals visit the pair in the hope of good fortune. Tradition says that one should make a vessel of laurel leaves, fill it with water from Cerne Abbas well, face south and make your wish.

I have already described in Chapter Two how the ghost of a solitary Roman soldier was seen in Thorncombe Wood, Stinsford (see Plate 6). Another spectral tale comes from Ashley Wood, next to the Wimborne to Blandford road (grid ref: circa 925050). A man out walking his dog in the woods heard sounds not unlike galloping horses. He continued his walk but next morning returned to the spot, but could find no hoof marks. A similar tale comes from Down Wood, on the same road nearer Blandford. Of interest is the discovery that Ashley Wood lies directly on a ley alignment, running from a barrow south of Wimborne, via two stones at Pamphill and more tumuli, ending at a barrow south of Buzbury Rings (see *Ancient Stones of Dorset*, Fig. 39 for details).

A link between leys and unexplained phenomena occurs in the second case also, at Down Wood. The wood is on an alignment running from Child Okeford (a former stone at the cross-roads), Hod Hill, a long barrow next to the woods, on to Badbury Rings. Other ley-spooky tale links are described in my previous book.

At Sixpenny Handley a spectral soldier in armour mounted on a horse was seen near a large oak, at the junction of Newton Rd and Denehand Rd. He was seen on separate occasions by different people. A hoard of Roman coins was later found near where the tree stood, and locals thought that the ghost may have been the guardian of the treasure. He has not been seen since the coins were dug up! Another ghost has been see at Burnham Oak, Swanage (grid ref: 014800). It is thought to be that of a suicide victim.

There rose a tree. Oh magic transcendence!
Rainer Maria Rilke (1875-1926).

Plate 89. The sycamore at Tolpuddle

*Plate 90. The relationship of large tree and ancient stone cross, at Pimperne.
Many other places have this combination.*

The fruit and foliage of trees have featured strongly in Christian architecture. Across Dorset countless acorns, berries and leaves in stone and wood adorn churches. At Christchurch Priory, the misericords in the choir area display fine wood carvings of leaves and flowers. The misericords at Bradford Abbas church include a bird eating acorns.

Mans close relationship with trees has continued into modern times. Many pubs around the county are named after trees, several villages have taken their names from specific trees. For instance, the village of Hollow Oak is just south of Bere Regis, whilst Broadoak is a village west of Blandford. Broad Oak is situated NW of Bridport. It appeared as Brode Woke in 1493, meaning literally large oak tree.

Several Dorset trees have become well known. Amongst these is Monmouth's Ash, at Woodlands, near Cranborne. This former tree was where the son of Charles II was captured whilst hiding in it in 1685. The Damorty Oak was illustrated by Hutchins (see Fig. 72). It was 75 ft high with a cavity at the bottom that was 16 ft across and 17 ft high. In the Civil War until after the Restoration an old man sold ale in the hollow area! The makeshift inn even had a door and a window. Another hollow oak, at Alloville in Normandy, had a chapel built inside the tree, which was known as the sacred oak.

At Tolpuddle an old sycamore stands just south of the main road. It is said that the famous martyrs of the village would meet under the tree prior to their imposed exile. Plate 89 shows the tree, which is now smaller than in previous times.

At the centre of many towns and villages a large tree is often to be found, frequently accompanied by an old stone cross. At Winterborne Stickland the base of the medieval cross base rests beneath the branches of the Cross Tree, a huge lime (see Ancient Stones of Dorset, p 73-74). At Sydling St Nicholas the old stone cross used to stand under the shade of another Cross Tree, which had a hollowed centre capable of containing several people. It was a huge elm and was unfortunately blown down in 1880. At the Nine Stones circle a tall beech tree is the guardian of the locality. Plate 4 shows its long branches sheltering the megaliths. At Pimperne, NE of Blandford, another large tree stands next to the medieval stone cross, near to the church and at the heart of the village (see plate 90).

These trees were often the very hub of village life, and the gathering of people at large trees may be a subconscious link to our distant ancestors, who met in sacred groves, amongst trees deemed magical and full of wisdom. Standing beneath a large tree we are also standing at the Tree of Life, the axis mundi, symbolically linking earth and the heavens. The tradition of stones being placed next to trees (and vice versa) is an ancient one. In the Old Testament we read how Joshua took a great stone, and set it up under an oak (Joshua XXIV: 26). Trees, it seems, are part of our long spiritual heritage.

When a man plants a tree, he plants himself.
Naturalist John Muir (1838-1914).

Early Christianity certainly employed leaves and fruit on Celtic crosses and church architecture. This tradition was not just some distant memory of former nature worship times. Well into the Middle Ages pagan practices continued in Britain. Sometimes it was the actual clergy themselves who venerated the earth. For instance, in the 14th century the monks of Frithel Priory, in Devon, set up an altar in the woods and are said to have worshipped a pagan Goddess figure.

Trees and Dragon Lore

The dragon has been a linking element throughout these chapters, and the mythical beast is also associated with trees and woods. A dragon is said to have lived in Shervage Wood, Crowcombe, in Somerset. At Stratton, Gloucestershire, a dragon in the church is guarding the Tree of Life, an image is repeated at Wordwell, in Norfolk. At Burgh by Sands, Hertfordshire, a carving shows the tree accompanied by a winged dragon. At Cranborne, the 14th century wall painting mentioned earlier has demons and dragon-like creatures next to the Tree of Life. This image typical of anti-pagan doctrine. At Crowcombe Church, Somerset, is a quite different image. A 16th century wood carving shows a dragon with vine issuing from its mouth. This is a symbolic reference to the fertilising and beneficial attributes the dragon was seen to represent.

The Sacred Yew

What magic there is in the ancient yew trees!
George Trevelyan.

Yew trees are linked with pre-Christian and Christian ritual and mystery. Dragons are associated with these long-living trees also. At Brent Pelham, in Hertfordshire, a dragon dwelt in a cavern under the roots of a gigantic yew. This link between yews and the old religions of Britain is further enhanced by the well-established beliefs of Celts and other races that yews were thought to guard the dead. Recent excavations suggest some Bronze Age barrows were encircled with yews, confirming that the tree was a potent pagan image.

Plate 91. A naturally sculptured old yew in the churchyard at Lychett Minster.

219

It is probably the longevity of yews that link them to the dead. One in Clwyd, Wales, is over 4,000 years old. The yew is always in leaf, a symbol of death and resurrection, continuity of spirit. It was the custom in Mediterranean countries to plant evergreen trees in graveyards. The practice may have been brought to Britain by priests trained in Rome.

Some interesting folklore regarding yews in Dorset and neighbouring areas is to be found. The Highclere Grampus (a peculiar creature said to resemble a monstrous dolphin) lived in an old yew tree at Highclere, Hampshire. In Dorset itself, tradition has it that half a mile from Tarrant Gunville a silver table is buried beneath a yew. As mentioned previously, a yew forest on Hambledon Hill is said to have been planted by Druids. An import into the area was the Nordic runes. One of the runic letters is the OE name for a yew, Eithwaz, whose characteristics include patience, waiting and perseverance, which the yew epitomises.

Poet Walter de la Mare spoke of the mysterious yew thus:

> Build me a tomb the raven said,
> Within the dark yew tree,
> so in the autumn yewberries,
> Sad lamps, may burn for me.
> (from *The Raven's Tomb*).

The yew tree has given its name to some local villages. For instance, Iwerne Minster derived from the yew, as did Uley in Gloucestershire. They probably derived from a large yew or a wood of yews in the area. Dorset's own Thomas Hardy was moved to write of the primeval yews and oaks of the County. Some of Cranborne Chase's ancient yews are at Knowlton (Plate 3).

Whenever I walk through churchyards now I always keep an eye out for large and old yews. They can be knarled and often form weird and wonderful sculptures. Plate 91 is an old yew in the churchyard at Lychett Minster. The weathered and ancient branches form skull-like features. I can but urge the reader to look at these ancient trees with new eyes, and you may find all manner of magical images in them.

An ancient yew is as important as Durham Cathedral, and a hell of a sight older.
Naturalist David Bellamy.

Tꞅee Spiꞅits

You are the forest,
You are all the great trees...
Why don't you show your face to me?
Mahadeviyakka, 12th C.

In this section we will look at trees which exhibit features which resemble dragons, animals, faces, eyes and more. Trees frequently display engaging zoomorphic and anthropomorphic forms. Such features have been recognised across the world in the mythologized landscape, and it takes but a change of perception and a mythical eye to discern them. Some may say that apparent faces and other features in trees and rocks are mere coincidences, chance arrangements that simply remind us of familiar things. Yet sceptics are missing out on much here. My own view is radically different from this, and it is a view shared by countless aboriginal cultures throughout time. I see faces and such like in trees as spiritual expressions of the Earth, of Nature, of the essence of Life itself. North American Indians and Australian Aborigines, to name but two races, see spirit in every atom and recognise ancestral spirits in rocks, trees and topographical features. It has been suggested that these forms could be the spirits and Devas of places, making themselves known to us.

The cracks, scars, twisted branches and weathered surfaces of trees can be likened to the lines and wrinkles developed during a human lifetime. The features of a person reflect his/her life, and so too with the tree. When we look at a persons body, or similarly a gnarled old tree, we look back through time.

Since Ghermaine and I started perceiving faces, vulvas and creatures in trees and rocks, the frequency of their appearance, and the way we often stumble on them, has increased my belief in the reality of a living planet, an all prevailing planetary spirit, the very Goddess of the ancients. Too many wondrous coincidences leave me in no doubt that we can all be guided towards something more than we are. If we open our minds to the Earth Spirit then every tree, rock, river and stone takes on new meaning and we can perceive Nature as magical and alive. Something reaches out to us, to connect with a spirit within us yearning to be set free.

Be still, my heart, these great
trees are prayers
Indian mystic.

221

Plate 92. Vulvic symbolism in a tree in Delph Wood, between Poole and Wimborne.

Plate 93. Face in a tree at Ulwell, near Swanage.

To align oneself with the spirit and power of trees is to reach beyond the ordinary. We reach towards greater truths. Things will never look the same again once such a seeing threshold is crossed. To start recognising faces starring out to you from trees to recognise a change within yourself.

I give the reader here but a small sample of creatures and faces seen in and around Dorset by Ghermaine and myself. It is hoped they will be the inspiration to others to follow this wondrous discovery of the secret life of trees. Remember, it is simply a question of seeing behind appearances to the essence beyond.

Some Dorset Tree Spirits

I do so love trees. I have thinks
I was once a tree, growing in the
forest. Now all trees are my brothers.
from diary of Opal Whiteley
(published in 1920).

Plate 94. The huge, wise face of a large oak at Delph Wood, north of Poole. My wife and daughter are dwarfed by the huge soulful features above.

224

*Top: Plate 95. Sycamore Spirit. Kingston Lacy. Bottom: Plate 96. Talking Sage.
Delph Wood, north of Poole.*

225

The first example is one commonly encountered in trees throughout the countryside of Dorset. In fact, one can find such forms along busy streets of towns, as we have done. Plate 92 shows a hole in a tree which is clearly the vulva of the Earth Goddess symbolically created by the tree. The hole is elongated, moist and dark, a place of mystery and the unknown.

These holes are similar in form to the cracks and crevices seen earlier in megaliths (Plate 69 for instance). I cannot believe our ancient ancestors did not also recognise such features, and likewise relate them to spirits and the Goddess. Another form of tree expression is that of facial features, and even entire heads. The range of forms is limitless, each tree on the planet being unique.

We came across a wonderful tree in 1996, by the roadside at Ulwell, north Swanage. Several vulvic cavities and heads are visible and Plate 93 shows just one. The image is one of kindness, with a half smile and large round eye. Another form on the same tree was that of a medusa-like creature, with several snake-like branches shooting off from the head, which displays a prominent eye socket. The whole appearance is dragon-like, yet not threatening.

On a trip to the grounds of Kingston Lacy, near Wimborne in 1997, I was drawn to take a look at a large sycamore. I circled the tree several times, knowing that there was something the tree wanted to show me. After a while I perceived the image in Plate 95. It is only 3 across, a tiny face with eye sockets, nose and mouth on the end of a branch stump. It is almost alien in nature and seemed to acknowledge my recognition of it.

As a family we often go to Delph Wood, north of Poole, an area of wonder and hidden treasures. We once visited the wood at dusk and while walking through the trees in the fading light we perceived forms in the trees not seen previously. Plate 94 shows one such form (rephotographed on a later trip when the light was more agreeable). A huge wise face can be discerned on the trunk of the giant oak, one of the tallest trees in the wood. The large clearing around the tree seemed to confirm the trees age and wisdom, the other trees keeping a respectful distance. Plate 96 shows another tree face seen at Delph Wood. To me the expression is one of sadness. It seems to yearn to be recognised and befriended. Perhaps it speaks to us on behalf of its brothers, to call a halt to deforestation, before it is too late.

We have photographed many incredible tree shapes and curious forms over recent years. We have found hugging trees, branches and resembling limbs and torsos, stretching legs and much more. And one need not go out into the countryside to see such wonders. Try walking along your own road, through your local park, or out into your own garden. Trees are expressing themselves in many ways which may well surprise you.

226

The next example is from a typical suburban street. I spotted this wonderful image outside a hotel on Charminster Road, Bournemouth. I call it Feline Tree. The features are that of a giant cat, panther or lioness. The eyes, nose and large lower jaw are in perfect proportion. Thousands of people hurry past the tree every day. I wonder how many have seen the feline features starring down at them?

Plate 97. Feline Tree. This incredible form stares at passers-by, next to a busy road.

227

*I must shape my life out of myself... or what
Nature brings to me.*
Carl Jung.

Dragon Trees

*Every appearance in nature corresponds with some
state of mind.*
Ralph Waldo Emerson.

The enigmatic dragon, that mythical and symbolic creature of pre-Christian pagan cultures, rears its head incredibly in the form of symbolic trees. The two examples we shall look at now were found as recently as 1997 by Ghermaine and myself. I would not be surprised if Dorset was not the abode of more.

The first is lying in Delph Wood, Poole, and can be located south of Broadstone Cricket ground. I was led to this tree whilst Ghermaine was in meditation next to another tree which has outstretched arms. The features are reptilian/dragon-like (see plate 98). Just out of the shot, to the right, several branches rise out of the ground, like multiple limbs or flames. On the right side of the picture a leg helps raise the body and head off the ground. The head is well-defined, with tight-shut mouth, dark round eye, nostril, even a sharp tongue at the extremity of the mouth. A straight, crest-like feature rises from the head, sweeping backwards.

I went to fetch Ghermaine to show her the dragon. As we walked back to it a large crow led the way, hopping from one branch to another until it came to rest above the dragon-like tree! Magic, indeed, was woven that day.

The second dragon-shaped tree is spectacular, not simply for the form it takes, but also because we have, once again, a link between a dragon and a ley line. The tree stands at Woodlands, near Cranborne, opposite a cottage at a road junction west of Sutton Holmes (grid ref: 052100). It is in fact the Remedy Oak of folklore, said to be where a young Edward VI came seeking healing for his illnesses.

We stumbled upon the tree by accident whilst looking at other ancient sites in the area. We turned a corner in the car and both exclaimed aloud. The gnarled, ancient oak is hollow and split, one side of the trunk having completely gone. Due to the

228

Plate 98. The Dragon Tree at Delph Wood, Poole. Note the eye, nostril, tongue and crest - like features.

Plate 99. The Dragon Tree at Woodlands (it is a healing tree, also known as the 'Remedy Oak'.)

Plate 100. A closer view of the head of the Dragon Tree, Woodlands.

Plate 101. The Antler Tree, Lambert's Castle. (Photograph by Ken Bailey, shown with kind permission.)

folklore regarding the king, the tree is now happily prevented from collapse by steel supports. The dragon leans across the road, and traffic and ramblers alike pass beneath the dragons head. Plates 99 and 100 show the tree from the north. It rises from the earth like some antediluvian serpent, with gaping jaws complete with tongue hanging out. The eye is deep and penetrating and eye brows bulge above. To the right of the eye is a nostril-like bump, whilst under the mouth a lower jaw growth suggests a beard or chin.

As if this were not enough, the tree had more surprises in store for us. I plotted the trees position on a map when I arrived home, in particular to see if by some wonderful chance it lay on a ley line, the dragon lines of many cultures across the earth. To my astonishment it stood exactly on a ley running from Winspit, on the Purbeck coast, right up to the temple of Stonehenge. This is one of many leys

232

Plate 102. The Green Man carving at Mappowder church.

233

Fig. 73. The Green Man-like image on a misericord in Wimborne Minster.

plotted by Gordon Harris some years ago, which he placed at my disposal. The ley is detailed in Fig. 76. Of particular interest is that the Dragon Tree lies just the other side of the road from another ley, running from Rockford Common, in the New Forest, to a hill west of Okeford Fitzpaine, via Knowlton, the Verwood stone and other sites. For details of this ley see Ancient Stones of Dorset, Fig. 32. The locality of the tree could mark a very ancient site at the intersection of at least two leys. The tree does possess folklore of a healing nature, not inconsistent with many other sacred sites situated on ley lines.

You rise from the earth, full of power and majesty.
Your eyes sparkle skywards, mouth gaping with the celebration of life.
Most do not notice you as they pass beneath,
Yet I hear you speak to me from another world:
Recognise my wisdom, see my face, feel my love,
I have been here awaiting your return.
Standing on the enchanted path to the temple,
I am guardian and healer of the earth and of men.
Feel my gnarled skin, and my eternal spirit,
And take me with you in your mind and in your heart,
So that when times of doubt and sadness arise,
You will recall how we shared this sacred moment in time.
The Dragon Tree by Peter Knight.

Plate 103. A Green Man in Christian style at Winterborne Whitchurch. A close inspection reveals what at first appears to be hair, is in fact foliage.

When one views these zoomorphic images in trees it is easy to see how, from prehistoric times right through to Medieval ages, people perceived magic, fairies and spirits, etc in the landscape. Tree images must have been particularly potent when they fitted in with myth and legend. The next one is one such example.

Somerset bard Ken Bailey has sent me a photograph of an amazing tree at the Iron Age enclosure at the top of Lambert's Castle, near the Devon border. He calls it, fittingly, the Antler Tree. It takes the form of the huge antlers of an old stag, reaching out into the clearing. It is as if the Celtic god Cernunnos himself was holding court. The place is one of peace and mystery, and, as Ken describes it a place of silent weeping for those who sought refuge and died there. The antlered Cernunnos was the spirit of the forest, a spirit which seems to still be with us. The gods of old never left, it is us that separated ourselves from them.

The Green Man and the Wodehouse

Very gay was this great man guised all in green,
and the hair of his head with his horses accorded:
fair flapping locks enfolding his shoulders,
a big beard like a bush over his breast hanging...
from *Gawain and the Green Knight,*
Geoffrey of Monmouth, 12th century.

The Green Man is one of the most powerful and enduring symbols of pagan mythology. The image of a male head with foliage issuing from his mouth and nose and possessing leaves for hair, is found in churches throughout Europe. The symbology is that of creative fertility, the spirit of the woods and woodland creatures. These characteristics make him closely associated with the Celtic god Cernunnos, whom we saw earlier. Like Cernunnos, the Green Man is connected with the spring festival of Beltaine, and we shall see later how he is still represented in todays May Day festivities.

Carvings with foliage features can be traced back to the 1st century AD, where they can be found in Roman art. The symbol spread to Britain with the Normans, although most carvings seem to date from the 13th century or later. Green Man heads can be found on capitals, corbels, fonts, misericords, indeed on a variety of church architecture. His survival into Christian times seems to have been due to the fact that he represents fruitfulness of the earth, which was vital to Medieval villages and towns. The crops had to flourish and the presence of Green Man images in churches was seen as Gods blessing and protection of the fields. The original pagan imagery was all but forgotten, except perhaps by those rustics who saw beyond the Christian hype.

In the South we have many Green Man images. One can be seen on the wooden misericords in Exeter Cathedral, dated 13th century. Others can be found in churches at the Somerset villages of Broomfield and Withycombe. Let us now turn to Dorset and see what unexpected treasures can be found.

The Green Man in Dorset

In my opinion the finest Green Man carving in Dorset is in the church at Mappowder, NE of Cerne Abbas. It is in a prominent position on a stone column, and the ledge above it usually supports the hymn board (this was removed for Plate 102). The foliage emanating from the nostrils is typical of the image.

The image of the Green Man evolved with other Church symbology over the centuries. Some later examples simply show male heads, often hairy and bearded,

Plate 104. One of two foliated heads on the outside of the cemetery chapel,
Charminster, Bournemouth.

237

Plate 105. The Green Man looking down on the streets of Southbourne, Bournemouth.

238

with foliage coming out of the chin or else surrounding the head. Fig. 73 shows a wood carving in the misericords in Wimborne Minster, and is dated 1608. The strong Celtic-like features have an accompaniment of foliage on either side, emanating from the chin.

At a lecture I gave in Weymouth in May 1997, an informant told me of a large Green Man image in stone on a wall at the south end of the Manor grounds at Abbotsbury, on the opposite side of the lane to the church. I have not been able to confirm this yet. Is it a Green Man image or not? I would welcome news of such a survival. At the church at Shipton Gorge, near Bridport, one of the capitals is of another male head with leaves growing out of his chin. The age of this image is Victorian, demonstrating an amazing resilience of the Green Man image. At the church of Winterborne Whitchurch five more capitals display male heads with foliage emanating from the sides of the face. One of these is shown in plate 103 and close inspection reveals leaves on his chin and below the cheeks. Inside Sherborne Abbey Church, carved misericord heads are surrounded by foliage.

A capital in the south arcade of Bere Regis church is a head with leafed branches protruding from it, another vestige of the Green Man tradition. At the chapel in Charminster Cemetery, Bournemouth, I unexpectedly found quite modern examples of how the Masonic tradition of foliated heads has continued. On both the SW and NW corners, where the roof meets the walls, sit modern carvings of pointed-eared creatures with leaves coming from their mouths. The one on the south side is the best, with accompanying acorns (Plate 104). The building is dated 1866 and the carvings are a testimony to the tenacity of the foliated head tradition.

Another Green Man is to be found in the suburbs of Bournemouth. Julian Court is the name of shops and flats on Seabourne Road, Southbourne. At the junction with Hosker Road a carving can be seen high up on the corner of the building (Plate 105). This image, like some other open-mouthed carvings, is a frightener, no doubt intended to ward off evil. Foliage grows from his cheeks and lower face. His features are full of strength and authority with deep set eyes.

The leaves of the trees are for the healing of the nations.
Revelations 22:2.

The Wodehouse - Wild Man of the Woods

Closely allied to the Green Man image is the Wodehouse, or Wodewose. He is the wild man of the woods, totally covered in hair except for his upper face. He has a long beard and wise, wizard-like features. He is the equivalent of the Greek satyr, and has modern parallels in the Yeti of Asia and Big Foot of North America, the difference being that the Wodehouse is almost human and, perhaps, has intelligence and wisdom at least on a par with ours. Although he is mythical, some would say he is a spiritual being of the forest, and many claim to have seen and interacted with such wild men.

The Wodehouse is well represented in Church architecture. A misericord at Hereford Cathedral shows him fighting with a beast. Several fonts in East Anglia depict him, and even stained glass windows show the Wild Man. A fine carving of

Plate 106. The Wodehouse at Aldbury, Hertfordshire.

240

him is at Aldbury, Hertfordshire. It shows his whole body, complete with club, underfoot to some Christian figure. No doubt this symbolised the oppression of paganism by the Church, which we have seen elsewhere.

I believe that at least two depictions of the Wodehouse have survived to modern times in Dorset, and my guess would be that others may yet be recognised. On the font at Stoke Abbot (see Plate 21) one of the carved heads is of a different style. The male head is bearded, hairy, with wild eyes, typical of Wodehouse depictions (Plate 107).

The other is in the misericord area of the Quire at Christchurch Priory. It is on a bench end and dates from 1515, showing the style of the Renaissance. As at Aldbury, he wields a club, and here appears somewhat aloof. The guide book on the misericords by K F Wiltshire, obtainable at the priory gift shop, states that the form

Plate 107. Carving on the font at Stoke Abbot. There is a marked similarity to Wodehouse depictions elsewhere.

to the right of him is a large profile of a human face... It is clear to me that the features are far from human, with foliage for hair, eyebrows and beard. Here we have the Green Man once again, interest-ingly in profile. I am not aware of another work that has the Green Man and the Wodehouse together in a single depiction.

Michael Hodges (see biblio-graphy) makes the interesting argument that the wodehouse is similar to the club-wielding Cerne Giant. He gives evidence to suggest that they may both represent the sun god Helis.

Fig. 74. The Wodehouse and Green Man carvings on a bench in Christchurch Priory.

Survivals

Surviving traditions of tree veneration, as well as the Green Man and the Wodehouse, can be found even in modern times. The Wild Man featured in many processions in Dorset, especially in spring. Someone would dress from head to toe in leaves as part of hobby horse, May Day and other spring festivals. Such characters are recorded from Bridport and Lyme Regis festivals, to name but two. Many Morris dance groups of today are often clad in strips of green cloth and paint their faces green, echoing the Green Man and Wodehouse myths of the past. In 1997 the author photographed such a group at the Wimborne Folk Festival (Plate 108).

The Green Man tradition survives in another form in Dorset. There are pubs named after him, such as at Wimborne and King Stag (4 miles SW of Sturminster Newton). The pub sign of the latter is shown in Plate 109, and although the face is of modern design, foliage still grows from his nostrils, ears and chin, reminiscent of the images made hundreds of years before. From our study of trees and their associated folklore, spirits and deities, I hope the reader will perhaps in future look at these sentinels of the Earth Mother with more reverence and respect than may have been the case before. Trees live, trees feel and woods are the abode of more beings than humans usually appreciate. When we place ourselves above Nature, then we do ourselves and Nature a great disservice. We are not above Nature, we are part of it.

242

Left: Plate 108. Morris dancers in green garb, echoes of the Wild Man.
Right: Plate 109. The pub sign at the Green Man pub, King's Stag.

243

When one tries to rise above Nature,
one is liable to fall below it.
Sherlock Holmes.

Chapter Twelve

Paths of the Dragon

All the country is lay'd for me.
Shakespeare, *Henry VI*, Act 2.

The subject of ley lines is a very controversial one. Most archaeologists are still in denial as to the existence of these straight alignments of ancient sites across the landscape. The ley flag has been kept flying by earth mysteries enthusiasts, geomancers and the New Age community. But, even amongst these people, differing camps with opposing views have become entrenched. Are leys alignments of sacred sites, or energy grids, or the symbolic transference of out-of-body trance experiences into the land? Perhaps they are more than all these. Perhaps they are none of them. What ever the outcome of the debate (if there ever is one!) leys perform, at the very least, the service of providing us with an enigma which has been instrumental in bringing many people into the earth mysteries and New Age theatre. Surely this cannot be a bad thing and, perhaps, this was the whole point of the exercise! Forces move in mysterious ways, often beyond our scope of comprehension.

In 1925 Alfred Watkins, an amateur photographer from Herefordshire, published *The Old Straight Track*, a milestone in modern earth mysteries research. His theory was that prehistoric trackways were layed down by ancient surveyors to form a network of straight tracks, which he termed leys. He argued that barrows, stones, trees, ponds, hill tops and other features marked out leys, and that ley alignments could still be traced today. He saw Christian crosses and churches as having evolved from older ley markers on many sites, a phenomena which has become known as site evolution. Immediately the academic backlash was brutal, and this wave of hostility towards the existence of ley lines has continued to this day. One of the main objectives was that a ley may suddenly go over a cliff, or cross a wide stretch of water or through difficult terrain when an easier route was available. Eventually earth mysteries researchers had to face up to this anomaly. This is not to say that many leys did not evolve into trackways, as we will see below, but it implies that some other primary process must have been involved in the origin of leys.

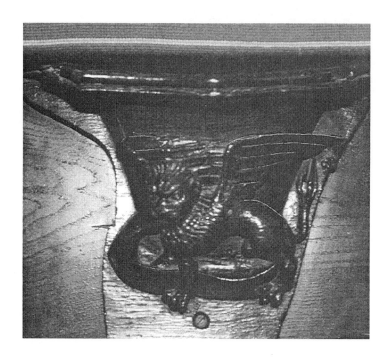

Plate 110. Dragon-like misericord at Christchurch Priory
(see also Plates 8 and 9).

In the 1970s and 80s many saw a connection between leys and earth energies crossing landscape. Unfortunately, the term ley gradually became synonymous with an energy line, so we had energy leys. Leys by definition are alignments of sacred and other sites in straight lines, and nothing to do with energy lines or grids. This is not to say that earth energies are not detected at sites on ley lines, but this is a different kettle of fish. Just because dowsable energies are detected at individual ley marker sites, we should not automatically assume that energies pass along leys, at least not in most cases. I myself, in my previous book, have cited folklore that would seem to suggest some sort of flow along a ley. But we must not apply this possible link to all ley lines. Perhaps at this point we can look at another theory which may or may not encompass earth energies.

Paul Devereux, through his many fine books and as former editor of *The Ley Hunter*, suggests that leys are spirit paths, routes along which shaman and priests may have travelled whilst in out-of-body trance flights. Many cultures speak of flying across

Plate 111. St Mark's emblem is the pagan symbol of the dragon, Gussage St Michael (see also Plate 16). The church stand on the intersection of two leys.

the landscape as part of hallucinagenically induced ecstatic rituals. The tradition of straight line movements is well documented. The shaman of the Selk-nam, of Tierra del Fuego, leave their bodies travelling in a straight line to a destination on the landscape. The spirits, or Rai, of the Aborigines of Australia travel along aerial rope through the air. In Siberia, the Tunguska tribes believed an invisible thread linked them in a straight line with their god of fate. Mayan shaman spoke of flying through the air when in a trance state. In Europe we have the old folklore of witches flying on broomsticks, which probably derived from the experiences wise women had during out-of-body magical rituals. In Norse legends, the goddess Freya sat on a pillow of bird feathers, symbolising divine flight.

These lines of flight mimic the fundamental component of the Universe - The Path Of Light Itself! Perhaps a ley is a symbolic representation of an out-of-body event which proved useful to a tribe, bringing back information from the spirit world. A celebration may have ensued, with stones and other markers being placed on the

Plate 112. Two tiny dragons inside the church at Cattistock. Other dragon symbology can be seen inside and outside the church, which stands on ley lines.

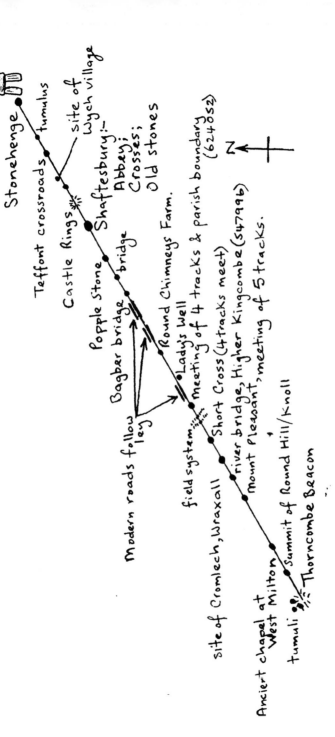

Fig. 75. *Ley running from Thorncombe Beacon to Stonehenge. The line is on the winter solstice sunset and summer solstice sunrise directions.*

landscape to either mark out or symbolise the event. Perhaps the ley was already present and subsequently developed or extended as a result of new flights.

If we have a line of sacred sites across the landscape we can assume that they would be visited by people, probably in the form of pilgrimages. Over many generations paths, and then tracks, would naturally evolve, due to plodding feet, chariots, wagons and horses hooves. And this, I believe, is where Alfred Watkins comes into the equation. This is the stage which he interpreted to be the original primary design of leys, as merely ways of getting from A to B. His book traces the development of leys through the Christian era, with the replacement of ancient stones and other markers with Christian stone crosses and churches.

I am not dismissing the concept of energy leys completely, as others have unfortunately done (too prematurely by my thinking). I am simply saying that many leys probably do not follow energy lines, and one should be wary of the energy school of thought that has been influencing all and sundry, my self included for a time.

I do believe in a living planet, personified as the Earth Goddess. I also believe that dowsable energies, so often detected as sacred sites, and ley alignments may come together now and then, as would only be expected. Both are part of the whole, but perhaps belong to different processes and derive from different origins. An arm and a leg of the human body operate independently from each other yet they are connected by other bodily parts. Despite their own independence, the act of walking requires synchronistic movements of the arm and the leg. It may be that leys and earth energies sometimes converge, both being part of the body of the Earth Mother.

In my own experience, the study of leys has provided me with the motivation to explore the landscape and its ancient sites in a way I may never have done. Following a ley across the land and visiting in turn its ancient markers, I feel I am partaking in a pilgrimage, and one that may have been acted out many thousands of years before me. It is, after all, the journey which is the lesson, not the destination.

And proclaim unto mankind the Pilgrimage,
That they witness things that are of
of benefit to them....
The Koran, Surah 22:27-28.

250

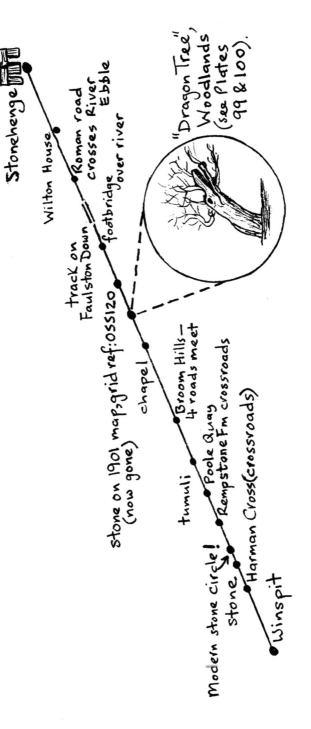

Stonehenge

Wilton House

Roman road
crosses River
Ebble

footbridge
over river

track on
Faulston Down

stone on 1901 map;grid ref:OS5120
(now gone)

chapel

Broom Hills –
4 roads meet

tumuli

Poole Quay

Rempstone Fm crossroads

Harman Cross(crossroads)

Modern stone circle!
stone

Winspit

"Dragon Tree",
Woodlands
(see Plates
99 & 100).

Fig. 76. Ley running from Winspit to Stonehenge, via the 'Dragon Tree' at Woodlands (after Harris, with amendments).

Of Leys and Dragons

In ancient China the power of the dragon was symbolic of earth energies, which were channelled through dragon lines across the landscape. The Chinese dragon is often fiercely portrayed yet is rarely harmful. Like the dragon lines, leys are vestiges of ancient cultures who believed the earth had a spiritual dimension. Time and time again across Wessex I have found evidence linking leys to dragon folklore and church architecture. A connection has also been discovered linking leys with wells and springs with curative traditions. Of further interest is the siting on several leys of churches dedicated to St George and St Michael, the two chief Christian dragon-slayers. Some Dorset examples will be cited below. In addition to this, I do not believe it to be coincidence that countless Dorset churches have demon/dragon-like gargoyles and stonework and that many of them have been found to stand on ley alignments.

We have already discussed the dramatic folklore of a fiery dragon at Christchurch in Chapter Three. A well known ley runs from Hengistbury Head, through the priory, along Fairmile Road to St Catherine's Hill (see *Ancient Stones of Dorset,* Figs. 21 and 22). Is this folklore a memory of the ley, the dragon line of old? Or perhaps it is even an exaggerated account of phenomena witnessed on the ley. Unusual phenomena have been seen in the Priory, as well as in the Castle Tavern, very close to the ley. Numerous depictions of dragons can be seen in the Priory, such as carved misericords (disguised as the emblem of St Mark - plate 110), stone dragons at the foot of Norman columns (Plate 8), tiny images on the rood screen, and dragon-like gargoyles.

At Gussage St Michael, the church of St Michael (and a stone cross nearby) stand at the intersection of two leys. One runs from Pimperne to Wimborne St Giles, the other from Knowlton Circles to a tumuli on Earls Hill. The dragon-slaying saint is seen with dragons on stained glass windows in the church, as seen in Plates 16 and 111.

Other churches displaying dragon stonework lying on leys can be found at Cattistock, Durweston, Batcombe, Mappowder, Holwell, Child Okeford, Maiden Newton, to name but seven of numerous occurrences. Cattistock church lies at the intersection of two leys (see my previous book - Figs. 12 and 36). Dragon depictions can be seen on the pulpit (accompanied by a winged bull), up the tower, on a giant mural, and at the foot of a stone column (see plate 112). Near the church a large stone can be seen set into the corner of the Fox and Hounds Inn, which could be further evidence of ley alignments.

Parts of the chancel of Cattistock church date from around 1630, but most of the church was rebuilt in the 19th century. I am not saying that the presence of dragon architecture on a ley line church means the architects were aware of leys. But forces

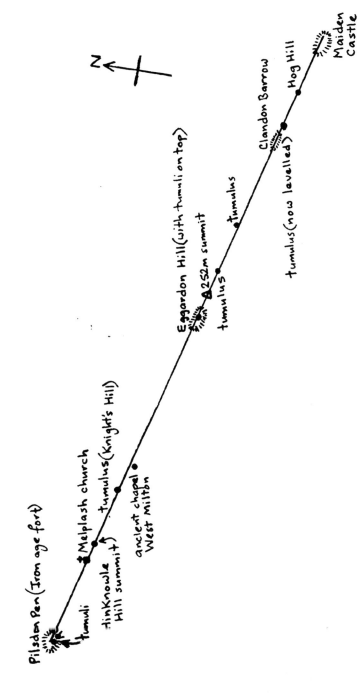

Fig. 77. Ley running from Pilsdon Pen to MAiden Castle.

work in mysterious ways. Perhaps sacred sites, which the Church often build on, communicate with us on many levels. Subconsciously, it is possible that church builders connected with the essence of the sites and fitting stonework and architecture was the result.

In *Ancient Stones of Dorset* I describe many leys that cross the Dorset landscape, over 50 of which are illustrated. I see no need to repeat any here, so I have selected a few that either did not come within the scope of my previous work, i.e. they do not have stone sites on them, or else were not illustrated.

An instructive ley is one that runs from Thorncombe Beacon, on the coast, across Dorset up to Stonehenge itself. It was plotted by Gordon Harris who placed much useful material at my disposal. It is a typical Watkins-type ley, one where tracks developed along sections of it (see Fig. 75). It has tumuli, crosses, old stones, and an ancient chapel on its route. The Popple Stone (grid ref: 823200) sits in a lonely field near Shaftesbury directly on the ley. The name derives from the Dutch word popelen, meaning to throb. This could be a relic of the sensations that were once felt at the stone. The stone is flat-topped, to enable seating. The ley also passes close to two holy wells, at Hermitage and Holwell (the latter unconfirmed). There are instances of bridges, cross-roads and modern roads following the ley, just as Watkins cited as proof of ancient trackways.

Of further interest is the alignment of the ley on the directions of the winter solstice sunset and the summer solstice sunrise. This astronomical association of leys has been demonstrated elsewhere in Dorset and across Britain (Fig. 35 in Ancient Stones of Dorset shows another ley aligned with the solstices, running from White Horse Hill to the Dorset Cursus). Leys are not solely features of the landscape. They link landscape with the cosmos, Man with the skies.

Cross-roads are among the most magical
spots in the whole of folklore.
From *Wayland*, D Hand.

Another ley running down into Dorset from Stonehenge is shown in Fig. 76. This ley is interesting, for on it stands the Dragon Tree described in Chapter Eleven (see Plates 99 and 100). the ley is again one plotted by Gordon Harris, with amendments by myself. I find it incredible that such a dragon-like tree should stand on a dragon line to the sacred temple of Stonehenge, and is one of the many magical coincidences I have encountered around Dorset over the years. It would appear that a magically inclined imagination reveals a magically empowered landscape.

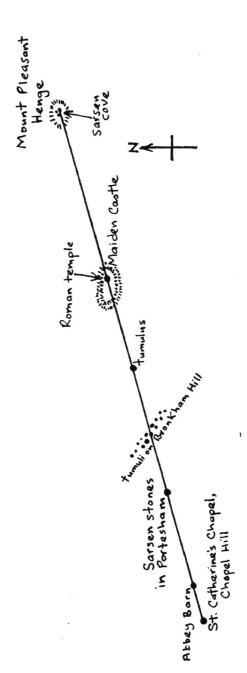

Fig. 78. Ley alignment between Chapel Hill and Mount Pleasant.

Also of interest is the fact that the ley passes within yards of the circle built in the 1970s near Bushy House, west of the Bronze Age circle at Rempstone. It is as if ley consciousness, mentioned above, was again at work, with the site of the new circle being selected by forces not human. South of Bushy House the ley runs up the track to the top of the Purbeck ridge, passing a small stone on the way (east of bridlepath).

The next two leys show several ancient sites closely situated to each other. Each has three major spiritual and cultural localities on their course. The first is a ley running from Pilsden Pen to Maiden castle, passing through Eggardon Hill on the way (Fig. 77). Clandon Barrow, between Eggardon and Maiden Castle, yielded many gold and bronze ritual objects, such as the ceremonial mace head inlaid with gold shown in Fig. 23(A). I think the alignment of three major prehistoric and Iron Age centres is significant and a major piece of evidence in the search for proof of the existence of leys.

Fig. 78 shows another ley running from the chapel on top of Chapel Hill up to the site of the Mount Pleasant henge, via the Roman temple on Maiden Castle (see Plate 56). This is a good example of a tight ley, with close, often intervisible sites. Standing at the Roman temple one can look NE and see the site of Mount Pleasant henge, the tree-covered Conquer Barrow marking out the locality on the landscape. Maiden Castle and Mount Pleasant were major spiritual centres from the Neolithic right up to Iron Age times, and both sites have several leys radiating from them (see *Ancient Stones of Dorset*, Figs. 82, 95 and 98).

Many more leys crossing Dorset have been uncovered by several researchers and the reader can take an active part in ley discoveries. Mapwork, patience, a keen eye and field plodding are all that is required. When I check out or walk a ley I never fail to be amazed at what other things I discover or experience. Incredibly trees, hidden stones and much more come to light. Leys are, if nothing else, a means Mother Earth is using to inspire us to visit sacred sites. More than that, they encourage us to interact with the landscape.

One phenomena of leys is the evidence of site evolution, where a sacred locality has literally evolved over countless generations, very often from a prehistoric stone or barrow. Knowlton henge stands at the focus of several leys involving primarily prehistoric sites. A Norman church was built within the centre henge to Christianise the locality. The church at Child Okeford stands at the intersection of several leys, as too is the church at Cattistock. At Whitcombe, south-east of Dorchester, a stone rests within the wall of the churchyard. The church stands on a ley running from Mount Pleasant Henge to a tumulus south of Broadmayne. (For details of all the leys mentioned in this paragraph see diagrams in my previous book).

At Sydling St Nicholas there is a very convincing example of site evolution on a ley. Fig. 79 shows the medieval stone cross in the foreground, whilst across the road is a

Fig. 79. Medieval stone cross and markstone (arrowed) at the crossroads at Sydling St. Nicholas.

257

3 ft long stone. A ley runs up through the village passing the stone and the cross, following the N-S village street for a while. The ley runs from Maiden Castle to Yetminster church, passing sites on the way such as the Sydling markers, Stratton and Chetnole churches and tumuli.

Remnants of the former importance of leys to our ancestors can be found around Dorset, and I shall give two examples here. A ley alignment links Pilsdon Pen, Lambert's Castle, Broadwindsor, Halstock and Stonehenge (plus some other minor sites on route). Halstock comes from the Old English, meaning holy place. The village church stands on the ley to Stonehenge. Of interest is the fact that it also stands on another ley running from West Bay up to Ansford, via Corscombe church, Sutton Bingham, Barwick and Marston Magna (see Ancient Stones of Dorset Fig. 123). Ghostly folklore is associated with Halstock and the holy place tag may be connected with the ley.

At Muckleford, near Stratton, is a small stone just north of the bridge over the Frome (grid ref: 643936). In my previous work I showed how the stone and the bridge stand at the intersection of two leys, one of which goes all the way, once again, to Stonehenge. The name Muckleford derives from the OE Mycel ford, meaning great ford. I believe that this lonely spot tucked away in the Dorset countryside was once an important locality, at the meeting of two leys.

Clues that might lead us to conclude that ley awareness survived into Saxon-Medieval times is plentiful. The British camp at South Cadbury is one of the favourite contenders for the site of Arthurs Camelot. Is it coincidence that it lies midway between Hambledon Hill and Glastonbury, and on a straight line alignment with them?

An incredible story comes from Whittle, in Lancashire. Leyland Church should have been built at Whittle, but every night building materials were moved to a site at Leyland. The villagers eventually built the church at the latter site and afterwards found a marble tablet on the church wall. It read:

> *Here thou shalt be*
> *And here thou shalt stand*
> *And thou shalt be called*
> *The church of Ley-land.*

The words 'Ley' and 'Land' were separate yet hyphenated, giving us a mysterious, yet tangible case for ley consciousness in post-Norman times.

Ley lines will no doubt continue to incite controversy and perhaps this is a necessary step along our evolutionary track back to a more earth-conscious mind-shift. Ley hunting provides us with impetus to go out into the landscape and view it with the

258

new eyes that I spoke of earlier. Tales of dragons, leys, earthlights, unusual phenomena and so forth help jog our subconscious memories into releasing the deeply concealed ancient wisdom that I believe is inside each one of us, just waiting for the magical key that unlocks the gate of the inner mind. Perhaps for many it is what may lie beyond the door that stops them turning the key, even though they know it fits the lock. to study earth mysteries, leys, ancient sites and the like without a sense of wonder, magic, imagination and humility, is like never even getting the key out of ones pocket.

...their minds were wrapped up with
notions of primeval giants and dragons,
which kept a jealous watch over their
hidden treasures.
T Wright, *The History of Ludlow*, 1841.

Chapter Thirteen

Awakening The Dragon

The world is a divine dream.
Ralph Waldo Emerson, *Nature*, 1936.

As we arrive near the end of our tour of magical Dorset, I hope the reader has by now attained the realisation that the landscape and its sacred sites are impregnated with a life-force that we can contact and interact with. The Earth is the teacher and we Her privileged children in a beautiful classroom. This planet possess consciousness and we can connect with that spirit to enhance our own lives and the well-being of our fellow human beings. In this chapter I will hopefully dispel any lingering beliefs that the earth is simply a rock spinning through the void of space. This planet has a spiritual dimension which is constantly reaching out to us.

I will also aim to give a few pointers which have proved valuable to myself in how to approach the landscape and its sacred sites, trees and so forth, so that we can open up the channels of dialogue between us and the Earth Spirit.

The Dragon Stirs

...a great dragon, which those of
Babylon worshipped.
The Apocrypha Scriptures.

Phenomena of the unexplained kind have been witnessed since prehistoric times, and these were firmly laid at the door of gods, goddesses, demons, devils, fairies, dragons and the like. We have already discussed several throughout these pages, many inside Dorset. Yet despite the romantic metaphors and folklore exaggerations we must remind ourselves that unusual events did take place, in some form or another. These events are still happening today and perhaps we just need a change of perception to see the dragon awakening all around us.

Buddhists have a term called The Shining. They apply it to a consciousness change within a person that enables them to perceive the Earth as having consciousness, and of the person being actually part of it. George Russell once said "...perhaps most of what has been said of God has in reality been said of the Earth". This is a telling phrase and one that will ring true for todays pagan community. If the Divine is omnipotent and everywhere in the Universe, then there cannot be a place where It is not. The Earth Goddess is that force on this planet, enabling us to connect with divine forces through the Earth Spirit.

Plate 113. Double-headed snake carving in porch at Broadway church, dated as 12th century Norman.

When you know nature as part of yourself,
You will act in harmony.
When you feel yourself part of nature,
You will live in harmony.
Lao Tzu, from *Tao Te Ching*.

The dragon has been a key figure in many nature-based cultures and has frequently been used as a metaphor for unusual phenomena and earth energies. A link between the land and these dragon energies can be found in the legends of the Greek goddess Ceres. She was the goddess of the land and of harvests, and she rode a chariot drawn by two flying dragons. The Chinese dragon frequently dwelt on a hillside near running water, symbolising the flowing of benevolent energies across the land. One type of dragon called the Wyvern derives its name from the Gaulish word wouivce, meaning spirit. In France it is often depicted as half-snake/half-woman, an appropriate image for the goddess energies that snake across the landscape.

Plate 114. Dragon gargoyle at St. John's church, Weymouth
(one of two, on the east and west sides).

The old dragon has been stirring and puffing fire since at least Biblical times. In the Book of Job, Chapter 41, we read Out of his mouth go burning lamps, and sparks of fire leap out...he maketh a path shine after him. This powerful verse links earth energies and leys (paths), be it a controversial connection. In Samuel 28:13 we are told that a ...woman said to Saul, I saw gods ascending out of the earth. This is a direct contradiction to most biblical accounts of gods and angels, who usually descend from the skies above. It is usually demons, not gods, who are associated with subterranean regions. Was the woman in the account telling Saul of earth energy phenomena she had witnessed?

The above account is complimented by a Japanese haiku which goes:

The earth speaks softly,
To the mountain,
Which trembles,
And lights the sky.

This may well be, as Paul Devereux concludes in *Earthlights*, a reference to earthlights phenomena which, he goes on, may be the origin of many UFO reports. Strange lights have been seen at many Dorset sites, notably at the Burning Barrow, Bincombe, and the Cross-and-Hand Stone, Batcombe (see plate 85 and Fig. 29). Perhaps the tale of the fiery Christchurch dragon originated from unexplained earth-generated processes. A spectacular example of lights issuing from the earth was witnessed by two women walking on cliffs near Weymouth on a sultry August day in 1876. Over the crest of a hill they saw numerous balls of light, the size of snooker balls, which moved up and down independently to a height of three feet above the ground. It is reported that they eluded being grasped, a bit like soap bubbles. Various charming colours were displayed and the phenomena lasted for around an hour. Strange lights have also been seen over Maiden Castle and near sacred sites at Eggardon Hill.

Leaving the county briefly, we travel up to Warwickshire. In 1923-4 strange lights were seen in the skies around the church at Burton Dassett. Inside the church can be seen a number of dragon/serpent carvings, similar to those we have encountered around Dorset (see Plate 113 and 114 for instance). I have discussed earlier the possible connection between sightings of earthlights and faults in the earths crust, first advocated by Devereux. He noted that every stone circle in England occurs within a mile of faulting,. Interestingly, Burton Dassatt church stands in an area riddled with faulting, as does the Burning Barrow at Bincombe. The cliffs where the women saw the bubble-like lights is close to where major faulting occurs between Cretaceous and Jurassic strata.

Perhaps certain regions are more prone to light phenomena, and out distant ancestors built stone circles and other sacred sites where they witnessed apparitions of what

263

they saw as dragons, fairy lights, etc. At these place the pulse of the Earth Goddess would be strong, in the form of earth energies.

Returning to the Bible again, Exodus 1 II, 2 tells us that ...the angel of the Lord appeared to him in a flame of fire. This passage was written by a Christian within a Christian belief system, but can easily be translated as the dragon flew across the land or even earthlights/UFOs/earth energies issued from the ground skywards. It should always be remembered that old folklore and legends were written within the framework of the language, literacy, dogma and general mentality of the day. Todays UFO may have been yesteryears dragon, and so forth.

In 1981 a woman was driving down Knapps Hill at Duntish when she saw a bright light, which she perceived to be a coach drawn by four horses. The apparition passed through a hedge and vanished. This tale has an interesting combination of earth energies phenomena (the light) and earth memory (the coach and horses). Earth memory is thought to be the transference and storage of events of a strong emotional manner onto a locality. Events may be mysteriously replayed at some later date, sometimes centuries later, when conditions are right. Roman soldiers seen at Thorncombe Wood and Maumbury, and the Duntish spectres, could be examples.

Sometimes landscape phenomena can be even more dramatic than just lights in the skies. Years ago, before Knowlton henge was cleared of trees and undergrowth and

Plate 115. At Wimborne folk festival, dancers dressed in green garb and leaves echo former fertility rites.

264

the church renovated, a man was out walking there. He suddenly heard crashing sounds like something coming violently through the undergrowth. He was apparently very shaken up by the experience, as one can well imagine. Knowlton is at the centre of several ley lines and members of both Wessex and New Forest Dowsers have revealed an active site of spiralling energy lines and risers, columns of dowsable energy which may mark the position of former megaliths. Paul Craddock has mapped many of the lines of force, most of which touch the church at some point. Many comment on the strange feel of the place. The site has atmosphere, but more than this, it has presence!

We do not need to go to India, Stonehenge, Egypt or the other famous mysterious places of the world. Dorset's own landscape is infused with ancient magic and wisdom, if we would but have the eyes to see it.

Seeking Out Dragons and Goddesses

Many things that have been hidden will arise and
expose themselves to view.
Thomas Sprat, Bishop of Rochester, 1667.

A constant thread running through the pages of this book has been to look at familiar things with new eyes. By a shift of mind-view and perception hills can be transformed into the breasts or tummy of the Goddess, lines and holes in the bark of trees reveal faces, and eyes stare back at us from rock outcrops, where weathering reveals the spirit of the place. Church architecture can be viewed in a new way, revealing all manner of characters and symbols of pre-Christian origin, such as dragons, fairies, the Green Man and so on.

Our link with the land is closer than we might imagine, and this connection is primarily a spiritual one. In a sense we are the land, for we are creations of the earth. Yet we constantly try to remould and enhance and alter our mothers body. The results of this madness are for all to see. Jose Ortega Gassett (1883-1955) once said "Tell me the landscape in which you live and I will tell you who you are." When we westerners survey our domain, with its pollution, road networks and urban decay, then this landscape is surely telling us who we have become.

We are entering time now, as we approach the new millennium, when at long last many people are connecting with the Earth in a way that they have not done for hundreds of years. The Goddess went underground, awaiting a time when She would be recognised again. Merlin predicted a time when the Goddess shall lie hidden within the closed gateways of her sea-beaten headlands. William Blake saw the decline of Albion's spirituality, yet spoke of its rebirth. Many of the worlds religions are largely guru-centred, evolving from one persons illumination, such as Christianity, Islam and Buddhism. The earth religions of the past, such as paganism and other nature-based spiritualities had nothing to kill or die for, as John Lennon put it. They held no dogma nor had egos to defend. Nature was the guide and inspiration, as it can be today.

Plate 116. The slaying of the dragon on the war memorial outside Wimborne Minster.

In Dorset (as in places across the world) trees, animals, birds and mythical breasts have inspired generations of religious architects. The 13th century font at Stinsford, near Dorchester, has carved animals on it. A squirrel can be seen clinging to the walls inside Wimborne Minster. There are reptile gargoyles at Long Crichel church, and elsewhere around the county. A large carved bird watches over the churchyard at Lillington, its outstretched wings casting shadows over the tombs below. In many Dorset churchyards sacred yews guard lonely graves.

These are but remnants of former times when Nature was us, and we were Nature. Symbols intended for the veneration of the earth eventually came to represent Mans dominance of it. Today we can still find vestiges of Nature veneration in festival and procession activities, such as morris dancing, well-dressing, hobby horses and beating-the-bounds ceremonies. In these forms the dragon, the Green Man and Cernunnos still survive, be it in barely recognisable forms (Plate 115).

I would urge you to seek out church architecture, museum exhibits, etc., and to explore buildings around town for signs of ancient symbology (such as in Plates 104 and 105). The carving of Michael slaying the dragon outside Wimborne Minster Plate 116) reminds us of dragons that need to be slain today, such as famine, wars pollution and global warming, to name but a few. The fiercest dragon may be our own pride and ego, which foolishly tells us we are above Nature and its laws. To revere the Earth Goddess, as our ancestors did, is to place ourselves within Nature, a part of Her, with all the respect and humility that is encompassed by such veneration. The following Gaelic hymn was written in earlier Christian times, when it was clearly recognised that the Earth Spirit, the Goddess (Brighid) and the serpent were beneficial to Mankind and were, in fact, essential for their everyday survival. Here there is none of the Biblical damnation of the serpent, but a tender acknowledgement of its power and life-force coming from the Earth:

Early on Bride's [Brighid's] morn,
Shall the serpent come from the hole,
And I will not harm the serpent,
Nor will the serpent harm me.

Awakening the Dragon Within

Anywhere is the centre of the world.
Black Elk

The dragon we are seeking to awaken here is not the ego side of our nature spoken of above, but our recognition of the Earth as our sacred physical and spiritual mother. Black Elk is telling us that wherever we are we create our own universe, our own world-view. Our perception of the planet may be an individual one, and prone to the culture we live in, yet it is true that a change in personal perceptions also changes the world. We can develop an attitude whereby we place ourselves in the frame of mind to be receptive, to pay attention to what the Earth has to teach us. Imagination is an important step to bridge the gap between the logical 20th century mind and that of the prehistoric shaman.

Trees, rocky outcrops, hills, pebbles in a stream, driftwood on a beach, even the clouds in the sky can all take on magic and new meaning when we open our heart, mind and soul to the Earth spirit. Let your imagination play with shadows in the moonlight. Take your soul for a walk into the landscape.

I recommend the reader to spend some time in a wood or forest after dark, preferably on a moonlit night. Let ones imagination run riot. Share the Dreamtime of the place. I personally feel that a forest comes alive after the sun sets. My wife Ghermaine reflects this perception in an extract from one of her poems about the nightime forest:

> The air slumbers, the forest rests,
> And yet in their dreaming
> The trees feel more active than when they awake.

Perhaps it is time for a sacred journey, a pilgrimage no less, across mother Earth. After all, an outer journey can be the trigger, the release, for an inner one.

Pilgrimage

> The simplest way to explore Gaia is on foot....
> how else can you reach out to her with all your senses?
> James Lovelock.

In his latest book *Re-Visioning the Earth*, Paul Devereux makes the suggestion that we go on a pilgrimage across the landscape, preferably to a sacred site. He urges us to study up on the site first, getting to know it, so to speak, on a subconscious level. But it is the journey which holds as much magic as the destination itself. Feel and hear the crunch of footpath gravel under our feet. Smell the scents that drift through

Plate 117. The author taking time out to rest on a tree branch. Tree-hugging is an uplifting pursuit.

the air into our minds. Sense what messages bird song and bird flight have for us. Note the shapes of trees we pass, feel their presence and perhaps stop and hug a few. Resting under a tree can be the start of a lifelong friendship.

As you get near your sacred site, your pilgrimage destination, note the apprehension and adrenaline that you feel. It is a good practice to pause a while before entering the site, be it a henge, stone circle, barrow chamber or whatever. Ask if you may enter. Tell the guardians of the site, for there will be ones there, that you come in peace, to learn, and to venerate the place. Let your intuition guide you, for visiting sacred sites is not about logical thinking, it is about feeling and love. Find a spot that draws you to it and stand or sit...listen...be still...smell the place...feel the place...perhaps you could meditate or simply daydream, asking yourself am I dreaming or is it the earth that is dreaming me? Am I experiencing the site, or is it experiencing me?

There was a time when meadow, grove and stream,
The earth, and every common sight,
To me did seem
Apparelled in celestial light,
The glory and the freshness of a dream.
William Wordsworth.

At sacred places the forces of spirit link with the physical world. This has the effect of enhancing our imagination and opens up our intuitive nature. For we are part of these forces. We are, ultimately, part of the sacred site.

269

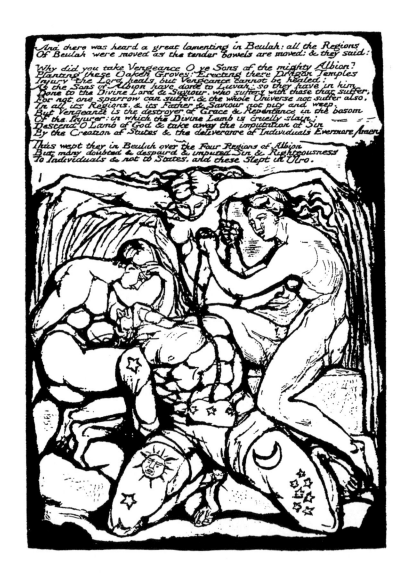

Fig. 80. In this depiction by mystic William Blake, Albion (England) lies in a comatosed sleep, whilst the triple Goddess laments his demise and awaits his re-awakening.

Ghermaine and I frequently leave an offering at a place, be it a sacred ancient site or even a tree in a wood. This may take the form of a crystal, a flower or some other object. This is important to us, and we feel we are not only leaving part of ourselves at the place, but we are also taking a very personal memory away with us, a memory that forges a close bond between us and the spirit of the place. We recently placed crystals discreetly and with great care within the bark of the Dragon Tree, at Woodlands. I could feel the appreciation of the tree, as a closer bond was made between us and the trees spirit.

My earnest wish is that the reader open his or her heart and soul to the wonders of our sacred landscape. If you do I have a feeling that you will never fail to be amazed at the wonder and sanctity of it all. I believe Albion is rising again, as Blake predicted, as a long slumber nears its end.

He will delight the company of every fairy knoll,
He will be a dragon before the hosts at the onset,
He will be a wolf of every great forest,
He will be a stag with horns of silver.
Kuno Meyer, *The Voyage of Bran*, 1895.

Appenòix One

Ancient Stones of Dorset - Supplemental

---

*The presence of a sacred stone will protect
you from misfortune.*
Lone Man, Sioux Indian, 1918.

It was inevitable that some new stones, interesting quotes and other stone related material would come to light after the publication of *Ancient Stones of Dorset*. In that very book I said they probably would, such is the wealth of material and scope for the amateur in Dorset. I welcome the opportunity here to do a brief addenda, to accompany the previous volume. Some discoveries such as the stone face at Rempstone and the Goddess Stone have already been discussed. Below are items that did not fit into previous chapters.

Biblical Accounts anò Folklore

I have come across several more old accounts that give us clear indications that megaliths have been erected for spiritual means for thousands of years. Hebrews and early Christians alike saw nothing wrong with marking events or localities with stones. The following passages are noteworthy:

Where are their gods, their rock in whom they trusted? (Deut. 32:37)
And Joshua...took a great stone...that was by the sanctuary of the Lord. (Joshua 24:26)
The Ebenezer stone was erected to remind people that God helped the Israelites defeat the Philistines. (1 Samuel 7:12)

In the Anglo-Saxon tale of Beowulf we read the following passage:

Fare thou with haste now,
To behold the hoard neath
the hoar-greyish stone.

An old Welsh proverb tells us Good
is the stone together with the Gospel,
which is an amazing admission of
Christian beliefs blending with pagan
sacred places. In Wiltshire sarsen
stones are also known as Bride
Stones, which probably derived from
the goddess Brighid.

Some Dorset Place Names

In my previous work I commented on
such places as Broadmayne,
Littlemayne, Stone, Grimstone and
other localities as having been named

Fig. 81. Megalith outside Toller Porcorum church.

after megalithic sites (mayne comes from the Welsh word maen, meaning stone).
Others have been uncovered, probably referring to former stones. Graston House,
near Burton Bradstock comes from the Middle English, meaning grey stone. The
O.E. element *han* means boundary stone, probably giving rise to Redhone Hundred.
Hanford, on the river Stour, comes from the OE ford at the stone. The O.E. element
har means grey, hoar, boundary, giving rise to Hargrove and Hartgrove.
Bellingstone and Ellingstone are two more Dorset examples, both possibly
associated with the old sun god Helis.

Additional Dorset Stone Site Information

In *Ancient Stones of Dorset*, and in this volume, Cattistock church has been cited as
being on several ley lines. The church architecture reflects this with dragon
stonework and paintings. Just east of the church is the Fox and Hounds Inn. Built
into the corner of the building is a large stone, over 3 ft in length. I believe it could
be one of the original ley markers.

The village of Toller Porcorum lies two miles west of Maiden Newton. Just outside
the main churchyard gate are two large stones, reset on modern bases. The
churchyard is roughly circular and, according to the church booklet, has the
appearance of a Llan, or sacred site. On the north side, the churchyard rises over 6 ft
above School Lane. When an older wall was exposed two upright stones were found
standing against it. The booklet goes on to suggest that the churchyard site may

273

have once been surrounded by a circle of stones. The stones were moved to the east gate and were given the names of Peter (the rock) and his brother Andrew. Fig. 81 shows one of the stones.

The Toller Porcorum site lies directly on a ley running from Powerstock up to Old Sarum, on the outskirts of Salisbury. The church and stone at Cattistock lie on the same alignment, as do other stone sites (see Ancient Stones of Dorset, Fig. 12). I was unaware of the existence of the Toller Porcorum stones when plotting the ley. Stones have also been uncovered in a bank in the churchyard at Hordle, Hants.

John Bush, of Winterborne Zelston, informs me of two stones west of Winterborne Kingston, close to the River Winterborne (grid ref: 85169790 and 84839816). He describes them as being of an attractive pink, fine-grained rock, out of place amongst the flint and chalk of the neighbouring land. They are up to 5 ft in length. By coincidence my wife Ghermaine spotted a stone less than a mile east of the above stones on a recent visit to the area. The stone, a sarsen, is around 4 ft long and sits in a field opposite North House (grid ref: 860975). It lies just a few hundred metres

Plate 118. Sarsen stone in field opposite North House, Winterborne Kingston.

Fig. 82. The Bellingstone, next to the ridgeway track south west of Cerne Abbas.

SW of one described previously outside Winterborne Kingston village hall.
Martin Driscoll informs me of a stone on Black Down, north of the Hardy
Monument. the area is littered with barrows and apparently the long barrow at grid
ref: 604883 aligns with the stone.

A stone can be seen just outside the north gate of the churchyard at Bere Regis. It
lies next to Stable Cottage, but does not appear to be a wall protector. The stone
could be yet another example of site evolution, being situated as close as it is to the
churchyard.

One mile SW of the Cerne Abbas Giant is Hog Hill, over which an ancient north-
south path crosses. Just east of the path (at grid ref: 647008) stands the little-known
Bellingstone. It is a solitary megalith standing about 6 ft above the ground. During
summer months it is practically lost amidst the hedgerow bushes. The stone stands
on the parish boundary of Cerne and Sydling, and was mentioned in records of
rogation ceremonies 700 years ago. The name may derive from Belenus who was an
Iron Age god. Rodney Castleden, in The Cerne Giant, considers it possible that the
stone may date back to the Neolithic or Bronze Age. Of interest is the fact that the
stone would have at one time been visible on the skyline from the vicinity of the
Giant, who in fact faces directly towards it. The stone may have been connected to
rituals associated with the Giant.

In February 1998 I located two stones (2ft +) in a hedge bank on the PFP North East of Hampton Hill stone circle. They lie next to a gate going into woods at grid ref: 598867. The stones may help confirm both the proposed processional route, and a ley that passes just north of the stones, both proposed by myself previously (*Ancient Stones of Dorset* Figs. 76 &82).

In my previous work I referred to a large megalith that once stood at one entrance of Maumbury Henge, at Dorchester. The stone was subsequently buried and later destroyed. More evidence has come to light regarding further stones at the site. In the 1903 OS map of the town two stones are shown on the ramparts of the earthwork. No traces of them appear in reports of the 1908-13 excavations and the stones now appear to have been lost.

Members of the New Forest Dowsers have been doing site work at the large fallen megalith at Verwood, a locality I have described previously. They have uncovered another stone in the earthern bank on the edge of the clearing around the stone, and dowsing suggests more may be present.

Mr D Partridge of Corfe Mullen informs me of two stones in his area, one at grid ref: 979955, at Naked Cross, the other at home Farm, grid ref: 977970. Work remains to be done regarding their authenticity or any possible ley associations.

Michael Hodges, of Christchurch, corrects me by informing us that the stone on the ley going from Hengistbury Head past St Catherine's Hill, in fact IS an old boundary stone marking out the old Borough of Christchurch.

An informant at a recent talk I gave told me that he had seen a menhir, or megalith, marked on a 1590 map of the Lulworth area. He could not remember the exact position. I have already given details of a former stone circle in the area.

Recent work by New Forest Dowsing Society members suggests an avenue of megaliths may have ran NEE from the church at Knowlton towards the flattened break in the henge bank, north of the two yews. Dowsing by them further suggests former outer and inner circles of megaliths and a path that may have followed the lines of the yew trees which skirt the central henge. They also confirm the powerful energy nodes, risers and blind springs that have been described elsewhere (see Ancient Stones of Dorset Fig. 26 and plate 16). Work on the site by members of the New Forest Dowsing Society and Wessex Dowsers is on-going and contacts for both groups can be found in Appendix Two.

Belinda Lopez, of Bournemouth, informed me of three stones, up to 2ft high and 3ft long, near Shaftesbury. They lie in a field between Quoits Copse and Motcombe House (at grid ref: 855242). The naming of the nearby copse may be relevant as a quoit is another name for the remaining stones of a Neolithic chambered tomb. Plate

Plate 119. Stones north west of Quoits Copse, near Shaftesbury. Photo by Belinda Lopez, shown by kind permission.

119 shows two of the three stones, which are pot-marked. Of further interest is the reporting in 1954 of stones of another possible chambered barrow less than one mile to the east, on the Shaftesbury to Motcombe road (grid ref: 862244). Alignments between the two sites may be revealed by further study.

I am grateful to the people who have contacted me prior to and since the publication of Ancient Stones of Dorset. I would welcome any further information on sacred sites from around Dorset. My address is in Appendix Two.

I am indebted to Dave Partridge for informing me that the modern stone circle at Bushy House, west of the ancient Rempstone Circle, has been demolished by the owners. On a lighter note, Val Ghose confirms the survival of Jackman's Cross, on Grimstone Down, stating that it is easier to find when vegetarian is low.

We may never get to find all the remaining stones around the county, many of them being virtually hidden now by hedgerow, earth and development. But with each one that is recognised and recorded we have another valuable piece in the jigsaw of our spiritual and cultural heritage.

...the standing stone or Druidic circle
on the heath; here is an inexhaustible fund of
interest for any man with eyes to see, or
tuppence worth of imagination to understand with.
Robert L Stevenson, *Notes Concerning Treasure Island.*

Appendix Two

Further Information

The following information may prove useful to the reader who wishes to pursue aspects of this book further. The local groups listed are particularly recommended, and welcome beginners and people of all levels of knowledge and experience.

WESSEX DOWSERS
holds monthly meetings in Wareham.
Members have many years experience in dowsing, including work on stone sites.
Beginners welcome and instruction given.
Write to: Paul Craddock, 6 Library Road, Parkstone, Poole, BH12 2BE.

CELTIC CONNECTIONS
The quarterly magazine on Celtic and related subjects, such as sacred sites, holy wells, etc.
Write to: David James, Sycamore Cottage, Waddon, nr Weymouth, Dorset, DT3 4ER.

EVENTS BY THE AUTHOR
The author gives regular talks to groups and societies across the South. Field trips and workshops also take place.
For details of these events write to: Peter Knight, 14 Maxwell Road, Winton, Bournemouth, BH9 1DJ.

WESSEX RESEARCH GROUP
Holds monthly meetings and workshops on subjects such as UFOs, earth mysteries and sacred sites.
Write to: Pat Law, Flat 8, Western Court, Western Road, Branksome Park, Poole, BH13 6EP.

NEW FOREST DOWSING SOCIETY
Holds regular meetings and field trips. Issues lively Newsletter.
Write to: Mike Clark, 30 Hobbs Park, St Leonards, Ringwood, BH24 4PU.

Bibliography

Ashe, Geoffrey. *Mythology of the British Isles*, Methuen, 1990.

Bailey, Ken. *A Bardic Offering*, Unique Publications, 1993.

Bellingham, David. *An Introduction of Celtic Mythology*, Quantum, 1996.

Bord, Janet and Colin. *Mysterious Britain*, Garnstone, 1972.

Bord, Janet and Colin. *The Secret Country*, Paul Elek, 1976.

Bord, Janet and Colin. *Earth Rites*, Granada, 1982.

Bord, Janet and Colin. *Sacred Waters*, Granada, 1985.

Bord, Janet and Colin. *Ancient Mysteries of Britain*, Grafton, 1986.

Branston, Brian. *The Lost Gods of England*, Thames and Hudson, 1974.

Brown, Mary. *Dorset Customs, Curiosities and Country Lore*, Ensign, 1990.

Bryce, Derek. *Symbolism of the Celtic Cross*, Llanerch, 1994.

Calkin, J.B. *Ancient Purbeck*, Friar Press, 1968.

Carr-Gomm, Philip. *The Druid Way*, Element, 1993

Castleden, Rodney. *The Cerne Giant*, Dorset Publishing Co., 1996.

Chadwick, John C. *Folklore and Witchcraft in Dorset and Wiltshire*, N.J. Clarke.

Cooke, Grace and Ivan. *The Light in Britain*, White Eagle Publishing, 1971.

Cross, Joy. *Imagery in the Churches of Dorset, Hampshire and Wiltshire*, (local study group publication), 1988.

Devereux, Paul. *Places of Power*, Blandford, 1990.

Devereux, Paul. *Earth Memory*, quantum, 1991

Devereux, Paul. *Symbolic Landscapes*, Gothic Image, 1992.

Devereux, Paul. *Re-Visioning the Earth*, Simon and Schuster, 1996

Devereux, Paul, and McCartney, Paul. *Earthlights*, turnstone Press, 1982.

Field, N. *Dorset and the Second Legion*, Dorset Books, 1992.

Forbes, J.F. *The Unchronicled Past*, Simpkin Marshall, 1938.

Friar, Stephen. *A Companion to the English Parish Church*, Alan Sutton, 1996.

Graves, Tom. *Needles of Stone Revisited*, Gothic Image, 1986.

Grinsell, Leslie. *Dorset Barrows*, Dorset Nat. Hist. & Arch. Soc., 1959.

Grinsell, Leslie. *Barrow, Pyramid and Tomb*, Thames and Hudson, 1975.

Harte, Jeremy. *The Christchurch Dragon*, self-published, 1985.

Harte, Jeremy. *Cuckoo Pounds and Singing Barrows*, Dorset Nat. Hist. & Arch. Soc., 1986

Harte, Jeremy. *Haunted Roads*, in The Ley Hunter, 121, 1994.

Heselton, Philip. *The Elements of Earth Mysteries*, Element, 1991.

Heselton, Philip. *Secret Places of the Goddess*, Capall Bann, 1995.

Hodges, Michael. *Helis, The Cerne Giant & His Links With Christchurch*, Self Published, 1998.

Hutchins, John. *The History and Antiquities of the County of Dorset*, 1861-70 ed.

Kelly, Eamonn P. *Sheela-na-Gigs*, Town House (Dublin), 1996.

Knight, Peter. *Ancient Stones of Dorset*, Power Publications, 1996.

Laird, M. *English Misericords*, John Murrey, 1986.

Legg, Rodney. *Mysterious Dorset*, Dorset Publishing Co., 1987.

Legg, Rodney. *Cerne's Giant and Village Guide*, Dorset Publishing Co., 1990.
Meaden, George Terence. *The Goddess of the Stones*, Souvenir Press, 1991.
Meaden, George Terence. *Stonehenge - The Secret of the Solstice*, Souvenir, 1997.
Mclahan, T.C. *Cathedrals of the Spirit*, Thorsons, 1996.
Michell, John. *Megalithomania*, Thames and Hudson, 1982.
Miller, Hamish and Broadhurst, Paul, *The Sun and the Serpent*, Pendragon Press, 1989.
Mills, A.D. *Dorset Place Names*, Roy Gasson, 1986.
Molyneaux, Brain Leigh. *The Sacred Earth*, Macmillan, 1995.
New Forest Dowsing Society. *Newsletter, No7*, Sept 1997 (article on Knowlton).
Osborn, George. *Exploring Ancient Dorset*, Dorset Publishing Co., 1985.
North, John. *Stonehenge*, Harper Collins, 1996.
Palmer, Kingsley. *Oral Folk-Tales of Dorset*, David and Charles, 1973.
Pearson, Michael Parker, *Bronze Age Britain*, English Heritage/Batsford, 1993.
Piggott, Stuart. *Ancient Britons and the Antiquarian Imagination*, Thames and Hudson, 1989.
Pitfield, F.P. *Dorset Parish Churches*, Dorset publishing Co., 1980.
Pollack, Rachel. *The Body of the Goddess*, Element, 1997.
Pope, Alfred. *Old Stone Crosses of Dorset*, Chiswick, 1906.
Readers Digest. *Folklore, Myths and Legends of Britain*, Readers Digest, 1973.
Royal Commission on Historical Monuments, *Inventory of Historical Monuments of Dorset*, HM Stat. Office, 1959-75.
Rudd, Chris. *Cernunnos, Celtic God and Christian Devil*, in The Dorset Year Book, 1986.
Scott, George Ryley. *Phallic Worship*, luxor Press, 1966.
Shaw, Phillip. *The Hidden Face of Stonehenge*, New Horizon, 1982.
Simpson, Jacqueline. *British Dragons*, Batsford, 1980.
Sjoo, Monica, and Mor, Barbara. *The Great Cosmic Mother*, Harper Collins, 1987.
Skelton, Robin, and Blackwood, Margaret. *Earth, Air, Fire, Water*, Arkana, 1990.
Stewart, R.J. *Celtic Gods, Celtic Goddesses*, Blanford, 1990.
Stone, J.F.S. *Wessex Before the Celts*, Thames and Hudson, 1989.
Streep, Peg. *Sanctuaries of the Goddess*, Bulfinch, 1994.
Thomas, Nicholas. *Guide to Prehistoric England*, Batsford, 1976.
Udel, John. *Dorsetshire Folk-Lore*, Hertford, 1922.
Wainwright, Geoffrey. *The Henge Monuments*, Thames and Hudson, 1989.
Waring, E. *Ghost and Legends of the Dorset Countryside*, Compton, 1987.
Watkins, Alfred. *The Old Straight Track*, Methuen, 1927, Abacus ed,. 1974.
Whitlock, Ralph. *In Search of the Lost Gods*, Phaidon, 1979.
Whitlock, Ralph. *Here Be Dragons*, George Allen and Unwin, 1983.
Whittle, Jane. *Twenty Wessex Walks Exploring Prehistoric Paths*, Hobnob, 1988.
Wiltshire, K.F. *Christchurch Priory, The Choir Stall & Misericords*, 1991 ed.
Wood, John Edwin. *Sun, Moon and Standing Stone*, Merrivale, 1978.
Yorke, Barbara. *Wessex in the Early Middle Ages*, Cassell, 1994.

Index

Abbots Bromley, 96
Abbotsbury, 13, 116, 186, 239, 256
Aborigines, 5, 10, 98, 120, 138, 183,
    193, 221, 247
Acropolis, 185
Affpuddle, 41, 50
Agglestone, 190-191
Albion, 5, 265, 270-271
Amerindians, 34, 63, 82, 98, 138, 221
Anchoret's Well, 108, 112
Anderson, 37
Anglo-Saxons, 47, 100, 140, 175, 181,
    198, 204, 272
ankh, 42
anthromorphic stones, 171-173
Anu, 185
Artemis, 82, 156
Arthur, King, 19, 41, 103, 122, 126, 258
Ashley Wood, 211, 214
At;hena, 185
Aubrey, John, 74
Avebury, 8, 11, 64, 74, 142, 165-166,
    171, 185, 192
Axis Mundi, 45, 75, 217
Aztecs, 35, 136

Bacchus, 136
Badbury Barrow, 64
Badbury Rings, 126-127, 196, 214
Ballard Down, 75
Barnes,William, 95
barrows (see 'long' and 'round')
Batcombe, 74, 252, 263
Bath, 5, 13, 106
Bayford, 27
beasts (mythical), 19-27
Beating the Bounds, 41, 94, 267
Beelzebub, 96
Belcalwell, 50

Belenos, 138, 275
Bellingstone, 273, 275
Beltaine, 79, 84, 106, 138, 144, 148,
    150, 155, 202, 204
Beowulf, 195, 198, 272
Berend's Barrow, 143, 158
Bere Regis, 108, 196, 208, 217, 239,
    275
Bettiscombe Skull, 50-51
Bible, 7, 37, 120, 124, 136, 155, 164-
    165, 195, 217, 239, 262-263, 272
Bigfoot, 240
Bincombe, 158-159, 199-200, 263
Bindon Abbey, 23, 41
Bisterne, 20-21, 101, 195
Black Down, 206, 275
Black Elk, 267
Blackmoor Vale, 26
Blake,William, 32, 135, 161-162, 265,
    270-271
Blandford, 27, 38, 82, 210, 213-214
Blue Pool, 103-104
Bockhampton, 104
Bokerley Dyke,198
Bottlebush Down, 30-31, 144, 202
Bournemouth, 9, 28, 37, 42-43, 126,
    181-182, 227, 237-239
Bourton, 74, 101
Bradford Abbas, 23, 217
Bradford Heads', 51
Breamore, 59
Bridport, 41, 77, 95-96, 112, 189, 242
Brighid, 102, 128, 138, 267, 273
Broadmayne, 256, 273
Broad Oak, 217
Broadstone,the, 74
Brockhampton Green, 102, 198

Bronze Age, 5, 11, 42, 55, 58, 63, 65,
71, 73, 81, 85, 105, 134, 136, 159,
164, 195, 218, 256, 275
Bryce,Derek, 66, 70
Buckland Newton, 107
Buckshaw, 28
Buddhists, 34, 63, 68, 77, 261
Bugley, 28
Bulbarrow, 84, 101, 116, 126, 154
bulls, 81-84, 86, 91, 94, 101, 147, 176
Burley, 21, 27, 195
'Burning Barrow', 200-201, 204, 263
Burton Bradstock, 96, 128, 273
Buzbury Rings, 214

Cadbury, 49, 122, 133
Cadham Oak, 212
Campbell,Joseph, 174
Castleden,Rodney, 50
Castle Frome, 8
Catherine Wheel, 67, 110
Cattistock, 36-37, 39, 82-83, 95, 168,
248, 252, 256
caves, 18, 35, 53, 72, 81, 133, 135, 155,
163-164,193
Celts, 4, 7, 18, 47, 49, 51, 66-67, 71, 76,
78, 81, 86-88, 104, 136, 138, 160,
165, 180, 185, 212, 218, 235
Celtic crosses, 6, 7, 24, 42-45, 47, 160,
218
centaurs, 6, 7, 24-25
Cerne Abbas, 67, 70-71, 78, 82, 90, 95,
102, 110-112, 198, 214, 236, 275
Cerne Giant, 70-71, 78-79, 88, 106,
152, 155, 242, 275
Cernunnos, 5, 71, 73, 78-79, 81, 85-90,
96-97, 124, 235-236, 267
Chalbury Hill, 104, 190
Chalice Well, 68, 116
Chaldon Herring, 81
Chapman's Pool, 28
Charborough, 40 Charminster, 31, 55,
61, 91, 93, 175
Chartres, 67

Chaucer, 19
Cheselbourne, 176, 178
Chesil Beach, 26
Chetnole, 258
Chettle, 141, 208
Chideock, 84-85
Chilcombe Hill, 151
Child Okeford, 38, 214, 252, 256
Chimaera, 24-25
China, 35, 98, 135, 252
Christchurch, 21-23, 25, 32-33, 38, 66,
101, 113, 187, 217, 241, 246, 252
Christianisation (of sites), 7, 13, 74,
106, 116, 175, 186, 250, 254, 256
Christianity (early), 6-8, 42, 51, 54, 68,
89, 112, 165, 175, 180, 218, 267
Christian phallicism, 79-80, 82
Church Knowle, 13, 1S
circle symbology, 62-70
Clandon Barrow, 65, 138, 253, 256
College Down, 153
Colliton Park, 54, 66, 77, 165
Colmer's Hill, 189
Compton Valence, 155
Conquer Barrow, 204, 256
Corfe Castle, 16, 31, 40-41, 50, 106,
188
Corscombe, 166, 149, 258
Cornwall, 25, 55, 58, 70, 96, 116, 192,
197
County Museum, 6, 16, 22, 24, 48-49,
53, 72, 77, 82, 85, 98
Cranborne, 91, 110, 141, 176, 198, 208,
217-218
Creechbarrow, 188-189
Cripplestyle, 110, 208
Crone Goddess, 180
crop circles, 68
crosses, 6-7, 37, 42-47, 54, 66, 74-76,
216-218, 250, 252, 256-258
Cross-in-Hand Stone, 74, 263
Crowcombe, 218
crusades, 37, 41
Culliford Tree Barrow, 199-200, 202

Culpepper's Dish, 192-193
cup and ring marks, 63-64
Cursus, Dorset, 65, 73-74, 81, 140-147,
   158, 195, 198, 202, 206, 254

Damory Oak, 213, 217
Danes, 37
Delph Wood, 222, 224-226, 228-229
Delphi, 10, 63
Devereux,Paul, 10, 67, 147, 192, 246,
   263, 268
devas, 210, 212, 221
Devil, 32-34, 36-37, 41, 89, 96, 98, 101-
   102, 104, 116, 124, 128, 157, 175,
   190
Dewlish, 98, 101
Dorchester, 13, 17, 27, 39, 54, 66, 70,
   73, 77, 89, 103, 133, 200, 276
dowsing,, 13, 55, 101, 114, 184, 212,
   250, 264, 276
dragon folklore, 7, 19-23, 35, 98, 100-
   103, 106, 120-122, 195, 218, 262-
   264
dragon gargoyles, 23, 89, 252, 262
dragon lines, 232, 252, 254
dragon symbology, 8, 22, 35-41, 79, 82,
   96, 163, 176, 228-232, 246-248, 252,
   262, 265-267, 273
dragon trees, 226, 228-232, 234, 251,
   254, 271
Dreamtime, 10, 193
Druids, 5, 11, 18, 82, 122, 156-157,
   164, 190, 210, 212, 220
Dudsbury, 126
Dungeon Hill, 107
Duntish, 264
Durotriges, 78, 88
Durweston, 39, 86, 103, 124, 252

earth energies, 13, 23, 34, 36-37, 55, 65,
   108, 112, 114, 134, 197, 246, 250,
   252, 263-265

Earth Goddess landscapes, 3-4, 6, 10,
   13, 17-18, 148, 151, 163-164, 182-
   193
Earth Goddess symbology, 35, 53-54,
   68, 74, 76, 98, 105, 116, 120, 148,
   149, 164-194, 206, 222, 226, 250,
   265
Earth Spirit, 4, 8, 10, 184, 221, 260-261,
   267-268
East Chelborough, 67
East Stour, 45
Edward IV, 21
Edward VI, 228
Egbert's Stone, 100-101
Eggardon Hill, 126, 134, 152, 253, 256,
   263
Egypt/Egyptians, 10, 20, 42, 63, 73, 75,
   81, 84, 98, 101, 136-138, 157, 265
Eleusis, 10
Ellingstone, 273
energies (see earth energies),
Epona, 5, 180
equinoxes, 112, 143, 149, 150-152, 158-
   159, 193
Evershot, II6
Excalibur, 103
exhibitionism, 177-179
Eype, 65, 77

fairies, 27-34, 100, 133, 138, 185, 207-
   208, 235, 263, 265
faults,geological, 112, 263
fertility rites/festivals, 41, 71, 73, 79,
   81, 84, 89, 94-96, 101, 264
Fifehead Neville, 102, 112
Flagstones, 73
flights (shamanic), 246-247
Flower's Barrow, 126
'Flying Angel', 51-52
Forbes,J Foster, 9, 29, 131
Fordington, 204

Gaia, 193

gargoyles, 9, 23, 31, 41, 51, 55, 85, 89-90, 175, 252, 262, 267
Gawain, 207
Geoffrey of Monmouth, 19, 157, 236
giants, 131, 195, 197-198, 207-208
Giant's Grave, 197-198
Gillingham, 42, 45
Glastonbury, 11, 55, 58, 68-69, 116, 122, 133, 186, 210, 258
goblins, 28
Goddess, Earth (see Earth Goddess)
goddesses, Celtic, 5, 106, 128, 180, 185, 267, 273
    Egyptian, 63, 75, 156-157, 210
    Greek, 100, 103, 180, 185, 262
    river, 100, 102
    Roman, 5, 54, 165, 180
    solar, 138
Goddess Stonees, 165-170, 174-175
Goddess,Triple, 119, 179-182, 193, 270
gods, Celtic, 5, 71, 73, 78, 81, 85-90, 96-97, 122, 124, 138, 204, 235-236, 242, 267, 273, 275
    Egyptian, 73, 84, 136-137
    Greek, 81, 120, 136, 210
    lunar, 135, 136, 138
    Norse, 105, 203-204,210
    Roman, 16, 81, 85-86, 94, 98, 136, 138, 21Q
    Saxon, 78, 204
    solar, 135-138, 242, 273, 275
Golden Cap, 152
golden coffins & tables, 107-108, 124
Gog and Magog, 210
Greece, 4, 10, 23, 25, 35, 63, 81, 98, 100, 185
Greek mythology, 25, 59, 103, 181, 185, 262
Green Man, 9, 28, 32, 181, 209, 233-240, 242-243, 265, 267
Grey Mare and Her Colts, 62, 147, 168, 170-171, 187, 206-207

griffins, 22-23, 25-26, 40-41
Grimes Graves, 73
Grim's Ditch, 198
Grimstone Down, 152, 155, 273, 278
Gundestrup Cauldron, 7, 87
Gussage Hill, 144, 146-148, 158
Gussage St Michael, 37-38, 73, 143-144, 247, 252

Halloween, 138
Halstock, 258
Hambledon Hill, 121, 123-124, 152-153, 210, 220, 258
Hampton Hill Stone Circle, 126, 151-152, 276
Hardy, Thomas, 128, 220
Harpstone, 74, 102, 168, 170
Harte, Jeremy, 280
Hawkchurch, 94
head cults, 49-51, 106
Heedless William's Stone, 74, 104-105
Helis/Heil, 78, 242, 273, 275
Hellstone (cromlech), 128, 170, 174-175
Helstone (standing stone), 168, 170
Hengistbury Head, 139, 187-189, 276
heraldry, 40-41, 85, 89
Hermitage, 116, 254
Herne the Hunter, 97, 204
Hethfelton, 101, 109
Highclere, 220
hills, as sacred places, 17, 120-134, 193, 265
Hilton, 90
Hindu myth, 20
Hinton Parva, 65
Hinton St Mary, 24-25, 66
hobby horse, 41, 70, 96, 103, 267
Hod Hill, 121, 124, 214
Hog Hill, 253, 275
holed stones, 168
Hollow Oak, 217
Holt Heath, 110
Holwell (Cranborne), 110

Holwell (near Cerne), 109, 252
Holwell Farm (near Broadwey), 109
Holy Stream, 101, l09
holy wells, 13, 16, 106, 108-115, 119,
    254
Hopi, 194
Hordle, 274
horned fertility cults, 81-84
Horton, 102
Hutchins, John, 22, 40, 60, 112, 217

Imbolc, 151-152,159
Inca, 136
India, 73, 75, 265
Isis, 63, 75, 156
Islam,100, 165
Isle of Sheppey,ll9, 179
Isle of Wight, 178-179, 188, 190
Iwerne Minster, 220

'Jerusalem', 161-162
Jordan Hill, 16, 202
Jung,Carl, 228

Kabalah, 164
Karnac, 75, 84
Kilpeck, 179
King's Stag, 242-243
Kingston, 16
Kingston Lacy, 75, 225-226
Kingston Russell, 126, 168, 171, 205
Knossos, 59
Knowlton, 11-12, 141, 147, 149, 151,
    1.93, 207, 220, 234, 252, 256, 264,
    276
Kogi (tribe), 120

labyrinths, 58-59, 131
Lady's Well, 116, 249
lakes, 98, 103-104
Lambert's Castle, 124-125, 232, 235,
    258
Lammas, 106, 144, 148, 150, 185, 202

landscape symbology (see Earth
    Goddess landscapes)
Lao-Tse, 119, 163, 184, 261
Lawrence, D H, 10
Leigh, 37, 60
Leyland, 258
ley lines, 9, 36, 76, 102, 104, 109, 110,
    116, 134, 153, 168,198,202, 214,
    232, 234, 245-259, 264, 273-274,
    276
Littlemayne, 75, 168-169, 171
Lillington, 267
Litton Cheney, 187
Loders, 93-94
long barrows, 62, 138, 142-155, 158-
    159, 168, 174, 187, 195, 196-208,
    214, 275
Long Bredy, 102, 155, 159
Long Crichel, 267
Longham, 26-27
Lullington, 37
Lulworth, 81, 126, 276
Luna, 155-156
lunar standstill, 159
Lychett Minster, 82, 219, 220

Mabinogion, 51, 87, 207
Macbeth, 181
Maiden Castle, 16, 53, 65, 82, 128-134,
    158-159, 165, 193, 255-256, 258,263
Maiden Newton, 23, 85, 91-92, 252,
    273
Mappowder, 39, 90, 233, 236, 252
Mars, 81
Martin's Down, 155, 159
'Matres', 180
Maumbury, 13, 70, 73, 264, 276
Mayans, 42, 98, 247
May Day, 70, 84, 97, 138, 155, 242
maypoles, 70, 79, 95, 140
mazes, 58-60, 131
Meaden,Terence, 5, 53, 73, 140, 142,
    146-147, 164-165, 168
Mecca, 100

Melbury Bubb, 8, 85
Melbury Osmond, 96
Melcombe Bingham, 198
Melplash, 253
Merlin, 19, 85, 103, 106, 157, 265
mermaids, 24-26
midsummer (see Summer Solstice)
midwinter (see Winter Solstice)
Milborne Port, 66
Miller, Henry, 16
Milton Abbey, 38, 112
Minerva, 165
Minotaur, 59
Minterne Parva, 74
mistletoe, 212
Monmouth's Ash, 217
Moon Goddess, 42, 155-157
moon,   risings/settings, 143-144, 150,
         158-159, 160
         symbolism, 53, 62, 64, 135-
         136, 160-161
moots, 207-208
Morcombelake, 112
morris dancing, 96, 242-243, 267
Moses, 73, 120, 156, 165
Mount Pleasant, 64, 73, 81, 140, 204,
         255-256
Muckleford, 102, 258
musical mounds, 198-200

Nature, sacred places of, 17-18 120, 221
Neolithic, 5, 11, 13, 53-55, 62, 71, 73-
         75, 81-82, 105, 124, 126, 128, 131,
         134, 141, 146-147, 155, 158, 164,
         175, 180, 185, 195, 275-276
New Forest, 21, 157, 234
Newgrange, 53-54, 62, 135, 180
Nine Stones, 11, 14, 74, 101, 148, 150,
         165, 167, 173, 217
Norden, 16
North, John, 64, 140, 142, 144

Oakley Down, 196, 206
Odin, 198, 204, 210

Odysseus, 35
Okeford Fitzpaine, 234
Old Sarum, 64
Ooser, Dorset, 93, 94, 96

Pamphill, 168, 214
Pan, 81, 85-86
Parkstone, 168
Parkwood, 104
Penbury Rnoll, 143-144,147
Pentridge, 141, 145
phallic symbolism, 13, 35, 42, 55, 71-
         80, 88, 136, 147, 155, 210
Piddletrenthide, 90
pilgrimage/pilgrims, 250, 268-269
Pilsdon Pen, 9, 51, 1.26, 134, 253, 256,
         258
Pimperne, 60, 207, 216, 252
Plato, 184
Plush Hill, 153
ponds, 19, 103-104, 110
Poole, 168-169, 222, 225, 228, 229, 251
Poor Lot Barrow Group, 204-205
Pope Gregory, 7, 118
Popple Stone, 249, 254
Portesham, 48, 50, 147, 151, 175, 255
Portland, 26, 126, 151-152, 158, 200
Portman Lodge, 86
Powerstock, II6
Poxwell Cairn, 126
Preston, 22, 37, 189, 190, 198
Puck, 27
Puckstone, 28
Puddletown, 59
Pulham, 90
Puncknowle, 8, 16
Purbecks, 28, 126, 188, 234, 256
Purewell, 113
Pyramids, 10

Rampisham, 37
rams, 81, 84-85
Rawlesbury Camp, 153-154
Remedy Oak, 228, 230

Rempstone, 9, 104, 168, 171-172, 192, 251, 256
Rhiannon, 180
Ringwood, 27
rivers, 98-102
Robilgalia, 94
Rogation, 41, 94
Romans (and relics of), 4, 5, 13, 16, 18, 23-25, 35, 37, 49, 54, 59, 63, 65, 67, 76-78, 81-82, 86, 89, 98, 101-102, 104-106, 110, 112, 118, 124, 128, 132, 134, 155-156, 165, 180, 196, 202, 210, 214, 251, 255-256
round barrows, 30-31, 65, 81, 85, 104, 127, 133, 147-149, 152, 159, 174, 189, 195-208, 214, 218, 251, 253, 255
runes, 46-47, 210, 220
Russell, G W, 3, 4, 13, 183, 261
Ryme Intrinseca, 31, 107

'sacred marriage', 73, 142, 146
sacredness of place, 10-18
sacred time, 18, 140
St Aloan's Head, 151-152
St Augustine's Well, 106, 110-111
St Andrew's Well, 112
St Catherine's Hill, 13, 186, 255
St Catherine's Well, 112
St George, 36-38, 106, 252
S t Luke's Chapel, 102
St Michael, 7, 8, 36-39, 41, 122, 252, 247
St Wite's Well, 112, 115
Samford Courtney, 37
Samhain, 138, 151-152, 159
satyrs, 4, 81, 240
Saxons, 19, 45, 51, 54-55, 85, 110, 112, 126, 160, 179, 188, 258
Shafteshury, 55-56, 109, 249, 254, 276-277
shamanic flight, 246-247
sheela-na-gigs, 90, 177-179
Sherborne, 25, 239

Shillingstone, 95, 160
Shipton Gorge, 48, 50, 94, 239
Shipton Hill, 151-152
Shroton, 23, 38, 47
Silbury Hill, 64, 122, 133, 185, 207
Silvanus, 81
Silver Well, 110
Singing Barrow, 200
site evolution, 13, 15-16, 245, 256, 275
Sixpenny Handley, 65, 74, 214
Skara Brae, 53
solar (see sun),
Sorcerer of Trois Freres, 81
springs, 49, 98, 101, 104-114, 116-119, 184, 252
spirals, 52-58, 70, 180
stags, 7, 26-27, 81, 85-87
Staple Cross, 66
Staplehill, 110
Stinsford, 18, 37, 74, 90, 214, 266
Stoke Abbot, 49, 51, 82, 116-117, 183, 241
stone circles, 11, 14, 63-64, 75, 101, 104, 126, 135, 148, 150-152, 164-165, 168-169, 256, 263, 276
Stonehenge, 9, 11, 64, 102, 109-110, 116, 135, 138, 168, 171-173, 234, 249, 251, 254, 258, 265
Stourpaine, 29, 31, 124
Stratton, 258
Studland, 16, 28, 46, 50, 66, 90, 160-161, 179, 190-191
Sulis Minerva, 5, 106
Summer Solstice, 138, 140, 143-145, 147-148, 150, 152, 154-155, 187, 249, 254
sun deities, 135-138, 242, 273, 275
symbology of, 45, 53, 62-63, 67, 135-138, 160-161
risings & settings of, 111-112, 139-155, 160, 187, 193
Swanage, 19, 198, 214, 223
Sydling St Nicholas, 217, 256-257

'Symbolic Landscapes',Devereux, 10, 192

Symondsbury, 41, 96, 112, 189

Table Mountain, 10
Taranis, 5
Tarrant Gunville, 220
Terminus, 94
Thirkthorn Down, 142-143, 145, 196, 207
third eye, 79, 93, 96
Thor, 105, 204
Thorncombe Beacon, 124, 249, 254
Thorncombe Wood, 17-18, 214, 264
Tilly Whim, 18
Todber, 45, 54-55
Tolkien, 47
Toller Fratrum, 8, 45, 50-51, 176
Toller Porcorum, 56, 85, 273-274
Tolpuddle, 215, 217
Tongue-pullers', 90
Tree of Life, 37, 42, 75, 91, 106, 176, 181, 210, 212, 217-218
trees, 11, 13, 62, 75, 106, 1.10, 124-125, 157, 176, 184, 209-235, 242, 254, 256, 265, 268
tree spirits, 13, 209-210, 212, 221, 223-232, 236, 240
Trent, 66
Trent Barrow, 104
Triple Goddess, 119, 179-182, 193, 270
Troy Town, 59
tymparnums, 22
Tyneham, 126
Turnworth, 82
Tutton's Well, 113

Udel,John, 95
Uffington, 122
UFO's, 263-264
Ulwell, 9, 75, 110, 223, 226
unicorns, 77
Upwey, 112-113

Veasta, 24, 26
Venus, 54, 180, 212
Venus of Laussel, 155, 163
Venus of Willendorf, 163
Verwood, 37, 234, 276
vesica piscis, 68-69, 77
Vikings, 37, 47, 135, 204
Virgin Mary, 27, 106, 116, 128, 157, 175, 180
votive relics/deposits, 16, 102, 105, 116, 167-168
vulvic symbolism, 68, 79, 164-171, 178-179, 184, 221-222, 226

Walditch, 112
Wareham, 22, 24-25, 47, 67, 188-189
Warmwell, 112
water,   sites near to, 101, 102, 104-105
         as mystical, 98, 100-114, 119, 183 (see also wells & springs)
Watkins,Alfred, 104, 245, 250, 254
Weatherby Castle, 75 wells, 13, 34, 49, 68, 104-119, 184, 214, 252
Wessex, 19, 140
West Milton, 249, 253
Weymouth, 24, 26, 28, 37, 39, 96, 262-263
Whitchurch Canonicorum, 113
Whitcombe, 26, 45, 256
white harts, 26-27
wild hunt, 203-204
Wimborne, 41, 44, 82-83, 102, 116, 168, 222, 234, 239, 242, 264, 266-267
Wimborne St Giles, 31, 141, 252
Winchester, 23, 26, 59
Windsor, 96-97
Winspit, 18, 232, 251
Winterborne Kingston, 105, 274
Winterborne Monkton, 104
Winterborne Stickland, 217
Winterborne Whitchurch, 235, 239

Winterbourne Abbas, 101
Winterbourne Steepleton, 51-52
Winter Solstice, 96, 138, 142-143, 145-
    148, 249, 254
witches (trials of), 33
Witchhampton, 54, 56, 79-80, 93, 101-
    102, 116, 118
Wo$ehouse, 51, 209, 236, 240-242
Woden, 105, 198
wombs (tombs as), 174-5
Woodbury Hill, 13, 108, 112
Woodlands, 44, 217, 228, 231, 271
Worbarrow, 143
World Tree (see Tree of Life)
Worth Matravers, 50
Wraxall, 168, 249
Wyke Down, 143, 145-148
Wynford Eagle, 22
Wyrd Sisters, 181, 210
wyverns, 40-41, 262

Yeti, 240
Yetminster, 74, 96, 107, 258
yew trees, 11-12, 124, 210, 218-220,
    267
Yggdrasill, 181, 210
yin-yang, 63-64, 157

A selection of other Capall Bann titles. Free catalogue available.

Secret Places of the Goddess by Philip Heselton

This book is a practical and evocative encouragement to seek the Earth Spirit in those special places where it dwells, embracing a wide definition of Paganism to include all those inner yearnings towards a closer contact with the land. It will appeal to all who are drawn to visit such natural and archetypal locations in the landscape as tree groves, sacred springs, special rock outcrops, the seashore and the Wild Wood. All these are Secret Places of the Goddess. The author shows why certain locations have been considered numinous and magical and how we can each go about finding these special places in the landscape. He provides a vision of the variety of ways in which we might respond to the spirit present at such sites and thereby enter into a closer relationship with the Old Ones. ISBN 1898307 40 7   £10.95

Magical Guardians - Exploring the Spirit and Nature of Trees
by Philip Heselton

This is a book about trees, but a book with a difference, for it acknowledges trees to be wise beings who can teach us much if we approach them in the right way. This book shows how to go about it, revealing the origins of our awakening interest in - and love for - trees. Trees have a spiritual nature, and opening up to this spirit has been a constant feature in human society. Through practical guidance, this book gives hints on how we can make that contact for ourselves. The personalities of the ancient trees - our Magical Guardians - are explored, and the book reveals how we can start to acquire some of their deeper meanings. ISBN 1 86163 057 3   £11.95

Practical Spirituality by Steve Hounsome

Many people today struggle with attempting to blend a spiritual life with the demands of work, home and family. For many, the rampant commercialism, exploitation and consequent destruction of the modern 'developed' world is in direct conflict with the sacred ideals held so dear by those who seek to live the way of the spirit. This book addresses this problem, offering a means whereby the dedicated, serious practitioner can learn to live a practical, spiritual life, with what is sacred to them at its heart and as its focus. This is achieved by close association with the natural world, the wheel of nature round its annual cycle and the Elements that constitute its life. There are many practical exercises included to help you find your way. Indeed we may well find that it is by living this way that society is changed, since all effective change must come from within. ISBN 186163 015 8 £10.95

Dragons of the West by Nigel Pennick

For thousands of years fabulous serpents and dragons have been the stuff of myth and traveller's tales. The dragon has held the attention of people for centuries, and continues to do so. The dragon is more than a beast of tall stories, myth and folk-tale, for it is a symbol of the awesome power of nature which appears in many variant forms, but which we can understand only in symbolic or allegorical form. Thus, it appears in religious symbolism, alchemy, medicine and geomancy as well as in the more lyrical tales of bards and storytellers. Ultimately the dragon is a product of the human mind, for there are dragons of various kinds lurking deep within us all. This book explores Western dragon and dragonslayer traditions, not just legends, but living festivals and rituals surviving today. ISBN 1 86163 007 7   £10.95   Illustrated

FREE DETAILED CATALOGUE

A detailed illustrated catalogue is available on request, SAE or International Postal Coupon appreciated. **Titles can be ordered direct from Capall Bann, post free in the UK** (cheque or PO with order) or from good bookshops and specialist outlets. Titles currently available include:

Angels and Goddesses - Celtic Christianity & Paganism by Michael Howard
Arthur - The Legend Unveiled by C Johnson & E Lung
Auguries and Omens - The Magical Lore of Birds by Yvonne Aburrow
Book of the Veil The by Peter Paddon
Caer Sidhe - Celtic Astrology and Astronomy by Michael Bayley
Call of the Horned Piper by Nigel Jackson
Cats' Company by Ann Walker
Celtic Lore & Druidic Ritual by Rhiannon Ryall
Crystal Clear - A Guide to Quartz Crystal by Jennifer Dent
Earth Harmony - Places of Power, Holiness and Healing by Nigel Pennick
Earth Magic by Margaret McArthur
Enchanted Forest - The Magical Lore of Trees by Yvonne Aburrow
Familiars - Animal Powers of Britain by Anna Franklin
Healing Homes by Jennifer Dent
Herbcraft - Shamanic & Ritual Use of Herbs by Susan Lavender & Anna Franklin
In Search of Herne the Hunter by Eric Fitch
Magical Guardians - Exploring the Spirit and Nature of Trees by Philip Heselton
Magical Lore of Cats by Marion Davies
Magical Lore of Herbs by Marion Davies
Masks of Misrule - The Horned God & His Cult in Europe by Nigel Jackson
Mysteries of the Runes by Michael Howard
Patchwork of Magic by Julia Day
Psychic Self Defence - Real Solutions by Jan Brodie
Runic Astrology by Nigel Pennick
Sacred Animals by Gordon MacLellan
Sacred Celtic Animals by Marion Davies
Sacred Grove - The Mysteries of the Forest by Yvonne Aburrow
Sacred Geometry by Nigel Pennick
Sacred Lore of Horses The by Marion Davies
Sacred Ring - Pagan Origins British Folk Festivals & Customs by Michael Howard
Seasonal Magic - Diary of a Village Witch by Paddy Slade
Secret Places of the Goddess by Philip Heselton
Talking to the Earth by Gordon Maclellan
Taming the Wolf - Full Moon Meditations by Steve Hounsome
The Goddess Year by Nigel Pennick & Helen Field
West Country Wicca by Rhiannon Ryall

Capall Bann is owned and run by people actively involved in many of the areas in which we publish. Our list is expanding rapidly so do contact us for details on the latest releases.

Capall Bann Publishing, Freshfields, Chieveley, Berks, RG20 8TF